HIGH LEVERAGE
REAL ESTATE INVESTMENTS

Inside Secrets
of Using OPM

HIGH LEVERAGE REAL ESTATE INVESTMENTS

Inside Secrets of Using OPM

OLIVER RAY PRICE

PRENTICE-HALL, INC.   Englewood Cliffs, NJ

Prentice-Hall International, Inc. *London*
Prentice-Hall of Australia, Pty. Ltd., *Sydney*
Prentice-Hall of Canada, Ltd., *Toronto*
Prentice-Hall of India Private Ltd., *New Delhi*
Prentice-Hall of Japan, Inc., *Tokyo*
Whitehall Books, Ltd., *Wellington, New Zealand*
Prentice-Hall of Southeast Asia Pte. Ltd., *Singapore*

© 1978 by

Prentice-Hall, Inc.
Englewood Cliffs, N.J.

All rights reserved. No part of this book may be reproduced in any form or by any means, without permission in writing from the publisher.

Library of Congress Cataloging in Publication Data

Price, Oliver Ray.
   High leverage real estate investments.

  1. Real estate investment. I. Title.
HD1379.P74   332.6'324   78-11280
ISBN 0-13-387597-0

Third Printing .... June, 1981

Printed in the United States of America

Dedicated to

Dorothy
Netah
Sandra
Marjorie
Brick
Lynn
Janet
Gregory
Tende

YOUR KNOWLEDGE, YOUR DRIVE, AND OTHER PEOPLE'S MONEY WILL MAKE YOU RICH

Are you ambitious? Do you want to become wealthy? Do you have a high drive? Are you a self-starter? Would you find making and managing real estate investments challenging? Are you willing to get started? If so, then this book is for you!

The *key* to making money in a real estate venture is *high leverage*. For example, using $1.00 of *Other People's Money (OPM)* for every 10¢ of your own to finance a venture, you get a high leverage of ten-to-one. And deals can be structured so that all of the profit (or most of it) on the entire venture, including profit on your money and OPM, is yours. Many techniques for setting up deals to multiply profits through high leverage are described in this book. Examples are given to illustrate each technique and to show how insiders use OPM in many different ways to increase the leverage of any cash they invest.

One example shows how to form a syndicate with no money of your own, buy an apartment building, make a profit, and share the profit on a 50-50 basis with other members of the syndicate. Other examples show:

- How to rezone a $50,000 property and double its value, using other people's money.

• How to bring a buyer and seller together and make use of their money to take a piece of the action.
• How to get an option on rezonable land, get it rezoned, and sell it for a profit.
• How to buy $1,750,000 worth of income producing property without a dime of your own.
• How to lease $1,000,000 worth of property, use other people's money, and purchase the property after 10 years of managing it for a fee.
• How to lease a $750,000 building for 50 years and pocket $40,000 per year.
• How to obtain an option using other people's money, and then sell the option itself for a handsome profit.
• How to net $100,000 or more using a progressive option and without using your own money.
• How to provide tax advantages for a seller and get him to let you use his money.
• How to use a wrap-around mortgage to buy a $240,000 suburban office building with no down payment.

YOU CAN DO IT BY USING OTHER PEOPLE'S MONEY

Thousands of individuals have made their fortunes by using other people's money in real estate with one or more of the approaches described in this book. Their backgrounds, educational levels, and experiences prior to involvement in real estate are quite varied. Educationally, they range from Ph.D.'s to dropouts from elementary schools. Plumbers, attorneys, retail clerks, professors, army privates, and senior aerospace engineers are but a few of these successful entrepreneurs.

What these newly wealthy individuals had in common was ambition, drive, and a determination to succeed. Even without a beginning stake, it can be done. Follow the techniques of using other people's money given in this book—read and reread the examples given—learn all you can about the real estate market in your area—study the success of others—and you can succeed also. And you can continue to use other people's money for even faster progress when you have money of your own after your first successes.

Real estate entrepreneurs by the thousands have disproved the old saying, "It takes money to make money." The successful ones are those who made use of the basic techniques of using other people's money revealed in this book. If they had waited until they had saved $20,000 to $50,000 from their nine-to-five jobs, most of them would never have started in real estate. In today's world of high prices going higher, of inflation, and of increasing taxes, accumulation of investment capital from ordinary income (such as from a job) is quite difficult. With knowledge of how to use other people's money, you, too, can gain financial security without first accumulating investment capital of your own.

As you are analyzing a possible real estate project, reread the sections of this book which apply to your proposed project. Think and rethink various possible ways of financing it. Among other approaches considered, be sure to consider the examples given in Chapters 3, 4, and 5 on the option approach versus using other people's money by syndication as described in Chapter 2. Ask yourself whether to approach the seller with a proposal using his money for financing. It may be that an example in Chapter 17 fits your situation; it shows how an entrepreneur made $50,000 profit with an option which allowed him to put the property to its highest and best use. Don't zero in on the first financing approach which you think of or which is suggested by someone else. Analyze the various approaches described in this book. Above all, don't rely on the seller or a third party for structuring the financing. You can be the creative and innovative one and increase your profits by using other people's money and the techniques described in this book.

PROFESSIONAL APPRAISER'S APPROACH

You will, upon occasion, find yourself competing for a given piece of real estate with an individual similar to yourself; your competitor may even have money of his own to invest. If you have learned all the various approaches described in this book, you should have the edge on your competitor. Your competitive advantage and profits will be increased by learning the professional appraiser's technique of "highest and best use" approach to evaluating property. Take a look at the example in Chapter 17, where an entrepreneur realized that a $50,000 property would take a step increase in value if he could get it rezoned. He obtained the rezoning and the property's value increased to $100,000—a 100% increase in value. And he used other people's money to make his handsome profit!

DIVIDE AND PROFIT—USING OTHER PEOPLE'S MONEY

There is money to be made by buying well-located acreage and selling it in 1/2-acre to 5-acre parcels. The market for small outlying parcels has remained strong even though the government has spent tons of money to renew urban areas and to attract people to live near downtown. In Chapter 18, read how a 30 year old family man made a $10,000 profit and kept the best five acres for himself and family, all with the use of other people's money. But beware, there are pitfalls you may encounter. Above all, don't let your personal yens affect your judgment on the profitability of the project.

GET STARTED NOW

I will show you how to get started in real estate investment and how to use other people's money effectively in reaching your financial objective. Read every page and reread those sections which appeal most to you. Become familiar with every technique presented in these pages.

But, after reading, *take action*—take the steps described herein. It is action, based upon knowledge of how others have used other people's money, which will enable you to achieve financial success and security for yourself. If you choose the syndication approach, learn the principles described in Chapter 2 and study the examples given. A profit of $75,000 for you, the entrepreneur, is achievable; see the example in Chapter 2, which shows how it was done by another and how he used other people's money.

Almost every successful real estate investor I have known will sometimes take an action based, in part, upon what he calls a "hunch" or "intuition." You may be able to point out an individual in real estate investment who acted quickly, upon a hunch, and who made a large profit. It is my observation, however, that investors who are repeatedly successful in "acting upon hunches" are those investors with years of experience under their belts. I believe that it is their accumulated expertise, based upon several previous ventures, that enables them to reach their decisions so quickly. This book will show you how these successful men used other people's money to maximize their profits and speed progress toward their goals.

In Chapter 3, you will learn the powerful technique of using other people's money in the option approach. Read how a $50,000 profit was made by first obtaining an option.

This book reveals many, many techniques used by experienced and successful investors. You will learn the principles utilized in each technique. The concrete examples will clearly illustrate use of each technique. For instance, see the example in Chapter 12 which shows how to use leverage with other people's money to gain a tax-protected income for yourself of $15,000 or more per year.

Once you have learned the principles of the techniques given in this book and have studied the examples—go out and get started. You have to act in order to succeed, but act only after you have learned what is presented in Chapters 1 through 19 and then proceed with objectivity.

Oliver Ray Price

CONTENTS

Your Knowledge, Your Drive, and Other People's Money Will Make You Rich . 7

1 How to Use Other People's Money to Build Your Real Estate Fortune . 17

Entrepreneurs Make $30,000 Profit Using Other People's Money . Use Other People's Money to Build Your Fortune . The Most Powerful Techniques for Using Other People's Money . Principal Sources of Financing Using Other People's Money . Choose the OPM Technique Which Suits You Best . How to Approach Your Source of Money . How to Utilize Your Legal and Tax Counselors—Profitably . Taxes—Avoidance Will Speed Your Progress to Wealth . Remember These Points

2 High Leverage Syndicates: Using Other People's Money for Their Profit and Yours . 25

How One Entrepreneur Reaped 50% ($75,000) of Apartment Project Profits by Organizing a Syndicate to Finance It . Best Bets for Profits in Income Property—How to Maximize Your Profit . How to Find Syndicate Investors . How a Syndicated Commercial Property Put $20,000 Per Year in Pocket of Organizer . How to Set Your Real Estate Investment Goals . Choose Both the Property for Syndication and the Syndicate Investors to Suit Your Goals . The Insider's Secret of Building Net Worth with High Leverage and Without Incurring Taxes . A Successful Syndication Sets Stage for Larger Projects . The Biggest Inside Secrets of Syndicating— Nine Keys to Successful Syndication . Remember These Points

CONTENTS

3 Using Options to Gain Control of Apartments and Get High Profits . 41

Why Use the Option-To-Purchase Approach in Apartment Investment . How the Option Approach Netted $50,000 Profit on 60 Unit Apartment Building . How to Use an Option . How the Option Approach Minimized Risk and Returned Sixty-Five Percent on an Investment . Option on 45 Year Old Apartment Allows Investigation . How to Evaluate an Investment's Potential . When to Use an Option . Seven Keys to Successful Apartment Building Investing—and Insider Use of Options . Remember These Points

4 Secrets of Using Options to Gain Control of Land . 53

The Secret of High Profit in Land . How an Option Netted $60,000 With $1 Invested . How to Use an Option to Gain Control of Land . How to Use the Progressive Option to Develop Property with Little Money Down . How an Entrepreneur Used a Progressive Option to Reap $105,000 Profit . Remember These Points

5 How to Use Low Risk Options to Control Commercial and Industrial Property . 63

How an Entrepreneur Gained Control of $220,000 Shopping Center and Profited Without Investing His Money . How to Use an Option to Gain Control of Commercial or Industrial Property . How the Sale of an Option Netted $55,000 Profit on Option-Controlled $900,000 Industrial Property . Things to Watch For in Industrial Property Investing . Six Keys to Commercial/Industrial Property Investing—Insider's Use of Options . Remember These Points

6 Inside Secrets of Making Money on Property You Don't Own . 75

How the Sale of an Option on $1,100,000 Building Brought $60,000 Profit . How to Find a Buyer for Your Option . Checklist of Potential Option Buyers . Sale of Plan and $1,000 Option Nets $22,000 Plus 20 Percent of Medical Building . How to Make an Effective Presentation to a Possible Option Buyer . Sales Presentation Checklist . Be Careful—Your Optioned Property Could Slip Away From You . Five Keys To Making a Profit in Real Estate Without Owning It . Remember These Points

7 High Leverage Lease and Lease-Purchase Contracts Using OPM . 85

How an Investor Leased a $650,000 Building and Pockets $37,000 Per Year . Advantages of Sale-Leaseback to User and Investor . How Purchase-Leaseback Provides 278 Percent Return on Cash Invested by Small Investor . How to Use the Lease-Purchase in Lieu of a Down Payment . Lease-Purchase Gives Control of Apartment Building With no Down Payment . Six Keys to Use of Purchase-Leasebacks and Lease-Purchase Agreements . Remember These Points

8 How to Get the Money You Need for Your Real Estate Ventures . 97

Financing by Savings and Loan Associations . What Lenders Look For . Preview All Loan Documents Before Applying for Loan . How an Entrepreneur Obtained Financing for a $1,500,000 Building From His Best Future Tenant . Two-Step—Interim and Takeout . Master Sergeant Gets Insurance Company Takeout Commitment for $850,000 . Locating Private Investors for Your Project . Investment Review Checklist . How to Convince Individuals to Commit Their Money to Finance Your Project . How a $2,300,000 Special-Purpose Building Was Financed by Special-Interest Individuals . Six Keys to Success in Obtaining Financing From Private and Public Sources . Remember These Points

9 Using the Seller's Money to Finance Your Investments . 109

Look For Tax Advantages to the Seller—He May Finance Deal Himself . Checklist of Tax Advantages . How an Entrepreneur Structured for Financing by Seller—Seller's Ordinary Income Converted to Capital Gains Profit . Use Seller's Credit to Finance Real Estate Venture . How Andrew K. Used Seller's Credit to Finance Apartment Building and Pocketed $20,000 . Buyer-Seller Rapport Helps in Using Seller's Credit . Seven Keys to Financial Success by Using Seller's Money or Credit Rating . Remember These Points

10 More Key Sources of OPM to Finance Your Way to Wealth . 119

How to Use Limited Partner Approach With No Money of Your Own . Limited Partner Approach Finances Apartment Building . How to Use Contract-To-Purchase with No Money Down—Tax Advantages to Seller . How a Shop Owner Used a Contract-To-Purchase to Gain Control of Commercial Building with No Initial Cash . Use of Lease and Lease-Purchase Approach to Profits Using Other People's Money . How an Entrepreneur Used Lease-Purchase Contract to Gain Control of an Industrial Complex . Sharing Your Profit . Five Key Considerations on Sources for Money to Enable You to Profit Using Other People's Money . Remember These Points

11 How to Get High Profits Using Installment Land Contracts . 129

Land Contract Yields no Down Payment Deal for Apartment Building . Finance Deals with Little or no Money Down by Using Installment Land Contracts . Land Contract Review Checklist . How Entrepreneur Used Land Contract to Acquire a 21 Unit Building with no Down Payment; Tax and Income Benefits to Seller Helped Close the Deal . Senior Lenders Versus Installment Loan Contracts . Six Keys to Building Your Fortune With Installment Land Contracts . Remember These Points on Installment Land Contracts .

CONTENTS

12 Leveraging Your Way to Higher Profits and Income . 139

How to Use Leverage and Get Tax Protected Income of $15.000 Per Year . Why Use Leverage—Its Advantages . How a Forty Unit Apartment Building was Leveraged with no Down Payment . Disadvantages of Leveraging—Cautions . Analysis of Apartment Building Showed Negative Leverage; Deal is Rejected . Six Keys for Building Your Fortune With Leverage . Remember These Points .

13 Use Second Mortgages To Close More Deals and Put More Money in Your Pocket . 149

How a Second Mortgage Helped Buy a Twenty-Eight Unit Apartment Building with Nothing Down . Use Secondary Financing to Help Build Your Fortune . Why a 12 Percent Second Mortgage is Better than Refinancing at 8-3/4 Percent . Watch for Pitfalls—Don't Stretch Too Far . Why the Seller is the Best Source for Second Mortgages . Six Keys to Increased Profits and More Deals with Seller or Other Private Party Helping to Finance the Purchase . Remember These Points

14 How to Locate the Best Sources of Secondary Financing . 159

Secondary Financing—Does it Cost More? . The Best Sources for Seconds . How Second Mortgage Yields $14,500 Profit on Commercial Building . Shop Around—It Pays . A Hard Money Second Mortgage Saves the Day for Entrepreneur . Low Cost Seconds—Purchase Money Mortgages . Six Keys to Profitable Use of Secondary Financing . Remember These Points

15 Wrap Around Mortgages: A High Leverage, OPM Technique . 169

Why the Little Known Technique of Wrap Around Mortgages is a Powerhouse . Buyers Use Wrap Around Mortgages for Their Benefit . How a Wrap Around Mortgage Allowed Purchase of $240,000 Suburban Office Building with Zero Initial Payment . How to Find Investors to Finance Wrap Around Mortgages . Advantages of Wrap Arounds for Lenders—Leverage! . How an Entrepreneur's Tenant Financed a $40,000 Wrap Around Mortgage . Use of Wrap Around Mortgage Approach Gives Important Edge in Real Estate Investment Field . Eight Keys—Building a Fortune with Wrap Around Mortgages . Remember These Points

16 How to Sell Second Mortgages and Get Top Dollar for Your Real Estate . 181

Selling a Second Mortgage—Those Discounts Hurt . Low Interest Second Discounted Heavily . How to Sell a Second Mortgage . Entrepreneur Enlists Real Estate Broker's Aid for Commission of Only 2-1/2 Percent . How to Dispose of a Second Mortgage without Discounting . How Trading

16 **How to Sell Second Mortgages and Get Top Dollar for Your Real Estate** *(cont.'d)*

in a Second Mortgage Filled gap in Financing . How to Bargain with a Second Mortgage . Nine Keys to Better Dealing in Selling Second Mortgage . Remember These Points

17 **Buying and Rezoning for High Profit . 193**

Zoning—What it is and How it Controls . Rezone for Profit? . How Rezoning Doubled Market Value of $50,000 Property . Zoning in your Community . A $1 Option, Syndication, and Rezoning Puts $30,000 Profit in Entrepreneurs' Pockets . The Future in Zoning . Seven Keys to Fortune Building Through Rezoning . Remember These Points

18 **High Leverage Methods for Making Profits on Outlining Property . 205**

How a Family Man Made $10,000 Profit and Kept Five Acres . How to Close Outlying Property . How to Choose the Right Outlying Property . Dividing Your Land—Legal Cautions . How to Go Fishing and Boating and Make Money in Raw Land . Living Better—Environmentally and Financially . Six Keys to Making High Profits on Outlying Property . Remember These Points

19 **How Tax Avoidance Helps You Use Other People's Money . 217**

Use of Tax Avoidance and Avoidance of Tax Evasion Will increase Your Profit . Sixteen Ways to Take Advantage of Tax Factors in Real Estate . How a Seller Structured a Lease With Purchase Option To Allow Seller To Defer Taxes . Legal Tax Avoidance—Use The Government's Money . How To Use an Installment Sale to Defer Taxes . Seller Defers Tax Payments and Avoids Higher Tax Brackets by Installment Sale . How to Optimize Use of Services of Your Tax Counselor . Nine Keys to Use of Tax Benefits to Speed You on the Road to Wealth . Remember These Points . Special Note

Index . 231

HIGH LEVERAGE REAL ESTATE INVESTMENTS

Inside Secrets of Using OPM

1

HOW TO USE OTHER PEOPLE'S MONEY TO BUILD YOUR REAL ESTATE FORTUNE

It is essential that every ambitious entrepreneur make use of other people's money (OPM) in order to build a fortune in real estate. Any experienced investor familiar with the insider's secrets of real estate investing automatically analyzes the financing of available property with the intent of using other people's money to the extent it is wise and possible; he will hold on to as much of his own cash as he can to use in another future deal. The dozens of case examples given in this book show the many techniques for using other people's money to build a fortune through real estate investing.

ENTREPRENEURS MAKE $30,000 PROFIT USING OTHER PEOPLE'S MONEY

A young man with no money, for example, combined two fundamental techniques known to experienced investors and made a $30,000 profit from his first venture. He realized that changing the use of a property was one way of increasing its market value. He negotiated an option (to gain control of the property) and obtained a zoning change to convert the property's use from a single family residence to a site for eighteen apartments. The option period was sufficiently long to get the property rezoned. He combined the option approach with the formation of a small syndicate so successfully that his own cash investment was only $1. After the property was rezoned he sold the option itself for a $30,000 profit. His share of the profit was $15,000. Details of this venture are given in Chapter 17.

USE OTHER PEOPLE'S MONEY TO BUILD YOUR FORTUNE

The most common way of using other people's money in real estate investing is simply to borrow as much as possible on a purchased property from one of the public lending institutions, such as savings and loan associations or insurance companies. Many of today's successful entrepreneurs started out by buying a house for their personal residence and borrowing from a savings and loan association.

An entrepreneur with the drive and determination to make a fortune in real estate can use money borrowed from the aforementioned sources. However, he will also learn the insider's secrets of using other people's money, obtained from many other sources, in many other ways. Those who will attain their financial goals are those who learn and apply these insider techniques. The following chapters describe the most important techniques being used by experienced investors today. The case examples illustrate *how* investors have applied them for excellent profits using other people's money. Each technique is described in detail. A creative and innovative investor may vary the details of an approach or may, of course, use combinations of two or more techniques to increase his profits and travel faster on the road to wealth.

THE MOST POWERFUL TECHNIQUES FOR USING OTHER PEOPLE'S MONEY

Syndication

To form a syndicate is to form a group of people for investment purposes. Syndicating is a powerhouse approach for an ambitious entrepreneur who has very little or no money of his own to invest. Many highly experienced (or beginning) entrepreneurs use the syndication approach by taking a share of future profits and investing none of their personal cash. Their share of profits is earned by locating a good investment opportunity and managing it to make a profit for all. Many entrepreneurs who are familiar with the insider's secrets of real estate investing use the syndication approach over and over again during their building of a fortune. See how others have applied this approach in Chapter 2.

Options

An option to purchase gives you temporary control of a property. Real estate insiders use it for various purposes and their purpose may vary from one deal to another. One may use the option approach to see if he really can get a property rezoned to allow the "highest and best use" of the property. Another investor may use it to allow time for arranging financing, perhaps by forming a syndicate. A third may be uncertain about his fast analysis of the property and needs time to determine the advisability of proceeding. In all cases, the holder of the option is not obligated to purchase the property; he can surrender the option or simply let it expire. Options are such an important subject, for anyone wishing to learn the insider's secrets of real estate investing, that four chapters (Chapters 3, 4, 5, and 6) of this book are devoted to options.

Lease

Entrepreneurs' use of leases to make money in real estate has increased in recent years. The varieties of ways to make money by use of leases is limited only by an investor's knowledge of the leasing approaches used by others and his own creativity and innovativeness. For example, one entrepreneur with management experience generated an income of $37,000 per year for himself by negotiating a fifty-year master lease and improving the rental income from the property. His out-of-pocket investment was zero! A full description of this case is given in Chapter 7.

A different approach was used by a fifty year old owner of vacant property who had planned to sell it. His cost basis was very low compared to the market value; his capital gains tax would have been high. Instead of selling, he leased the ground for thirty-five years to a tenant who improved it with a large building and parking lot. The owner then had a lifetime income and, thirty-five years hence, his heirs would have an improved property with some residual value in the building.

Lease-purchase

Whether an entrepreneur is young and just beginning a career of real estate investing or older and semi-retired, a lease purchase for certain properties may be the best deal for him. An entrepreneur familiar with the insider's secrets of the various ways of structuring a lease or a lease-purchase has an advantage over his competitors. Suppose, for example, an owner is vacillating with respect to selling because of tax consequences in a period when his other income is high. If you are the one who presents an offer to lease his property for a period of years and purchase it then, you will likely be the one who gains control of the property. How to structure and use a lease-purchase for your increased profits with no initial investment is described in Chapter 7.

Use of seller's money or credit standing

One of the best possible sources for financing a real estate venture is the seller, provided, of course, the seller is in a position to carry the financing. In many deals, the seller's desire or need to sell means that you can get more liberal terms and conditions (and even a lower interest rate) than is obtainable from conventional lenders. Consequently, an experienced buyer will always probe for financing by the seller if he believes there is even a remote chance that the seller will finance the deal.

A variation is for the seller to borrow money on the property before you buy it. Then it is the seller's credit rating which is examined by the lender instead of yours. Double check with your tax counsel, however, especially if you are the seller and are selling for less than thirty percent down with the intent to postpone a part of your tax on profits to future years. The danger is that the IRS may rule that the amount a seller borrows shortly before a sale is "really" a part of the down payment on the property.

Chapter 9 describes in detail the various ways of using the seller's money or credit standing to finance your next venture.

Limited partners

Most individuals who are potential sources for financing your real estate ventures are familiar with the concept of "partner." The meaning of "limited partner" and case examples showing how to use limited partnerships to your advantage (and theirs) are given in Chapter 10. If your potential partners in a venture are not familiar with the financial and legal implications of a limited partner position, it will be to your advantage to learn the fundamentals and to be able to describe them in your presentation of a proposed venture to them.

Installment land contract

The beginning or experienced real estate investor with very little or no money available for a down payment should become acquainted with the Installment Land Contract (sometimes called "Contract for Deed"). It is one of the most powerful and effective of insider's secrets. In Chapter 11, read how a mechanic who, after learning the details of land contracts, used this technique to gain control of a six unit apartment building with no money down. He leveraged to infinity!

The complex aspects (see Chapter 11) of installment land contracts require study, but the advantages to a buyer with little cash make the effort well worthwhile. I rate knowledge of the technique as a must for beginning or experienced investors.

Leverage

As implied by the title of this book, the use of leverage in real estate investments is of paramount importance to anyone with a goal of building a fortune through real estate ventures. The concept of leverage is described and a simple, straightforward numerical example is given in the second paragraph of Chapter 12. The money makers are those who learn the insider's secrets of how to use leverage and, most important, how to use it in combination with other techniques described herein and illustrated by case examples.

Second mortgages

Entrepreneurs familiar with the insider's secrets of real estate investing will have learned to regard and use second mortgages as another opportunity to make money. It is the mark of a naive investor to speak of "seconds" as a necessary evil—something to be avoided as the plague. For instance, one example in Chapter 13 shows how an investor creatively used a purchase money second mortgage to buy a twenty-eight unit apartment building with nothing down. He leveraged to infinity (!) with the aid of a second mortgage.

Wrap around mortgages

In effect, a wrap around mortgage is a sophisticated variant of a second mortgage. It is a powerhouse technique. Although many entrepreneurs have made fortunes without using (or even understanding) the wrap around technique, you can use it to accelerate your progress toward wealth. In fact, Mr. M. (see Chapter 15) almost surely would not have closed a deal on a suburban office building without a wrap around mortgage approach.

PRINCIPAL SOURCES OF FINANCING USING OTHER PEOPLE'S MONEY

Entrepreneurs must, of course, know how to locate sources of capital for financing. Their goal in each venture is to obtain optimum financing. The nature of the real estate venture being considered and their personal goals determine the most desirable type of financing and the type of lender they approach.

The seller is such an important potential source of financing that all of Chapter 9 is devoted to this subject. Many entrepreneurs have obtained more money and on better terms and conditions from a seller than they could have obtained elsewhere. Others have closed deals, which otherwise might have fallen through, by structuring deals which gave the seller tax benefits by financing the transaction.

I have found that an organized, structured cataloguing of information (done as a continuing, ongoing project) on potential sources of money pays off when a new property becomes available. Chapter 2 describes this cataloguing procedure in detail for candidates for joining a syndication. The procedure, once used, can easily be broadened to include sources of capital described in Chapters 8 and 10.

CHOOSE THE OPM TECHNIQUE WHICH SUITS YOU BEST

My "natural approach" is first to locate a property with a profit potential and, second, as a part of analysis, decide which type and what source of financing is most desirable. I recommend, however, that everyone consider not only the objective aspects of using other people's money, but also consider which approach suits best on a personal, subjective basis. For example, some entrepreneurs appear to be natural "loners"; they will tend to use sources of capital which do not require an ongoing, personal relationship with the money supplier. General partnerships, or even limited partnerships, are not suited to loners.

Ideally, of course, an entrepreneur will consider all possible ways of using other people's money and use the particular mode most suitable to the type property and his personal goals. If you have tended to use only one source, then this book has a possible huge benefit for you by helping you become acquainted with a broad spectrum of ways to use other people's money for your profit.

HOW TO APPROACH YOUR SOURCE OF MONEY

In effect, an entrepreneur is selling when he approaches a source of money to finance a proposed venture. Anyone seeking money needs to know who has money, what kind of financing each source likes best, what the terms and conditions are likely to be, and whether the source has money available at the time. You will know the answers to these questions if you have followed the organized cataloguing procedure mentioned in the second preceding section and described in detail in Chapter 2.

Examples throughout this book illustrate approaches used by entrepreneurs familiar with insider's secrets of real estate investing. Doing your homework first is important in any approach. Suggestions for your preparation (your homework) are detailed in Chapter 8.

A part of your documentation for presentation to your selected source of money should be your personal financial statements. A sample Balance Sheet and Personal Data Form, suitable for an individual entrepreneur, are given in Chapter 19. Also, the financial sheets you present should include figures which show how you will be able to meet your loan obligations.

HOW TO UTILIZE YOUR LEGAL AND TAX COUNSELORS— PROFITABLY

In every expense connected with a real estate venture an entrepreneur is interested in the cost and in the benefits expected. And, of course, the costs and benefits expected from engaging legal and tax counsel are included. How to optimize the use of services by these professionals is described in detail in Chapter 19.

It is important, too, that your advisers act as devil's advocate on your proposed deals. A procedure I've tried and recommend is given in Chapter 19; it's called "Green Light"—"Red Light." An adviser who merely rubber stamps your attitudes and decisions can be very costly.

TAXES—AVOIDANCE WILL SPEED YOUR PROGRESS TO WEALTH

Obtaining the services of a good tax counselor can be the very best use of your money. Every taxpayer wants to minimize taxes, but the real estate investor is in a special position to do even more. Tax laws still treat real estate in a preferred way. Your tax adviser can help you structure deals to postpone or defer taxes. If you are buying, he can show you how to structure an agreement so as to allow the seller to get tax relief. You should be able to close more of your attempted deals and make more profit on each deal if you are knowledgeable in the tax area. Read Chapter 19 to learn how and to see how others have avoided taxes.

REMEMBER THESE POINTS

At the end of almost every chapter there is a summary and review of the keys to making a fortune in real estate and a list of points to remember. After you have read this book, I suggest that you reread the "Remember These Points" sections at the end of chapters. It is an excellent way to review; you may also be motivated by this review to reread certain chapters.

2

HIGH LEVERAGE SYNDICATES: USING OTHER PEOPLE'S MONEY FOR THEIR PROFIT AND YOURS

Whatever amount of money you may have on hand, whether it is $100 or $100,000, the use of insider's secrets to obtain high leverage will increase your profits and your rate of progress toward financial independence. You could, of course, use $100,000 to buy a five or six unit apartment building for cash and get a return on your investment of perhaps 10 to 12 percent. But even a moderate amount of leverage will improve your return on investment. The ordinary way of getting a modest amount of leverage is to pay 25 percent down and borrow 75 percent from a savings and loan company. The leverage is then the use of $3 of other people's money for every $1 you invest or, simply, a leverage of three-to-one. The insider's secrets presented in this chapter show how to obtain truly high leverage by use of one of the most powerful approaches known to insiders in real estate investment, that is, by syndicating.

An example in this chapter will show how an entrepreneur obtained the use of other people's money for an apartment building by syndicating and leveraging to infinity! He obtained a 50 percent interest in any profits he could generate and a monthly management fee without having a penny of his own tied up in the venture. Another example shows how to achieve similar high leverage results in commercial property.

A third example shows how you can get high leverage and increase your net worth without incurring any immediate tax liability. Again, the approach is to use other people's money by forming a syndicate.

A real estate entrepreneur will occasionally learn of an investment opportunity which is beyond his own financial capability but which offers a good profit potential. At a time when Mr. Brick R. had no available cash on hand he learned of just such an opportunity. Fortunately, he was acquainted with the insider's secrets of using other people's money by syndicating and he made use of his knowledge to the fullest.

HOW ONE ENTREPRENEUR REAPED 50% ($75,000) OF APARTMENT PROJECT PROFITS BY ORGANIZING A SYNDICATE TO FINANCE IT

Brick R., an active pharmacist and the owner of four pharmacies, had used the same bank for his business for 20 years. He formerly owned and managed a triplex and a quadruplex but had sold them two years earlier when he opened his fourth pharmacy. His banker was acquainted with his interest in and past participation in apartments. The banker mentioned that a client of the bank was interested in selling his 90 unit apartment complex.

Brick R. contacted the seller and was told that the price was $1,700,000 and that it was firm. Records on the apartments were made available.

The records showed an existing loan balance of $1,450,000 with eighteen years remaining of a 20 year loan obtained when the seller built the apartments two years previously. Inspection showed that the building had received generally good maintenance although some painting and minor repairs were needed. The cash flow, however, was *only* $19,000 per year. Brick R. also learned that four or five other possible buyers had inspected the property but declined to purchase it.

It is at this point in a real estate analysis that the difference shows up between a creative, innovative entrepreneur familiar with the inside secrets of real estate investments and one with "blinders on." The seller wanted "cash to existing loan," or $250,000 in this case. A cash flow of $19,000 would not justify investing $250,000 even if Brick R. had had the cash on hand. The cash flow was less than eight percent of the cash needed to make the purchase.

After considering all the possibilities of structuring the financing, Brick R. set to work. Two factors in his analysis caused him to be highly interested in the apartments. His investigation had revealed that prevailing rents in the area were somewhat higher than those charged for the 90 units. The questions he asked of savings and loan organizations convinced him that he could refinance the complex for a larger amount and for a longer time period and hold the debt service monthly payments somewhat less or the same as for the existing loan. Brick R. had evidently carried his analysis one or two steps further than had the investors who had already considered and rejected the property. This extra creative thinking was the direct result of Brick R.'s deliberately considering all of the insider's ways of structuring and managing an investment to convert it from one with a cash flow much too low into one with both good profits and good cash flow. It was this effort which set Brick R. apart from other investors who had seen the property. Furthermore, Brick R.'s banker said he would lend $5,000 to him on a personal, unsecured note upon request.

Brick R. approached the seller on the basis of purchasing the property using a 60 day escrow, with a $5,000 deposit by Brick R., and with the purchase being contingent upon obtaining financing. The deposit was non-refundable if the purchase was not consummated. Brick R. told the seller that he did not have the remaining $245,000 but that he was confident he could form a syndicate with the investors paying the full amount into escrow within the 60 day period. Inasmuch as the seller was being offered the full purchase price and he had already failed to sell to previous prospects, he agreed to the terms.

Brick R. prepared a prospectus for the venture including a synopsis of the purchase, limited partnership agreement, financial factors on the property, and a letter of intent for the future partners. His attorney, a specialist in real estate, assisted Brick R. to ensure compliance with state law. The prospectus provided for a modest monthly management fee for Brick R. to manage the apartments and a provision for him to receive 50 percent of the profit when and if the property was sold. Brick R.'s tax attorney gave the opinion that Brick R.'s share of the profit would be treated as a capital gain if sufficient time elapsed between purchase and sale.

Brick R. made a presentation first to one investor, including the plan for refinancing. His reason for selecting only one investor was to test his approach, to see if it needed revision before presenting to others less well known by himself. A second presentation to four additional investors resulted in commitments for $50,000 each. The total of $250,000 was paid into escrow and Brick R.'s $5,000 was returned to him. Brick R. paid off his personal debt of $5,000. At this point, he had achieved the highest leverage possible. *All* money in the project was other people's money. The ratio of other people's money to his own was infinity!

The minor repairs and painting were done. A more extensive survey of rent levels in the area supported Brick R.'s preliminary determination that their apartments were being rented below market. The rents were raised accordingly. Based in part upon the increased rents, Brick R.'s application for a $1,725,000 mortgage for 30 years was approved. The longer term on the loan resulted in monthly payments of principal and interest being less than on the previous loan. The cash flow was increased to $28,000 per year.

Thirteen months after buying the property, it was sold for slightly more than $1,850,000. Brick R. received $75,000 as his share of the $150,000 profit. Each of the five investors had received his initial $50,000 back when the project was refinanced and each received $15,000 as his share of the profits. The project had yielded a 60 percent capital gains profit on the initial $250,000 invested. Each hard-cash investor had received a capital gain profit of $15,000 for $50,000 invested for seven months!

You, too, can use this approach and these insider's secrets. The essentials are to find a property with potential for capital gain, get control of it, and find investors for forming a syndicate.

BEST BETS FOR PROFITS IN INCOME PROPERTY—
HOW TO MAXIMIZE YOUR PROFIT

The "best bets" for a "fast" capital gain in income property are those properties which have been mismanaged. If a property is currently showing a low net income you should be able to buy it at a "right price." If you can then correct any mismanagement practices (or be an aggressive manager instead of a passive one) and increase the net income, you can sell for top dollar.

For example, mismanaged apartment buildings commonly show one or more of the following deficiencies in management.

1. Lack of paint and poor outside appearance—use decorator chosen "modern" colors; make it look sharp.

HIGH LEVERAGE SYNDICATES

2. Lack of repairs—get competitive bids; be able to show a well maintained building before you resell it.
3. Outdated or shabby lobby—remodel or renovate; with artistic creativity you can minimize the costs.
4. Covered parking—tenants will pay more rent if you add covered parking (versus parking in an open lot).
5. Excessive operating expenses—expenses can frequently be reduced by:
   a. installing a master electricity meter for your apartment complex and buy in quantity; charging your tenants based on their individual meters.
   b. getting competitive bids from lawn care companies, swimming pool services, and pest control companies.
   c. changing from service companies to a full time maintenance man (or conversely) to handle items listed in 5b; compare the costs.
   d. reducing the thermostat to deliver water at 90°F at use point if you're paying the bill.
   e. reducing lighting level in parking areas and other common areas. (The recommended level by the Federal Energy Administration is one foot candle for parking lots).
6. Underpriced rents—some owners or apartment managers simply do not increase rents as rapidly as others in their neighborhood. A well managed apartment building will have rent levels which are up to date and competitive.
7. Poor cash flow—both the net income (profit) and the cash flow generated affect the market value in selling your property. Refinancing a loan to get a longer term loan and/or a lower interest rate will improve the cash flow.

Note: In the previous example, note that Brick R. painted, repaired, and raised rents to market level to improve the net income. He then refinanced to increase the cash flow. And he sold for a handsome profit!

Also, note that Brick R. gained control of the property by entering escrow with a non-refundable deposit and with the purchase being contingent upon obtaining necessary financing. With this contingency he had no further liability beyond his initial deposit if he didn't consummate the purchase. An option to purchase is another powerful way of gaining control for a limited time period. Read Chapters 3, 4, and 5 to learn the insider's secrets of using an option.

How to find investors for a syndication is a whole subject in itself.

The next section will provide you with helpful guidelines and suggestions.

HOW TO FIND SYNDICATE INVESTORS

Before contacting anyone, check with your attorney—one who specializes in real estate—to become acquainted with the laws limiting and controlling real estate syndicates in your state.

Your friends, relatives, and acquaintances are prime candidates for investing in a so called "private" real estate syndicate. If you need only two or three syndicate investors and can identify them readily, then "flying by the seat of your pants" may suffice. A longer range outlook involves a methodical approach. If you have not already developed your own organized approach then this section will be of special benefit to you. The suggestions herein are intended only as an example. Alter or add to the example to suit your mode of operation.

Make a list—or better yet—prepare a 3" x 5" or 4" x 6" file card on every prospective investor. Estimate and record the amount each prospect might contribute to a real estate syndicated venture. Add names to your list by going through your address book, your personal telephone index, and Christmas card list. A particularly good possibility is anyone who has just sold his apartment house, shopping center, or other real estate holdings. Be sure to make use of the "ripple effect," i.e., at the appropriate time ask bankers, attorneys, fellow club members, and each prospect if he knows of others with a possible interest in syndicating.

Likely syndicate prospects

Even though you may have used the syndicate approach previously, read the list given below of likely prospects for investors in your future syndicated ventures. You may have overlooked whole categories of potential investors.

Don't hesitate to contact friends and relatives. We all have heard the old cliche about not doing business with close friends and relatives. If, however, you have found a good investment opportunity you are doing them a favor by allowing them to participate in the investment.

The list below is certainly not all inclusive; your own creative thinking can yield additional types of prospects for your list. Many of those on the list can also assist you by suggesting other prospective investors.

Accountants
Active investors in real estate

HIGH LEVERAGE SYNDICATES

Actors/Actresses
Attorneys
Automobile dealers
Bankers
Baseball players/other sports figures
Boat owners
Businessmen—many types
Certified public accountants
Club members
Corporation executives
Dentists
Engineers
Farmers
Friends
Golfers
Judges
Managers for professional people
Mortgage brokers
Musicians
Pharmacists
Physicians
Pilots
Professional people—many types
Professors
Ranchers
Real estate brokers
Real estate management companies
Relatives
Savings and loan companies
Scientists
Singers
Surgeons
Teachers

Organize investor information

Contact each prospect and determine his interest in investing. Check your estimate on the probable amount of capital the prospect has available for investment. Determine and record the nature of a venture which would appeal to him, e.g., whether he prefers to invest for income, or for a chance at long term capital gains, or to shelter current high ordinary income from taxes. Note his age, occupation, and family information (including the ages of his children). Determine whether each prospect is primarily a high risk/high gain or low risk/low gain investor. Note, particularly, each one's interest in high leverage.

Summarize your information on a file card. A sample card on "John Q. Doe" is given below. It is intended as a guide only; change the format and type of information to suit your mode of operation.

DOE, JOHN Q.	Born Approx. 1928
1000 Maple Drive	Dentist
Middletown, Ohio	Married 22 yr. (Jane)
Orig. Card Date _____	Children: Bart (21), Joan (19), Susan (18)

(orig.) (date)	Would invest appr. $20,000—$40,000 in new real estate venture.
"	Likes tax shelter, capital gains—not interested ordinary income.
"	Likes high risk with proportionate potential.
"	Likes high leverage.
"	Probably personally sign heavy obligation unless CPA (Paul Doakes) strongly objected.
"	Much too busy to participate in seeking/managing real estate investment.
"	Has money in blue chip stocks, silver bullion, and a shopping center, 4300 Main St.
"	Likes to diversify investments.
"	Probably retire w/i ten years and travel.
"	Checks investments with his CPA and makes own decision.
(New) (Date)	Just sold his shopping center for $340,000. He owned 50%; partner was Roger Stokes.
(New) (Date)	His attorney is Lawrence Cunningham.

As time goes on, it will benefit you to keep each card up to date. Each entry on the card should be dated. For example, if John Doe were to sell his blue chip stocks and put the money in more silver bullion, you need to know how this change in his investments affects his attitude in your future real estate ventures. At least, record the change he made on your file card even though you probably will not make an immediate effort to determine his updated interest in real estate.

If your list is long enough and if your potential investors differ enough in their interests and financial goals, you should be able to form

HIGH LEVERAGE SYNDICATES 33

a syndicate on almost any worthwhile venture you discover and structure.

Above all, always deliberately think through many possible ways of structuring a venture and financing it. Note in the prior example and the following one that the entrepreneurs sought out investors with similar interests and whose goals coincided with the potential of the proposed real estate venture.

HOW A SYNDICATED COMMERCIAL PROPERTY PUT $20,000 PER YEAR IN POCKET OF ORGANIZER

John P. was an automobile mechanic with an income barely sufficient to support his wife and two children and meet the monthly payments on their mortgaged home. He had developed an interest in real estate investment but had no capital with which to start.

He set as a goal the generation of sufficient personal income from a real estate venture to allow him to devote full time to real estate.

John P. located a small suburban shopping center priced at $1,250,000. It was less than five miles from his home. The eight year old center had an existing loan balance of approximately $800,000. The cash flow was $25,000 per year. After much talk, the seller agreed to give John P. a 30 day option for only $3,000 or a 60 day option for $6,000. John P. borrowed $3,000 on his personal assets and paid for a 30 day option to purchase. The agreement contained a provision that the option would be extended for another 30 days if an additional $3,000 was paid to the seller within the initial 30 day period. Said payments would be credited to the purchase price if the option were exercised.

John P. assembled financial and historical data on the shopping center. He prepared proforma statements showing projected profits and cash flow after making certain specified changes, made up his own personal financial statement, and applied for a $1,250,000 loan at the savings and loan association which held the existing mortgage. He was told that the property would probably qualify for the requested loan, but that he himself did not have sufficient financial strength for them to accept his signature on the loan.

John P. then approached three professional men who were experienced in real estate investments, but whose work would not permit their active involvement in seeking real estate investment opportunities or in managing them. He proposed that these men furnish $3,000 immediately to extend the option and (1) furnish enough capital (approximately $125,000) to qualify for a loan with slightly lower interest rate or (2) agree to sign for the full loan of $1,250,000. John P. also proposed that he would receive 50 percent of the cash flow as a fee for management and 50 percent of the profits when the center was resold. Two of the three investors were interested. They agreed to the second alternate proposal except that the three of them, including John P., would each receive 33 ⅓ percent of any profits realized and John P. would receive ⅔ of the cash flow as compensation for management. On the 28th day, the two investors signed an agreement with John P. and paid another $3,000 to the seller for the 30 day extension per the original option. A loan of $1,250,000 for 30 years was obtained and the property purchased within the option period.

The slightly lower payments for the longer term loan and a change in three tenants resulted in an increase in cash flow to the rate of $30,000 per year. Thus, John P. had an income of $20,000 per year without a penny of his own invested! He had accomplished one of his principal objectives. Even the $3,000 he originally paid for the option had been returned to him. He had taken an important step toward a full-time career in real estate investment and had no money tied up in the venture. He quit his job and began a search for another venture while managing the property just acquired.

The two investors were more than pleased. With the risk of signing the loan, they were in a position to realize long term capital gains and had not committed any cash to the venture. All three men had leveraged to infinity!

HOW TO SET YOUR REAL ESTATE INVESTMENT GOALS

Whether you are about to enter your first or twenty-fifth real estate venture, write out your goals for each project. In the previous example, John P. set a goal of generating enough monthly income to allow him to quit his eight-to-five job and devote full time to real estate. It was a difficult goal, but he achieved it by setting it and working toward it.

It is important that you do a *complete* job of writing down your goals. Some goals are directly related to the business of making money in real estate. Other goals are highly personal. For example, you may have had a desire for years to live near a beach or in the desert. If you want to satisfy a personal desire as well as make profits in real estate, include the personal goal in your list of written goals. The following list of goals includes both "business-like" and personal goals.

- Build fortune with other people's money
- Build net worth without immediate tax liability

HIGH LEVERAGE SYNDICATES

- Build up estate for children
- Diversify investments
- Enjoyment
- Generate long-term, permanent income
- Health benefits
- High leverage
- High risk/high gain ventures
- Income to allow full time effort in real estate
- Low risk investments
- Move to beach
- Move to desert
- Prestige
- Pride of ownership
- Profit
- Retire with income
- Syndication
- Tax shelter for high current income

Your own goals may be listed only in part in the above list. Making profits and building a fortune are, of course, prime goals. It's your life, your money and time—put in writing the goals you want.

CHOOSE BOTH THE PROPERTY FOR SYNDICATION AND THE SYNDICATE INVESTORS TO SUIT YOUR GOALS

As you are seeking property which you may decide to syndicate, keep your goals in mind. When you start to analyze a potential investment, determine whether it will help you reach your goals. If there is not a fit between the potential benefits of the project and your previously written goals, reexamine both the project and your goals. Whether your reexamination results in dropping the project or writing a new set of goals, you will have benefited by the exercise. If you rewrite your goals, you may have brought them in better alignment with the market place and kept them consistent with your needs and desires. If you drop the project, you will have avoided getting involved in a project not suited to your goals. This inside secret of time-tested, successful entrepreneurs is one of the reasons they became successful. A project which potentially fits your particular needs and goals is one which is more likely to be successful financially and to bring you increased personal satisfaction.

Your financial analysis of a project should include:

- Projection of total gross income (with annotations on the basis for your figures, e.g., "increase rents to make equal to prevailing rates").
- Vacancy factor (if you claim a better factor than the historical one, give your justification).
- Taxes (be sure your information is up to date).
- Maintenance (back up information is needed).
- Management fees (can you do better than the previous owner?).
- Debt service (you may need two columns on your analysis sheet—to show figures for servicing current debt and new figures for specified refinancing).
- All other expenses (cover them in detail with supporting information).
- Net income and cash flow projections (your projected net income (profit) and cash flow figures are subject to challenge by anyone you're asking to finance your venture; all items affecting these two quantities should be double checked).

Depending upon your goals and needs, added tax benefits from depreciation and future profit from selling the property may also be important. Once you have evaluated the financial potential of the project, determined its compatibility with your written goals and have decided to form a syndicate, turn your attention to choosing the particular type of investor needed and the form of syndication. It is essential that the goals of each investor be compatible with your own, with the goals of other investors, and with the potential of the venture. An investor with low, current income who wants to increase his income will be at odds with an investor who wants "tax shelter" for high current income and to defer taxes to a future year.

As an example, let's consider an entrepreneur who knew and followed the inside secrets discussed above.

THE INSIDER'S SECRET OF BUILDING NET WORTH WITH HIGH LEVERAGE AND WITHOUT INCURRING TAXES

Tom T. is an experienced, knowledgeable, and active real estate investor. His experience and extensive reading has made him aware of most of the insider's secrets in real estate investment and management. He recently sold his shopping center for a comfortable, long term capital gain. He is currently involved in two large apartment complexes

HIGH LEVERAGE SYNDICATES 37

which he had syndicated and is managing. His card files contain detailed information on more than 75 investors in the real estate field. Over the years, he has been involved in real estate ventures with several of them.

It was not until Tom T. sat down to rewrite his goals in real estate that he realized it had been more than five years since he had reexamined his goals. At the age of 52 and with his much improved financial position, he was overdue for the reexamination.

He set a goal of finding property with a good potential for appreciation in value. He did not set a requirement for current income. His search revealed a section (640 acres) of land which investigation showed to be in the path of urban growth. The price was $1,200 per acre or $768,000 for the parcel. Taxes on the agriculturally zoned land were low. The property had no buildings on it. It was being rented on an annual basis for agriculture. The owner (seller) was an elderly man who was not interested in cashing out. His objective was to sell and move to another state upon the advice of his physician. The seller offered terms of 29 percent down with the 71 percent balance to be paid in ten equal installments plus 7 percent interest. Tom T.'s offer of $10,000 for a 30 day option was accepted.

Tom T.'s further investigation indicated that the property would be "right" for development within 7 to 15 years, depending upon the degree of prosperity and growth in the area. He selected four names from his card files. All four were currently involved in real estate investments, but they had consistently avoided being involved in management of real estate. Each of the four had a net worth approximately equal to Tom T.'s and each had a high annual income. Until now, Tom T.'s goals had not been compatible with the goals of the investors under consideration; he had not been previously involved with them in a syndicate.

At a meeting with all four, Tom T. proposed a syndicate in the form of a five-way general partnership with each partner sharing equally in any future profits. Tom T. proposed transferring his option to the partnership in exchange for his one-fifth interest in profits. He also required that the four investors (1) provide $75,000 each to make the initial payment of 29 percent ($223,720) and provide a cash reserve for the partnership and (2) agree to make the 10 installment payments as provided in the option agreement. The four agreed after obtaining a commitment from Tom T. to (1) subordinate any profits to which he might have a claim (including profits from a possible sale of a portion of the 640 acres) until their cash inputs had been returned in full, (2) manage the property, (3) monitor the property for any changes in value, and (4) present an annual oral report. Tom T.'s attorney prepared the partnership agreement and they exercised the option.

At the second annual meeting of the partners, Tom T. reported that nearby smaller but comparable properties had recently sold for $1,600 to $1,750 per acre. Thus the net worth of the partners had increased by approximately $300,000. And they had the leverage provided by the seller's financing of 71 percent of the original value of the land. The original input of $300,000 cash and two subsequent payments of approximately $90,000 per year totaled $480,000 by the end of the second year. Their increase in net worth was more than 62 percent of the total amount they had invested over a two year period. Furthermore, they had realized tax benefits from the $38,000 per year interest and other deductible expenses they had paid. Their increase in net worth was not taxable since they had not yet sold the property. They decided to continue to hold the property.

What Tom T. did by syndication you can do also. With only $10,000 in the project, his net worth had increased by $60,000 in two years. Whatever the dollar level of your proposed syndication, note the key elements in Tom T.'s syndication. He (1) selected property in the path of urban growth, (2) determined that it met his new, revised personal goals, (3) gained control of the property with an option, and (4) selected fellow syndicators with desires, goals, and financial status comparable to his own. Tom T. also knew and understood the principle of leverage and used it to get high leverage with his original $10,000 invested.

A SUCCESSFUL SYNDICATION SETS STAGE FOR LARGER PROJECTS

In the example above, Tom T. was a highly experienced entrepreneur who was already established as a successful syndicator. On the other hand, John P. used the syndication approach in his first real estate venture for profit. Whatever your past experience has been in real estate ventures, consider syndicating as one of the possible alternates in financing real estate investments. In fact, if your analysis indicates that syndicating and some other way of financing a project rank approximately equal and if you have not used the syndicate approach, I suggest you syndicate your next venture. One successful syndication will establish your credibility as a syndicator. It will pave the way for even larger syndications in the future. Who knows—your analysis of the next large property you consider might strongly require the syndication approach. With your credibility already established in a

HIGH LEVERAGE SYNDICATES

small syndicated project you will be in a position for syndicating a large venture.

Also, if the investors in your first syndication are not interested in everyday management of real estate, they should become primary references for both other investors and for leads on properties.

THE BIGGEST INSIDE SECRETS OF SYNDICATING—
—NINE KEYS TO SUCCESSFUL SYNDICATION

1. Be sure to consider all possible alternate ways of financing a real estate venture. Consider syndicating as one of the alternates. Choose syndicating if it is the top choice consistent with your goals and desires.
2. Be sure to use the services of an attorney who specializes in real estate. Remember that an attorney primarily functions to insure your compliance with the laws of your state and to provide an easily understood, non ambiguous contract to keep you out of the courts; depend upon yourself for the business aspects.
3. Consult with a tax specialist with experience in real estate. Make sure your tax adviser understands your goals so he can advise you to your best interests. For example, if you want to shelter current high income he must know it; he can help you do a much better job with his intimate and up to date knowledge of tax regulations.
4. "Syndicate" is not a specific legal term. To syndicate simply means to form a group of people for investment purposes. Be sure to consider the various legal ways of forming a syndicate. The usual forms used are a General Partnership, Limited Partnership, Corporation, or Subchapter S Corporation. Consult with both your attorney and tax adviser before choosing the legal form.
5. Don't use the Tenants in Common form of syndicating. Because each tenant in common can select his own formula for depreciation, some syndicators have used this form. It is better to choose investors with compatible interests including the method of depreciation.
6. Don't use the Joint Tenancy form of syndicating. Your attorney can tell you the impracticability of this approach for holding title if there are non-related investors.
7. Choose investors with (a) comparable net worth, (b) similar incomes or lack of need for an income, (c) same age bracket, and (d) compatible personalities.

8. Choose the legal form of syndication which suits your investors. For example, if three potential investors are highly interested in depreciation for tax reasons and one is not, it would be advisable to find another investor rather than include the one who is not compatible.
9. A pre-formed syndicate with cash already in hand allows you to move quickly when a property is located. With the cash in, you can't get caught short by someone failing to come up with his pledged investment. On the other hand, locating the property first and perhaps gaining control with an option may have tax advantages for you and result in exceptionally high leverage on your part. It also allows you the freedom of seeking investors to suit the project. Choose the approach which fits your preferred mode of operation.

REMEMBER THESE POINTS

- Put your investment goals in writing. Include both business objectives and personal wants.
- Reexamine your written goals frequently and keep them up to date. They must be in accord with the market place.
- Consider syndication but always also deliberately consider other possible means of financing a real estate venture.
- Choose and use an attorney with real estate experience.
- Choose and use a tax consultant with real estate experience.
- You are responsible for all business decisions; you are the one who will enjoy or suffer the consequences.
- Choose between (1) a pre-formed syndicate and (2) finding the property before forming a syndicate.

3

USING OPTIONS TO GAIN CONTROL OF APARTMENTS AND GET HIGH PROFITS

Any ambitious entrepreneur who learns the many and varied possible uses of options will surely frequently use the option-to-purchase approach in investing in apartment buildings. Examples given in Chapter 2 showed that the syndication approach is one of the most powerful insider's secrets for the financing of apartments and other types of real estate ventures. An option itself is not a direct means of financing your apartment venture, but it does provide for the time needed to structure financing for your own high leverage goal and to obtain the financing.

In this chapter I'll describe how an investor wisely used the option approach to allow himself time to fully evaluate an apartment complex and how he cleared $50,000. A second example shows how a man with only $3,000 available used an option to ensure he could handle the conversion of a house to five apartments and how he earned 65 percent per year on the money he invested. For him, it was a substantial step along the road to financial independence. Still another example describes an entrepreneur who found an opportunity to get high leverage and a high return on investment in an apartment building. The building was in a segment of the real estate investment field in which he had no direct experience. The option he obtained allowed the needed time to make a full evaluation.

If you take the time to make a thorough evaluation before gaining control of an apartment building, you may find that you have lost an opportunity to another buyer. Also, many proposed investments are of such complexity that use of an option to purchase is a wise approach. The first example given in this chapter shows how Andrew K. used an option under such circumstances and how he made a big profit even though he never exercised the option.

WHY USE THE OPTION-TO-PURCHASE APPROACH IN APARTMENT INVESTMENT

An entrepreneur with very little or no money to invest in apartments or other real estate has a powerful tool in the option approach. The use of an option is not the only way for such a person to reach for profits, but it is a highly recommended approach. A key factor is that you can gain control of an apartment complex for a limited period of time with very little money committed and with no obligations or further liability if the option is not exercised.

There are several possible reasons for wanting to gain control. You may wish to gain control to allow needed time to structure the overall project and to line up the financing. Without having control of the property, you might find, after a considerable amount of work, that it was sold to another just before you arranged the necessary financing to purchase it.

Another important reason for using the option approach is to allow you to make a more thorough investigation. For example, the seller may have incorrectly stated that his property can be rezoned easily, say, to allow the construction of additional apartment units on the same site and that there is no filled ground on the property. Whether he has deliberately or innocently misrepresented, it is important that you, as an investor, find it out before completing the purchase. You might be able to recoup your money and the money you persuaded others to invest after closing a deal, but lawsuits are expensive and non-productive. An entrepreneur must maintain his reputation for ferreting out profitable deals. He must keep his attention on productive efforts only.

TO GAIN CONTROL OF APARTMENTS

Your time, money and reputation are all important; avoid non-productive encounters.

You should, of course, consider all possible uses of available real estate. Always consider the highest and best use of a property and analyze it with respect to profits for yourself. In many cases, you will need time to determine that there is a market for your planned use of the property. An option, tying up the property for a specified time period, will give you time to evaluate it thoroughly. And, of course, an option ensures that the property will be available to you if it stands up under your investigation. The risk you take is that the amount you pay for the option may be forfeited if you decide not to exercise it and not to consummate the purchase. In most cases, the money paid for the option is non-refundable.

HOW THE OPTION APPROACH NETTED $50,000 PROFIT ON 60 UNIT APARTMENT BUILDING

Five years earlier, Andrew K. had acquired an eight unit apartment building and a ten unit one located approximately two blocks apart. Both buildings were on his mail route. For the past six years of his 23 years with the U.S. Postal Service he had delivered mail in the same area. With the help of Mrs. K., he was personally managing the apartments on a part time basis and obtaining a good return on his investment. He was actively looking for an 18 or 20 unit building when he heard of a 60 unit one. It was priced at $1,050,000 and had been on the market for two months. Accounting records showed a gross income of $173,000 for the past year and a vacancy factor of four percent. The seller was the original owner of the nine year old apartment complex.

Andrew K. offered $5,000 in payment for a 60 day option with the $5,000 to be credited on the purchase price if the option was exercised. The seller granted the option. Andrew K. immediately approached two lending institutions. He found that the rumors he had heard about "tight money" were true. The conventional sources for borrowing were "short of funds." They had recently experienced "disintermediation," which is a seven syllable way of saying that depositors in savings and loan companies had withdrawn their funds to buy certificates of deposit and short term government bonds which were currently yielding appreciably higher returns. A credit crunch was in full swing. The bad news was not a complete surprise to Andrew K. but it was worse than he had anticipated. Even his offer to pledge his built-up equity in his other two apartment buildings did not help. By this time eleven days of the 60 day option period had passed.

Andrew K. approached three private investors with a proposal for sharing income, sharing any future profit from a sale, and a management fee for himself. All three investors were impressed by the quality of the venture, but were fully committed on previous investments. The fourth man he approached (on the seventeenth day) was a counselor and investment manager for a group of professional men. Andrew K.'s proposal to him was similar to the one he had presented to the first three. The investment manager took all information on the project and promised a prompt response. Three days later (the twentieth day of the option) he rejected Andrew K.'s offer, but offered to pay him $30,000 for the option with no further involvement by Andrew K. What had happened in this case was that Andrew K. had encountered a man who was at least a semi-competitor. The investment manager had evidently weighed the alternates of paying $30,000 to wrap up the deal for himself and his clients versus the possibility of Andrew K. locating other private investors during the remaining 40 days of the 60 day option.

At this point Andrew K. found himself vacillating. He had to choose between a sure and quick profit or gamble on lining up the financing within what remained of the time period in his option. One personal factor was that he had seven years to go before retirement from the Postal Service. He finally made a counter offer to sell the option for $50,000; it was accepted. When the investment manager exercised the option, Andrew K.'s initial $5,000 was returned to him. By tying up $5,000 for 25 days, Andrew K. had made $50,000 profit! His profit was more than five times his annual take-home pay from the Postal Service.

In this example, Andrew K. illustrates another characteristic of the successful real estate entrepreneur, i.e., flexibility. He had the knowledge and expertise to recognize a good investment and the entrepreneur's flexibility to accept an alternate way to profit when his original plan appeared to be bogged down.

You can benefit from this example. Do not freeze your thinking into a single-minded approach. If you gain temporary control of property by means of an option, keep your thinking open to alternates to the approach you have chosen as the most likely or desirable. Andrew K. had not even considered the possibility of selling the option until he received an offer, but he had the flexibility to accept it as a logical, profitable alternate to his original plan.

HOW TO USE AN OPTION

By definition, an option-to-purchase in real estate is a short term agreement between the owner (seller) of the property and a potential buyer wherein the buyer gains the right to purchase the property if he does so within the time period specified in the option agreement. The seller cannot sell to another during that same time period. It is important that the option agreement be as complete as an ordinary purchase agreement. It should specify the total purchase price, the terms of payment, and any other terms or conditions pertinent to the purchase. It must also specify the amount of money (consideration) paid by the buyer for the option itself and whether any money deposited is to be forfeited if the option is not exercised. Also, the agreement should specify whether the consideration paid is to apply toward the purchase price if the option is exercised. If an option is not exercised within the prescribed time period, it is automatically void and the seller is again free to sell to anyone.

An example, which illustrates legal format and words used in an agreement to cover the above key points (relating to an option to purchase), follows.

OPTION TO PURCHASE A PROPERTY

AGREEMENT made this _____ day of _____, 19__ between ____(name)____, ____(address)____, hereinafter described as Seller and ____(name)____, ____(address)____, hereinafter described as Buyer.

WITNESSETH,
1) that for and in consideration of the sum of one dollar ($1.00) in hand paid and other valuable considerations, the receipt and sufficiency of which are hereby acknowledged by Seller, Seller offers and agrees to sell and convey to Buyer, and hereby grants to Buyer the exclusive and irrevocable option, right and privilege of purchasing, under the conditions hereinafter provided, the following land with the buildings and improvements thereon, located in the ____(city)____ of _____ County, State of _____, described as: _____(legal description)_____
for the sum of _____ dollars ($_____); the amount being in addition to the one dollar ($1.00) above mentioned.

2) Notice of election to purchase hereunder shall be given by Buyer in writing by delivering said written notice in person or by registered mail to Seller on or before ___(time)___, _____, 19__.

The preceding two paragraphs are those which pertain to the option portion of the overall agreement. As mentioned previously, the balance of the agreement should be as detailed and complete as a purchase agreement without an option proviso.

There is one point which is sometimes overlooked even by investors familiar with the insider's secrets of real estate investment. If you obtain the optionor's (Seller's) approval to extend the optionee's (Buyer's) time period for exercise, have your attorney put it in writing. And be sure to pay an extra consideration for the extension, even if your payment is only $1.

Even though it is important for you, the entrepreneur, to be familiar with the insider's secrets of the application of options, use an attorney to prepare the legal document. Laws differ from state to state; an option agreement you may have used in California may not comply with the law in Florida even though the investment factors may be essentially identical. Even if all of your real estate is within a single state, laws change; a new or revised law may affect your project. A good attorney will also provide an agreement which is non-ambiguous and is easily understood and interpreted. A well written contract can avoid your getting involved in disagreements which lead to court action. You are the one who must make the financial and analytical judgments but use an attorney—one specializing in real estate—for preparation of all contracts, including options.

There is no better way to increase your knowledge of how to use the option approach than by studying examples of how others used options to their advantage. The following example shows how Mr. Richard S. used an option for self protection in what might well have been a losing investment. Follow his example if you unearth a similar investment opportunity or if in any real estate project you feel a double check is advisable.

HOW THE OPTION APPROACH MINIMIZED RISK AND RETURNED SIXTY-FIVE PERCENT ON AN INVESTMENT

Richard S. was a 42 year old carpenter with experience in rough carpentry and cabinetry. During a local lull in house building he worked an average of two days per week during the previous three months. He learned of a large old house, built the year he was born, which was for sale for $38,000. It was located on a corner lot three blocks from a major university. It appeared to Richard S. that the house could be divided into four apartments and that he could do much of the work himself. A large room with bath over a three car garage would become a fifth apartment. He learned that a larger house on the corner diagonally across the street had been divided into six apartments.

Richard S. had not had the experience of remodeling an older structure and was not familiar with plumbing, heating, and electrical costs. Knowledge of remodeling costs is, of course, absolutely essential in the analysis of a project of this type. He decided to attempt to gain control of the property for a long enough period to allow a thorough analysis. The attorney handling the sale for the estate which owned the property did not know whether the zoning department would allow conversion to apartment units. The attorney, who was not a specialist in real estate, declined to make any commitment and said he would prefer that Richard S. do his own checking. After summing up all of these factors, Richard S. decided to use the option approach.

Richard S.'s offer of $1,000 for a 30 day option was accepted. His purpose was to gain time to check (1) whether the city's zoning department would allow him to convert the house and garage room into five apartments, (2) the total costs of the conversion, and (3) the market for small apartments. The option was his guarantee that the property would become his if he decided to go ahead within 30 days. On the other hand, if he decided not to consummate the purchase for any reason, including the three listed above, he would not have to complete it and would have no further liability.

The university housing office assured him that there were students waiting for nearby apartments and that the demand was high even during the summer months. The Building Department verified that the property was already zoned for either new apartments or conversions. The estimates for costs of overall remodeling were within Richard S.'s expectation. He exercised the option and closed the deal. He hired tradesmen for some of the remodeling and did the rest himself. After refinancing the property he had only $3,000 of his own money in the property. He had achieved a high leverage of almost sixteen to one! Within a few months, his remodeled building was yielding an annualized net income equal to 65 percent of the cash he had invested. Richard S. had worked for others all of his life. After success on this small project he began aggressively searching for a similar but larger opportunity. He was on his way to financial independence.

Although the above example was for a "small deal," there are fundamental points involved. You, too, can protect yourself and at the same time gain temporary control of property as Richard S. did by using the option approach. An option gives you time to check out assumptions in your financial analysis, e.g., projected gross income, the vacancy factor, and pricing by your local competitors. If you plan to change the use of the property, such as conversion of a house to apartments, it is only prudent to double check government regulations. Do not assume that you can change the use of newly acquired property and use it in the same way as someone across the street or even next door.

Older apartment buildings or large, older houses (convertible to apartments) in some sections of a city can be excellent investments, but it is advisable to check them carefully. The following example describes Benjamin G.'s use of an option to allow time for a thorough investigation.

OPTION ON 45 YEAR OLD APARTMENT ALLOWS INVESTIGATION

Benjamim G. had purchased a quadruplex 12 years previously. He and Mrs. G. lived in one of the units. For 30 years he and Mrs. G. had owned and operated a small shop four blocks from their quadruplex. The government had condemned the commercial building, including their shop, for a new freeway right of way. They had sold their inventory and were looking for an income producing investment.

A 45 year old apartment building with 30 units was for sale for $320,000. The building was located ½ mile from Benjamin G.'s old shop. It contained ten two-bedroom apartments, ten one-bedroom units, and ten singles. There was off street parking for 12 cars.

Benjamin G. obtained financial records and rental history on the building from the seller's real estate broker. The broker stated that the seller would carry a large second mortgage at a desirable interest rate. The generous financing would enable Benjamin G. to get the high leverage which entrepreneurs strive so hard to get. Based upon the projected gross income and with a five percent allowance for vacancies, his analysis showed a return on investment of almost 25 percent! His natural caution led him to offer $1,000 for a 30 day option on the property at the full asking price. The seller, upon the advice of his broker, granted the option.

Benjamin G. called upon managers and owners of other income properties in the neighborhood. He found that the schedule of rents presented by the broker were, if anything, slightly below local prevailing rates. He also learned, by talking with the managers of a 28 and a 38 unit building, that they had started renting on a month-to-month basis with no security deposit within the past one and one-half years. One even had three units rented on a weekly basis. The managers were vociferous in their complaints about their newer tenants' treatment of their apartments. It appeared to him that the area had become less desirable within the past two years.

He then called upon senior loan officers of two savings and loan companies and a bank. Two of the three loan officers were of the opinion that the area was deteriorating. The third was hopeful that it would be upgraded.

Benjamin G. had seen another area of the city deteriorate in an amazingly short time once it started downhill. He informed the broker that he had reluctantly decided not to exercise the option. His use of the option approach to make an investigation saved him from making an investment which he might well have regretted.

Fundamentally, what Benjamin G. had done was to look ahead to predict the future of the neighborhood and of the property itself. Even though the property offered a good return in the near term and a highly leveraged investment, he decided it was too risky to depend upon the neighborhood upgrading to provide a good return in the future. He believed that the deterioration could well mean a much reduced profit in less than two years.

In fact, if you are investing in an apartment building to provide income for several years, the future quality of the neighborhood is extremely important. A general discussion of apartment area deterioration (neighborhood blight) is given in the following section.

HOW TO EVALUATE AN INVESTMENT'S POTENTIAL

Any knowledgeable investor considering low-priced, residential income property (whether it is a rooming house, duplex, or apartment building) should evaluate the future of a neighborhood. He will estimate whether the area is deteriorating, stable, or upgrading. A first step is to rate the property and area as of the present. A rating schedule used by some investors is: Excellent, Good, Acceptable, Marginal, and Blighted. Only marginal property will offer the high return on investment which Benjamin G. found in the previous example. If, however, the surrounding is deteriorating, such a high return will last only a short time.

If "creeping blight" is underway in a neighborhood it will change an acceptable neighborhood into a marginal one and a marginal one into an area wherein owners are losing money. Families whose standard of living is increasing will move from an acceptable or marginal neighborhood into a more desirable area as the deterioration continues. They will not accept the gradual decrease in cleanliness and maintenance. In comparison with tenants who leave, those who stay will be those who care less for the condition of the neighborhood. There will be a tendency for the vacated units to be filled by new tenants who also are not concerned about cleanliness and maintenance. As time passes there tends to be an acceleration of neighborhood blight. Then, "For Rent" signs tend to appear on every building even though there may be a shortage of available units in clean, well maintained buildings only a fairly short distance away. By the time blight has spread to this degree, your investment in a low-priced, high-return-on-investment building only two years earlier may well be in a money losing position instead of showing a profit.

In some cities the final blow comes when the city's Building Department issues an order to bring the building up to "City Standards" or to raze it. In such cases, some owners have simply let the lender foreclose. They lost all or most of the equity they had in the building.

Unless you can "see" into the future of your proposed investment for the next three to ten years and convince yourself that the neighborhood is and will continue to be a good one, stay away from it. The heavy costs of maintenance and management and increasing vacancies can cost you your equity. Your initial high return can change rapidly into losses.

WHEN TO USE AN OPTION

Any time you wish to use an option, have an experienced attorney prepare the document. He will ensure compliance with state law and that you have a well written contract. On the other hand, depend upon yourself for the business aspects to be written in the agreement. It is your time and money you are investing. You will be the one who bears the consequences of good or bad business judgments.

The key points to be covered in an option agreement were discussed previously in this chapter. Knowing when to use the option approach is also important. Fundamentally, an option should be used in those instances when you need additional time and when you wish to ensure that the property is yours if you choose to purchase it within the specified time limit. There should be many times when the option approach can be used to increase your profits in real estate.

One entrepreneur might use an option to gain time to secure advantageous financing with high leverage for himself, perhaps by forming a syndicate. Another may wish to carry out a more thorough investigation and analysis. You may have heard rumors of possible confiscation of the property by government for a school, highway right-of-way, or other use. If you plan to put the property to its highest and best use, you may need to check zoning, the possibility of a change in zoning, and other government regulations. The option approach gives time, if needed, to double check the market's future for your intended investment.

Additional examples in Chapters 4 and 5 illustrate other times when the option approach helps to increase your profits and how others did just that. The option approach is part of the insider's portfolio of techniques. Use it to increase your leverage and profits in real estate.

SEVEN KEYS TO SUCCESSFUL APARTMENT BUILDING INVESTING— AND INSIDER USE OF OPTIONS

1. The best bets in apartment investments are those which are being mismanaged in one way or another. For instance, a manager may have failed to increase rents (and hence, return on investment) at a rate at least equalling inflation rates. Another may have allowed some "junking" by tenants, e.g., automobiles being repaired in exposed parking areas or junk furniture on exposed balconies. The number of ways of mismanagement is large. Fortune builders look for such apartments, buy them, correct management's mistakes, and make big profits.

2. Leverage is the insider's key to building a fortune in apartment investing. Using leverage enables you to make profits with other people's money. It allows you to multiply the return on investment on your own money.

3. An ambitious entrepreneur will even leverage apartment financing to infinity—to the point where he has no money of his own invested.

4. The key to faster and more satisfactory progress to wealth through apartment investing is to select only those investments and modes of financing which meet your own goals and desires.

5. Compared with other types of real estate investments, apartment buildings are comparatively easier to finance and to get high leverage from. More money is available from a larger number of sources for financing apartment buildings.

6. An option to purchase an apartment building allows optimization of an investment on the "upside." It provides time to consider all possible ways to structure the project and time to optimize the details of financing for your own benefit.
7. An option-to-purchase allows protection on the "downside." It provides for time to evaluate the neighborhood's future, the rent being charged, and to find any other present or future negative factors which would adversely affect your investment.

REMEMBER THESE POINTS

- The option approach allows you to gain temporary control of property; use it to your advantage.
- Use time gained to check market factors of optioned property.
- Always consider possibility of obtaining an option if it is needed for any reason.
- An option allows time to structure a project.
- Option time can be used to ensure that desired financing is available.
- Option time can be used to check zoning and other government regulations.
- An option itself is a salable item.
- Increase your leverage in a project by using an option.
- Option approach can keep your position more flexible until it is exercised.
- Have an attorney, one with real estate experience, prepare the option document to assure compliance with law and yield non-ambiguous agreements.
- Laws vary from state to state and laws change with time.
- You, as an entrepreneur, must make the business decisions; you live with the consequences.
- Marginal areas tend to turn into blighted areas.
- Carefully evaluate the future quality of an area; avoid creeping blight.

4

SECRETS OF USING OPTIONS TO GAIN CONTROL OF LAND

If you are thinking about acquiring raw land (acreage) as an investment, double check to be sure that the financial potential of such an investment is consistent with your written goals. Investors in raw land are typically not looking for a tax shelter or for current income. Experienced investors, those who have become acquainted with the insider's secrets of investing in real estate, will not buy acreage unless they believe that the land will quickly appreciate in value. Most such investors are interested in profits which qualify for capital gains tax treatment. Be sure your goals are compatible with the potential profits in investment in unimproved land.

THE SECRET OF HIGH PROFIT IN LAND

If you are interested in fast turnover profits, a well chosen parcel of unimproved land ranks near the top of the list of possible real estate investments. The secret of profits does not lie in buying land in order to sell it later to a buyer who is interested in using it as unimproved land.

Instead, the "best bets" are acreage plots which you can convert to "higher usage" or which can later be sold to someone who will put it to higher usage. For example, if you buy land which is presently being used for farming or as pasture land and subdivide it into residential lots, then you have converted it to a higher usage. Another way of viewing it is that, in the language of a professional appraiser, the highest and best use of a property will change from its present usage to your advantage and profit at a future date.

In Chapter 2, you read about Tom T.'s experience investing in unimproved land which was in the path of urban growth. You saw how his net worth increased without current tax consequences and how he achieved high leverage. In this chapter, you will see how an experienced investor used the option approach to make $60,000 profit with only $1 invested! Another example shows how a grading contractor used a progressive option to minimize his risk and make a profit of $105,000.

The following example describes how Herbert L. used the option approach in a creative and innovative way to gain control of unimproved land and to get extremely high leverage. Note particularly the thinking process he put himself through when he considered various ways of financing the venture.

HOW AN OPTION NETTED $60,000 WITH $1 INVESTED

The owner of an unimproved parcel of real estate had just sold 320 acres of his 480 acres of land to a neighbor for $2,400 per acre. The seller was pleased with the sale. He had purchased the property many years before for $90 per acre. After payment of capital gains tax he was in a good cash position. He had almost simultaneously sold his local residence. He and his wife moved to their desert vacation home.

From the neighbor's point of view the portion he had just purchased was the more desirable acreage. The seller had offered the remaining 160 acres at $2,200 per acre, or a total of $352,000, but he was not aggressively promoting a sale.

When Herbert L. learned of the property, he drove by the 160 acres. Although he was not in a position to purchase the property by himself, he had previously formed successful syndicates and was confident he could do so for this new opportunity if it checked out well. His knowledge of the inside secrets of real estate investments was equal to that of Tom T., described in Chapter 2. He had been active in real estate investment for 22 years.

During his investigation, Herbert L. made a list of the advantages and disadvantages of the property. He planned to use the list as a part of his presentation to his intended syndicate partners.

He noted that a "college town" of 40,000 population was six miles east of the property. The college was a major branch of the state's university system; it offered bachelor's degrees in many subjects and graduate degrees in several. A major city was 65 miles to the west. An airport capable of handling large commercial jet aircraft was approximately equidistant (six miles) from the property and the university branch. He already knew that a six lane highway (freeway) was planned to pass within a short distance from the property. Upon checking details of the freeway he found that there would be an on-ramp and off-ramp approximately 2,500 feet from the property. The property would also be visible from the freeway. Herbert L. was thinking of it as an industrial site for some major manufacturing company.

There were only two disadvantages on his list of pro's and con's. One was that an outcropping of rocks on the property, which made the property less desirable to the neighbor who purchased the adjoining 320 acres, would increase construction costs for a plant. The other was the high uncertainty of the time required to find an industrial buyer for the property.

He reviewed the advantages and disadvantages of the investment and his list of potential investors for a syndicate. At this point he also opened his thinking to all possible ways of structuring the venture. He particularly recalled that the seller was not aggressively pushing for a sale and that he, the seller, had moved 120 miles to the desert. His creative thinking led to an unusual use of the option approach. He called the seller and drove out to present the following.

Herbert L. told the seller that he had thoroughly investigated the property and that he was convinced that the acreage could be sold within a year's time for more than the asking price of $2,200 per acre if it were properly promoted. The seller interrupted and offered to sell to him for 29 percent down with the balance to be paid in seven equal annual installments plus nine percent interest. Herbert L. admitted that he was short of investment capital but that he had two alternate plans which should be of benefit to the seller. He asked that the seller choose either (1) seller to grant Herbert L. a one year option at $2,500 per acre, or (2) seller to grant Herbert L. a one year option at $2,200 per acre with the provision that if the property was sold to another within one year from the date of the option, then the seller would be paid 50 percent of the amount in excess of $2,200 per acre plus, of course, the $2,200 option price.

Alternate number two had the greatest appeal to the seller. Three days later he granted the requested option based upon the second alternate and accepted a payment of $1 for the option.

To make a long story short, Herbert L. located a manufacturing company which expressed a serious interest. He offered the property to them for $500,000. After eight weeks of evaluation the company offered $475,000 ($2,968.75 per acre). Herbert L. accepted. The seller received $2,584.37 per acre from the three-way escrow which was $384.37 per acre more than his original asking price and $84.37 per acre more than he would have received if he had granted an option based upon Herbert L.'s alternate number one.

Herbert L., with an investment of one dollar, some creative thinking, and diligent work, had cleared more than $60,000! He had benefited by deliberately considering many possible ways of making a profit instead of proceeding unthinkingly down the path toward his original plan to syndicate He would also have made a profit by syndicating, but he made an even greater profit with the approach he used.

HOW TO USE AN OPTION TO GAIN CONTROL OF LAND

The technical aspects of using an option to gain control of unimproved land are similar to those for gaining control of residential income property or apartments. There are, however, some differences. The most successful entrepreneurs are those who know the differences and how to use an option in a manner which recognizes the differences. For instance, on the average, the owners of unimproved land are typically less experienced in the myriad possible ways of structuring a real estate contract. Any time you approach such a seller on the basis of something less than an all cash purchase you are, in effect, selling the other party on yourself. You will need to be able to show the seller that your proposal is in his best interest and may work to his financial advantage. If he knows very little about the option approach, you will hopefully be aware of his lack of knowledge and handle your approach accordingly. Don't overlook recommending that he touch base with his banker, attorney, or other adviser regarding your proposed option.

The time element in land options

If you are entering the area of unimproved land investment after using options in other types of ventures, take note of one other difference which is "statistical" in nature. If you could examine one hundred randomly selected options on unimproved land and the same number of options on apartments, similarly selected, you would find that the time element in the option is appreciably longer for unimproved land. No matter what type of real estate investment you are considering, it is, of course, in your best interest to obtain the greatest possible time period in which to exercise the option. If you are

TO GAIN CONTROL OF LAND 57

negotiating an option on unimproved land you will find it easier to get a longer time period because it is a common characteristic.

A special type of option, which typically has a very long time period, is the "progressive option." Its use is described in the next section. This type of option can and frequently does extend over a number of years.

HOW TO USE THE PROGRESSIVE OPTION TO DEVELOP PROPERTY WITH LITTLE MONEY DOWN

In some areas of the country the progressive option is called a "rolling option." It is typically used in the purchase of unimproved land for two primary reasons beneficial to the entrepreneur. It enables you to gain control of a sizeable parcel of land with comparatively little money and with high leverage. Furthermore, it is a pay-as-you-go plan which serves to minimize risk and to hold down your liability.

A progressive option is most often used in the purchase of land to be developed into residential sites or into a combination of residential, apartment, and commercial sites. Less frequently, it is used in the development of an industrial park or recreation/vacation areas.

A progressive option gives you, the optionee, control of a sizeable number of acres. The whole parcel might be divided, on paper, into two or ten or more smaller parcels. Recall from Chapter 3 that an option agreement should be as complete in all terms and conditions as an ordinary purchase agreement. Thus, each of the smaller parcels would have a dollar value assigned to it. Typically, the progressive option would call for purchase of parcel number one at the outset or soon thereafter and an option to purchase the remaining parcels in succession for their assigned values on or before a designated date for each parcel. The first time a buyer fails to exercise the option to purchase a parcel on or before its specified date, then the option to purchase it and the options on all the remaining parcels become void and the seller is again free to sell to anyone. This feature provides excellent protection on the "downside" for you as the optionee. If you find, during your management during the early stages of the development, that you were overly optimistic on the property's potential or if the economy takes a downturn, then you are not obligated to exercise your option on the next parcel. You also would have no obligation or liability with respect to the remaining parcels. On the other hand, if you had originally purchased the entire property then you would be liable for all of it. The progressive option can reduce your risk to a fraction of what it would be otherwise.

The progressive option document, as with all options, does not follow a fixed format. The goals and needs of sellers differ. Buyers and their partners also differ from project to project. And the goals of one project will be different from another. Progressive options do tend to be more complex than other options on real estate. They are pay-as-you-go plans. The portion of an overall option agreement which pertains to its progressive aspect is given in the following section. It is particularly important that your attorney for this type option be one who is experienced in real estate.

The following example shows how a man, who was previously involved in only a small segment of land development, used a progressive option to minimize both the risk and the capital required to carry out the project.

HOW AN ENTREPRENEUR USED A PROGRESSIVE OPTION TO REAP $105,000 PROFIT

Growth to the northeast at the edge of one of our country's top fifty cities (in terms of population) had been rapid the last three years. Eighteen miles northeast of the larger city was a smaller one with a population of nineteen thousand plus. In addition to being a bedroom community for the larger city, the smaller one had two manufacturing companies employing a total of 600 people.

Mr. Robert B. had been a grading machine operator for eleven years before starting his own grading contracting business five years ago. After building his business from only one machine to many, he wanted to enter the investment and real estate development field. At a Rotary luncheon, he heard that 367 acres near the northeast edge of the city were for sale. The land was owned by a corporation whose primary business was as an oil equipment supplier. Robert B. learned from the corporation's attorney that the price was a firm $1,000,000. The attorney said that the corporation would be willing to consider an offer of 29 percent down with negotiable terms on the balance. In answer to Robert B.'s direct question he said that the property had first been offered more than a year previously. The attorney gave Robert B. surveyor's maps of the property including a topographical map.

For his own use in negotiating the financing of the property, Robert B. prepared a development plan and map showing how he would divide the property into a commercial area, an apartment area, and the remainder into residential building sites of one-fourth acre each. He then prepared another map showing division of the 367 acres into ten parcels. Parcels one through seven were designated for residential sites. Parcels eight and nine were for apartments. Parcel ten was an

L-shaped strip with frontage along two existing streets; it was marked for commercial usage. Parcels one through seven were valued at $90,000 each, parcels eight and nine at $110,000 each, and parcel ten at $150,000.

Robert B. and his attorney then prepared a progressive (rolling) option agreement to present to the seller. The agreement provided for an option to purchase parcel number one within three months for $90,000 with a down payment of 25 percent and quarterly interest payments only for four years with the remaining 75 percent due and payable at the end of four years after exercising the option. The agreement further provided an option to purchase parcel number two at its designated value and on similar terms within six months after purchase of parcel number one and then each succeeding parcel, in numerical sequence and at their designated values, at six month intervals.

The portion of the overall option agreement (after amendments by the seller's attorney) pertaining to the progressive feature of Mr. B.'s option reads as follows.

> Ninety calendar days from the date of this agreement, providing Buyer has paid the sum of 25 percent of the assigned value of $90,000.00, Seller will deliver to Buyer title to Parcel One, said Parcel is described as Parcel One on the attached plat, which plat is a part of this option agreement. It is further agreed that each one hundred eighty calendar days thereafter, providing Buyer pays 25 percent of the parcel's assigned value on or before the end of each such period, Seller will deliver title to succeeding parcels Two through Ten, such title to be on parcels in numerical order. This procedure will continue until a total sum of $1,090.000.00 has been paid and titles to all parcels have been delivered to Buyer.
>
> In the event Buyer shall default on payments as prescribed herein and in the Payment Schedule, which Payment Schedule is attached and is a part of this agreement, this agreement shall be null and void and Seller will have no further obligation to deed any property to Buyer, nor shall there be any liability between Buyer and Seller.

Thus, if the buyer were to exercise the option on each parcel in succession, he would make an initial payment of 25 percent of that parcel's value and other payments per terms. Title to each parcel would pass to the buyer upon payment of the initial 25 percent with a clear title to be provided and delivered upon payment of the remaining 75 percent. In the event the buyer failed to exercise an option on any one parcel, then the option on that parcel and all remaining parcels would become null and void, with no further obligation by the seller to the buyer and no liability by the buyer to the seller for said parcels. The buyer would, of course, still be obligated for payment, per terms, on those parcels he had acquired to that date by exercising his option.

The proposed agreement called for payment of $2,000 for the option. This payment would be credited against the stipulated down payment upon exercise of option on the first parcel.

Over the years, Robert B. had noted that the successful investors were those who analyzed various ways of financing while they were investigating a property. While his attorney was preparing the option agreement, Robert B. obtained rough estimates of the costs of engineering the development, surveying, installing streets and utilities, and of advertising and marketing the building sites. He was primarily thinking of syndicating, but it increasingly appeared that he might have to sell his concept, preliminary development plans, and option to a buyer with the financial muscle to handle the development. By the time he presented the progressive option to the seller's attorney, he had decided upon the latter action plan. His judgment was that the potential profit and probability of success was worth the risk. His confidence was strengthened when he learned that agents of an out-of-town developer were looking for acreage for their client.

The seller's attorney shortened the time for exercise of option on the first parcel to sixty days, changed the payment for the option from $2,000 to $5,000 and added the provision that the option payment was non-refundable in the event of non-exercise of the option on the first parcel. Robert B.'s attorney required that the seller furnish a copy of a resolution by the corporation's board of directors authorizing the option agreement. Robert B. paid the $5,000 and was granted the progressive option.

Robert B. immediately started advertising the proposed venture in newspapers in his own city and in the city where the above mentioned developer was headquartered.

Special Note: In recent years, the federal government and many state governments have increased their control and intervention in the real estate area. The advertising and promotion of proposed land ventures is a particularly sensitive area. Have your attorney examine your proposed advertising *before* you advertise.

He was pleasantly surpised when one developer from his own city and two out-of-town developers were seriously interested in his project. It was not exactly a highest-bidder situation, but the multiple interest did work to Robert B.'s advantage. After considerable negotiation

TO GAIN CONTROL OF LAND

he and one of the out-of-town developers signed an agreement wherein the developer would pay Robert B. $15,000 upon exercise of option for parcel one and $10,000 whenever the option to purchase any succeeding parcel was exercised. Furthermore, they agreed to exercise options for parcels two through four not later than the starting of grading on parcel one.

The developer complimented Robert B. on his structuring of the progressive option. Although the developer was planning to and was partially committed to proceeding faster than the six months per step stated in the progressive option, he had the choice of slowing his pace if it became advisable. Also, the developer's initial outlay in purchasing the land was 25 percent of $90,000 plus $15,000 to Robert B. or a total of $37,500 instead of 25 percent of $1,000,000.

The standard way of calculating leverage does not apply in the case of a progressive option, but the developer had control of a $1,000,000 property with only $37,500 tied up at the beginning. Robert B. had fared even better in the low risk department. He had risked only $5,000 and had received a quick $15,000 profit with $90,000 additional profit to come as the project progressed.

Even with the advantages of using a progressive option, transformation of raw land into residential building sites is costly and many delays can occur. Extra care should be used to avoid underestimating costs or the time involved. In structuring the progressive option, try for the maximum time possible for each stage. You can always exercise such an option ahead of the time schedule, but there is no assurance that you could obtain an extension of time for exercise.

REMEMBER THESE POINTS

- Unimproved land ranks high on fast profit list if it is well chosen. Best bets are parcels in path of urban growth or industrial development.
- Option approach provides extra time to determine if unimproved land can be put to higher usage in near future.
- Double check your goals for compatibility with financial potential of unimproved land investment.
- Consider all possible ways of structuring a venture.
- Option on unimproved land should be for as long a time period as possible.
- Progressive (rolling) options can gain control of large parcels for little cost.

- A progressive option is a "pay-as-you-go" plan.
- A progressive option provides downside protection for you. If some adverse factor affects your optioned property, you are not obligated to purchase further parcels of the total optioned property.
- Have your attorney examine your advertising copy before you advertise a proposed venture. The federal government and many state governments have increased their control and intervention in real estate.

5

HOW TO USE LOW RISK OPTIONS TO CONTROL COMMERCIAL AND INDUSTRIAL PROPERTY

It is especially important to conduct a complete investigation of commercial or industrial property before making a full commitment on purchasing it. For instance, if I were considering investing in a shopping center I would want to know my competition for tenants for the property, both now and in the predictable future. A new development a short distance away could mean a loss of rental income and a negative cash flow. In the case of an industrial property opportunity, a thorough check of the lease and the lessee is as important as the finance-ability of the investment.

If you find a commercial or industrial property which is priced right and for which there appears to be a good present and future rental demand, then obtaining an option is the best approach. Without the protection of an option to purchase, you might find that someone else bought the property while you were conducting your investigation. And, just as important, an option gives down-side protection in that it provides you with additional time to discover possible negative factors which might mean you would not purchase the property.

A third reason for using the option approach in commercial or industrial property ventures is the same as for apartment or raw land projects. The time period in the option allows you to arrange for financing and, further, to structure the financing to maximize your own profit.

There tends to be an additional factor in real estate investing in the industrial area not usually present in other areas. I have found that one is frequently dealing with a corporation in either buying or selling industrial property. If a corporation is involved it is especially important to work closely with an attorney.

In this chapter, you'll see how an option was used by a high school teacher to make $26,000 profit on a small shopping center. He gained control of the $220,000 property first, then completed his investigation and arranged for financing. The total profit was $52,000 upon sale of the shopping center to a major new tenant.

You'll see how a profit of $55,000 was made by the sale of an option on an industrial building in the second example. It will also describe some of the differences in dealing with a corporation instead of individuals. Take special note of the key requirement imposed by the attorney who ultimately purchased the building.

HOW AN ENTREPRENEUR GAINED CONTROL OF $220,000 SHOPPING CENTER AND PROFITED WITHOUT INVESTING HIS MONEY

For the last five years of his fifteen years as a high school mathematics teacher Bruno W. had been "thinking about" investing in real estate. After his divorce, he had read several books on real estate and had passed the state examination for a real estate salesman's license. He was registered as a real estate salesman with a local broker but was not very active. He had made only one sale—a $40,000 house. He had decided that his strong points were not in frontline sales, but in areas where his analytical and research capabilities could be utilized. Bruno W. admitted frankly to his closest friend that he would like a career change to one more challenging and with greater financial rewards.

The owner of the realty firm with which Bruno W. was registered

COMMERCIAL AND INDUSTRIAL PROPERTY

listed a small shopping center only three blocks from Bruno W.'s apartment. The price was $255,000 for the corner property with seven small stores. It was located on a heavily traveled boulevard in an area where the shops were small and had very little off-street parking. The shopping center had once had a small, two-pump service station, but it had been razed and paved to provide additional off-street parking two years earlier. During the past 15 years the neighborhood had changed from mostly small and medium sized houses to apartment buildings.

Before listing the center, the seller had received notice from one of his tenants, the owner of a small convenience food store, that they would not renew their lease. The store was one of a four-store chain which was going out of business. One week after the listing, the convenience food store closed its doors.

Seven weeks after the shopping center was placed on the market, Bruno W. contacted the seller. As required by the realtor's code of ethics and by the law in his state, Bruno W. identified himself as a real estate licensee and as a possible principal. Coincidentally, another tenant went bankrupt and moved out. The seller admitted there was very little if any chance of collecting payments on the three remaining years of the lease by the tenant.

During their negotiations, Bruno W. pointed out that the store fronts should be made much more attractive and that most of the plumbing fixtures should be upgraded. The roof and parking area were in good shape except the parking lot needed to be restriped. Bruno W. also mentioned that he had insufficient capital to handle the purchase by himself and that he was thinking of forming a syndicate. Although Bruno W. mentioned the lack of two tenants, he was not too concerned about the vacancies because of a shortage of available commercial property along the boulevard and the fact that the shopping center had off-street parking. The seller required all cash or cash to a new loan.

After much more talking over a two week period and negotiations on the asking price, Bruno W. had his attorney prepare a 60 day option to purchase the property for $220,000 with a non-refundable $1,000 to be paid for the option. The payment for the option would be credited to the purchase price upon exercise of the option.

The seller stated he would have to have $3,300 as payment for the option if he were to take the property off the market for 60 days. Bruno W. agreed and the option was granted.

On the same day Bruno W. learned of the acquisition of one-half square block by a corporation which announced they would begin construction within five months on an eight-story office building. The location was just two blocks down the boulevard from Bruno W.'s optioned property. One tenant of a building to be demolished was a second-generation hardware store which had catered to family trade for 30 years. He found that the owner was still looking for a new suitable location and liked the idea of moving only two blocks.

Bruno W. had been looking for an apartment building for a client with $75,000 cash to invest. He suggested that the two of them form a general partnership to buy the optioned property with the investor furnishing as much as $75,000 if necessary. He proposed turning over the option agreement to the partnership in exchange for a 50 percent interest in profits from operation and/or resale and the refund of the $3,300 he had paid for the option. He would also manage the property for no additional benefits. He estimated that a loan of 70 to 75 percent could be obtained. If so, the difference between the down payment and the proposed $75,000 would be used for remodeling.

The proposed partner suggested that they have a talk with a friend, the president of a savings and loan association. Three days after their conference, the savings and loan officer said that he felt their loan committee would approve a loan of $160,000 provided (1) the vacant stores were leased for at least five years by responsible lessees, (2) the stores were remodeled as described by Bruno W., and (3) both partners assumed personal responsibility for the loan.

Bruno W. and his new partner signed a partnership agreement and both went to the seller to renegotiate the terms of the purchase. On the fiftieth day of the option period, the seller agreed to enter into a 60 day escrow provided an immediate additional, non-refundable $6,700 were paid into escrow with the balance to be paid by the close of escrow. Bruno W.'s partner agreed and the escrow was opened. The two men then made a formal application for a loan of $165,000 at the savings and loan association.

Events then happened fast. Bruno W. leased the two stores for five years plus a five year option to the hardware store owner after Bruno W. agreed to remodel per sketches he had made. There was no doubt as to their new tenant's financial capability and credit rating. They gave a copy of the lease to the savings and loan company. The loan committee made a commitment of a $150,000 loan plus an additional $10,000 to be added to the loan upon completion of remodeling. They closed escrow, Bruno W.'s $3,300 deposit was returned to him, and they completed the remodeling. At that time, Bruno W. and his partner were receiving a gross monthly rental 24 percent higher than the fully rented gross income of eight months previously.

COMMERCIAL AND INDUSTRIAL PROPERTY

Three months after occupying the new location, the owner of the hardware store opened negotiations to purchase the shopping center. They finally compromised on a sale price of $290,000, all cash to the existing loan. After incidental costs and $12,500 for remodeling, the two partners split a profit of $52,000 on a fifty-fifty basis.

By using the option approach Bruno W. had gained control of a desirable property and had used the time to structure the financing to his own advantage. He had made a handsome profit of $26,000 without having his own money invested. By risking $3,300 as a temporary but non-refundable deposit, he had leveraged to infinity.

Bruno W.'s partner had also fared well. He had realized $26,000 profit on an investment of $75,000 for a few months. With one successful venture behind him, Bruno W. was ready for a bigger venture.

HOW TO USE AN OPTION TO GAIN CONTROL OF COMMERCIAL OR INDUSTRIAL PROPERTY

The three major areas of real estate investment wherein options are used by those knowledgeable in the insider's secrets of investing are (1) apartments, (2) raw land, and (3) commercial/industrial property. Of the three, the commercial/industrial area offers the greatest challenge to those entrepreneurs who take pleasure in analyzing a project and structuring a venture as well as making a profit. I have found that the level of real estate investment expertise is generally higher for both buyers and sellers in the commercial/industrial area (in comparision with apartments or raw land). But there is plenty of room for creativity and innovative thinking on your part.

The "How to" in using the option approach depends upon the needs, goals, and circumstances of the seller, buyer, and those involved in financing. A buyer's goal in using the option approach is to gain control of a property. An insider uses the high flexibility of an option to structure a deal tailored to his own and the seller's goals. Variations in the needs and goals of sellers are shown in the following few cases along with suggestions for structuring a deal.

- *Elderly Seller with High Current Income*—Structure an option deal which allows him to defer tax consequences to future years when his annual income will be lower. You may be able to use his equity or credit rating for your own advantage (and his).
- *Widow Wants Monthly Income*—Seller may be receptive to an option deal with a specified very low down payment but relatively high monthly payments. An installment purchase should be

best for both buyer and seller; and it defers taxes for seller until payments are received.
- *Seller Wants to Move to Another Area*—Seller wants to relieve himself of the need to devote personal attention to his property. Seller may want a short time period for exercise of an option. An installment purchase with a low down payment may be the best approach. If you have exceptionally little, or no cash for a down payment, try a "lease with option to purchase" or a "lease purchase" approach.
- *Seller Wants All Cash*—An option to purchase gives you temporary control of the property and provides time for arranging financing for your best interest. The time period should be long enough for forming a syndicate, borrowing from an institution or private lenders, or whatever financial source your analysis shows is best for you.

In each of the examples given above, the option to purchase approach provides the time for further analysis to determine whether you want to proceed and for negotiation of financing which will optimize your position. The case examples given in Chapters 3 through 6 describe other situations wherein the option approach was used for the investor's benefit. Also the option approach allows time for the seller to become better acquainted with you and for you to learn about his goals and desires. It should allow you to structure a transaction which will be acceptable to everyone involved.

Note, in the following example, that Bill D. tried for as long an option period as possible and for a low payment for the option even though he originally thought he would not need a long period and the option payment was not made with his money.

HOW THE SALE OF AN OPTION NETTED $55,000 PROFIT ON OPTION-CONTROLLED $900,000 INDUSTRIAL PROPERTY

For the past eleven years Bill D. had been a merger and acquisition middleman. His clientele were the larger, acquisition-oriented corporations. Usually, he worked with a corporation's president or board chairman. Upon the advice of his attorney, he had obtained a real estate broker's license five years ago. The attorney had suggested that he preclude the possibility of being accused by the state of violating real estate license laws.

As growth by acquisition had progressively become less popular and less profitable, Bill D. had accepted consulting and other special assignments from executives with whom he had become acquainted.

COMMERCIAL AND INDUSTRIAL PROPERTY

He received a call from the president of an out-of-state company who had used Bill D.'s services as an intermediary in the acquisition of a manufacturing company. The president described a facility needed for light assembly, warehousing, and as a shipping center in the expansion of one of their subsidiary companies. He asked that Bill D. pin down the purchase price and tie up the facility in Bill D.'s name with assignability to a third party. Because the corporation was well known, the president felt a property's price would increase if a seller learned their identity. He set a limit of $1,000,000 for the property.

Three years ago, Bill D.'s arrangement with the company called for payment of a fee to Bill D. for a merger or acquisition per the generally used 5-4-3-2-1 scale, i.e., five percent of the first $1,000,000 of the acquired company's value plus four percent of the second $1,000,000 plus three percent of the third plus two percent of the fourth plus one percent of the value in excess of $4,000,000. The president said the usual 5-4-3-2-1 fee basis would apply in the new assignment. He authorized Bill D. to submit statements for reimbursement of out-of-pocket expenses. He also sent $5,000 to Bill D. as a retainer; the $5,000 was to be credited against Bill D.'s fee, if earned.

Bill D. contacted bankers, Realtors, real estate holding companies, investment companies, real estate investment trusts (REIT's), the financial vice-presidents of corporations, selected corporate attorneys, and others in his search for a facility meeting the specifications. An attorney and one of the REIT's expressed an interest in finding such a property themselves if there was a lease with a good lessee. One investment company had been managing an industrial property owned by three of their clients. It met the specifications even including a railroad spur for freight car service. The building was nine and one-half years old. The ten year lease on the property was expiring within six months and the building would be available at that time. The three owners had decided to sell for $950,000.

The president sent his Production Vice-President and Shipping Department Manager to inspect the property on the following weekend. On Tuesday, he called Bill D., approved the facility, and asked Bill D. to get an option on the property. He suggested that Bill D. try to get an option purchase price of $900,000 or less and stated that his company would furnish the money required for payment for the option.

Bill D. met with the head of the investment company and the three owners. Verbally, he asked for a 120 day option to purchase at $900,000 with a payment of $5,000 for the option and with this payment to be credited toward the purchase price. Bill D. called the president to describe the conference. Two days later the sellers verbally countered with acceptance of the $900,000 option purchase price but with a 90 day option and payment of $18,000 for the option. Bill D. called the president and obtained his approval. The president wired $18,000 to Bill D. to pay for the option. Bill D. was granted the option upon payment of $18,000.

The president presented the option agreement to the company's board of directors and requested a resolution authorizing purchase of the property and payment of a five percent fee ($45,000) to Bill D. The board chairman, a specialist in corporate finance, had been growing increasingly concerned about the amount of the corporation's indebtedness, the recent and predicted future increases in the cost of money (interest rates) and in the need for improved liquidity for the corporation. The corporation was far from being in jeopardy, but he was looking ahead. He had not discussed his concern with the president or other board members, but did so at this meeting. After prolonged discussion, the board decided to sell and lease back another property they owned and not to purchase Bill D.'s optioned property. The chairman complimented the president on his aggressive follow through and the board ratified his expenditure of $18,000 for the option and $5,000 to Bill D. There was an implied apology for not making this change in policy two months earlier. They decided to try to lease the optioned property or find another similar property to lease.

This change in direction was totally unexpected by Bill D. He was now in a position of not getting an expected fee of $45,000. He was, however, familiar with the insiders' secrets of real estate investment. His eleven years experience in mergers and acquisitions had often involved him in overcoming or working around unexpected events in order to close a deal. He deliberately reviewed every way he could think of to make a profit on the optioned property. His fundamental thought was that he had something of value, an option on desirable property, and that he should be able to turn it into cash for himself. Furthermore, he had an A-1 potential lessee, almost "in his pocket." He chose either to form a syndicate himself or to sell the option.

He contacted the attorney and REIT which had expressed an interest in finding similar property. Both had stated that they sought a 12 to 13 percent return on investment. He presented a proposal to both and mentioned that he was approaching others and was also considering syndicating. He described the proposed ten-year lease and emphasized that it showed a return of 13.1 percent on a $900,000 investment.

COMMERCIAL AND INDUSTRIAL PROPERTY

To make a long story shorter, the attorney offered Bill D. $50,000 for the rights to his option if and only if Bill D. could obtain the proposed lease. The attorney was quite specific about the necessity for the lease. Bill D. obtained a firm offer to lease (non-revocable for 60 days) from his original client and closed the deal with the attorney. The attorney then had $950,000 invested (his own money and borrowed money) including the $50,000 he paid to Bill D., but he was still getting a return of 12.4 per cent on investment. The corporation's $18,000 was to be credited against their first payments on the lease.

Bill D. had proven himself to be a true entrepreneur in real estate investment. He had the resourcefulness to overcome a setback and the creativity to choose another roadway to profits in real estate. At no time did he have a penny of his own capital invested or even temporarily tied up. Yet he showed a profit of $55,000 with $50,000 resulting when he had to change directions suddenly. His profit was even $10,000 greater than his anticipated fee of $45,000 from his corporate client.

THINGS TO WATCH FOR IN INDUSTRIAL PROPERTY INVESTING

When an industrial building becomes vacant it remains vacant longer than any other type of building. The attorney who bought the rights to Bill D.'s option in the prior example was 100 per cent right in insisting that his purchase was contingent upon a long term lease being signed by an A-1 lessee. If you are considering investing in industrial property, check and double check all leases.

Note, too, that a lease is only as good as the people who signed it. The tenant's financial status and credit rating are of the utmost importance. A long lease with a financially shaky tenant is of dubious and uncertain value. If a tenant closes his doors it is unlikely that you will collect any of the remaining obligations per the lease agreement.

In general, if you are considering investing in an industrial building of special purpose design and construction, look for an exceptionally long lease with a financially sound tenant. Before investing, estimate the effect on your investment and cash flow if your A-1 tenant vacates the property at the end of his long lease and if your building remains vacant for one or two years.

Lenders are especially cautious in lending money on industrial buildings. They are fully aware of long vacancies, weak lessees, special purpose buildings, and other risks involved with investments in industrial buildings. Before risking your own money be sure that financing is fully arranged.

The main factors to be considered before investing in an existing industrial building were presented briefly in this section. Discussion of the many factors for construction of an industrial building on speculation is beyond the scope of this book.

SIX KEYS TO COMMERCIAL/INDUSTRIAL PROPERTY INVESTING—INSIDER'S USE OF OPTIONS

1. Both commercial and industrial properties must be investigated thoroughly. Insiders use an option approach to gain control of the property while using the additional time involved for a *thorough* investigation and analysis.
2. In small shopping centers your ability to compete for renters must be evaluated. Insiders invest only in properties where new tenants will readily select their stores to lease rather than a competitor's vacant store a block away.
3. Invest in commercial property with the realization that a tenant may go bankrupt and that usually you will not be able to collect further payments on his lease no matter how tightly it is written. Use the option approach to allow time to determine existing tenants' financial soundness and credit rating.
4. Experienced investors in industrial buildings will invest only if there is a long term lease by a financially sound tenant with a good credit rating. They search until they find one meeting these requirements as well as their required return on investment.
5. A financially sound corporation is an excellent tenant for your industrial property. You have a good chance to collect per the terms of the lease if your building is vacated. A good attorney is worth several times his fee in such a case. Before buying, get the seller's permission to talk with the corporation's officers if you need to determine their plans for leasing beyond the expiration of a current lease.
6. An important key to successful investing in both commercial and industrial property is to find a property which will appreciate in value as time passes. Look for property in growing and/or upgrading areas. For instance, a small shopping center could become the site for a ten story medical building a few years later.

REMEMBER THESE POINTS

In investing in commercial or industrial property keep the following points in mind.

- Investigate thoroughly.
- Know your competition for tenants.

COMMERCIAL AND INDUSTRIAL PROPERTY

- Use the option approach to gain control of the property while you investigate further and arrange for financing.
- Determine the financial stability and credit rating of a possible new tenant before you lease to him.
- Predict future rental demand for proposed property.
- Ask your attorney about your possible need for a real estate license.
- Negotiate for lowest possible payment for option.
- Negotiate for longest time possible in which to exercise an option; it is particularly important for commercial and industrial property.
- Get confirmation of corporate executive's instructions and commitments in writing.
- Verify that corporation's board of directors has authorized executive's actions. Get a copy of board's resolution if possible.

6

INSIDE SECRETS OF MAKING MONEY ON PROPERTY YOU DON'T OWN

It is, of course, possible to make profits in real estate without ever actually owning any land. The three most commonly known ways are 1) by earning a commission for selling property owned by another, 2) by leasing a property and then subleasing at a higher price, and 3) by obtaining an option on a property and assigning (selling) your rights as the optionee for a profit or for a share in profits.

The first alternative, i.e., the role of Realtors and real estate brokers, is outside the scope of this book. In Chapter 7, I'll show how the second approach (leasing then sub-leasing) has been used and how handsome profits have resulted.

This chapter is devoted to discussion of earning a profit in real estate by obtaining an option and selling the option itself. In legal terms you are assigning the option, but in effect you are selling it.

In most states you are not required to have a real estate sales or broker's license in order to assign an option which you hold. You are not actually selling real estate property, but instead you are assigning an exclusive right to purchase a given property. But the law in your state should be checked. Check with your attorney before selling an option.

A good profit can be made by selling an option in any area of the real estate investment field. I have already described how a merger and acquisition consultant assigned his option on an industrial building and made a profit of $55,000 without ever having any of his own money tied up, even temporarily, and without owning the property. In Chapter 4, I told how a grading contractor who lacked the financial muscle to develop raw land into building sites assigned his option to a developer and made $105,000. He profited by developing and selling a plan and including his option. In some parts of the USA there are men who specialize in putting together package plans for development, including the land or option-controlled land. Colloquially, they are called "packagers."

Whether you are active in raw land, apartments, commercial buildings, or industrial buildings, consider obtaining and selling an option as a step in building your fortune. It might be your best bet for a fast and big profit especially if you are not in a financial position to handle large deals yourself.

In this chapter, I'll show how a creative investor obtained an option on a building, worked out a plan for a three story medical building, and did a professional job of marketing the plan for a handsome profit. The first example in this chapter shows how another creative entrepreneur made $60,000 profit on a commercial building by marketing his option and his plan for handling the venture.

HOW THE SALE OF AN OPTION ON $1,100,000 BUILDING BROUGHT $60,000 PROFIT

Upon his graduation from college with a B.A. in marketing Elliott U. had joined a major real estate company as a salesman in their leasing department. He was one of three salesmen whose work was to find tenants for commercial and industrial buildings managed by the realty firm. After five years with the firm he was promoted to manager of the leasing department. Two years later he resigned and became an independent leasing agent. During the following year his major accomplishment was the obtaining of a master lease on a commercial building; he was earning a comfortable income from subleasing. Then he was called by three owners of an office building to advise them on managing their property and finding tenants to lease their vacancies. They also discussed the possibility of selling the building. The building was generating barely enough income to pay operating expenses, taxes, and to service the debt. Even though the owners had an equity of more than 30 percent of the building's value, they were receiving virtually no cash flow. After much talk the sellers granted Elliott U. a 120 day option to purchase the building for $1,100,000. The sellers stipulated "all cash to the existing loan or new loan." Elliott paid $5,000 for the option with the non-refundable payment to be credited toward the purchase price if the option were exercised. The option was assignable.

At the same time, the sellers hired Elliott U. to work part time for $1,500 per month to resolve some management problems and make changes he had suggested to them. They also agreed to pay Elliott U. a fee for each new tenant he obtained on leases of five years or more.

Elliott U. had happened upon and recognized a good opportunity. The sellers did not have the expertise or the time to manage the office building themselves. They had been unsuccessful in finding a capable and effective manager to make the building show even a minimally acceptable return on investment. They had had three different managers in the four year life of the building since construction was completed. They fired the third manager upon reaching agreement with Elliott U.

Elliott U. did not have the financial ability to handle the venture by himself. He had, however, the confidence that he could quickly resolve the existing problems and find tenants for the vacant suites. The previous manager had limited his efforts at leasing to an "Offices for Lease" sign on the front of the building and a small, bland classified advertisement in the local newspaper. There was not even a brochure giving pertinent and promotional information on the building.

Elliott U. had not been seeking an office building, but he had found what professional insiders in real estate investment actively seek. He had found income-producing real estate which was being mismanaged, in this case by being "undermanaged." The previous manager apparently had not had the motivation and/or knowledge to aggressively manage the property.

Very briefly, Elliott U. prepared a four-color brochure, made a direct mailing to potential tenants, ran attention-getting advertising in the local and metropolitan newspapers, and began making in-person calls on possible tentants. At the same time, he contacted selected potential investors and proposed a joint venture or syndication including himself as a participant. Elliott U.'s banker put him in contact with a potential buyer who had recently moved into the city from out of state. The buyer had owned and managed an office building for nine years. He had sold it for $720,000 before moving to Elliott U.'s city. By the time the buyer completed his investigation of the office building, Elliott U. had the building occupancy up to 91 percent. The buyer said that he was not interested in a partnership. He offered Elliott U. $45,000 for the option rights. Because he was new in the city he offered, as a part of their contract, an additional $15,000 to be paid contingent upon Elliott U. increasing the occupancy rate to 96 percent within 90 days. Elliott U. accepted the offer and qualified for the entire $60,000 within 60 days.

Elliott U. had made a profit of $60,000 by, in effect, selling an option he held. He had utilized his knowledge of a highly specialized area of real estate, i.e., leasing of commercial and industrial buildings, to help make a far greater profit than he could by obtaining leases for others on a commission basis.

HOW TO FIND A BUYER FOR YOUR OPTION

I have found that professional, experienced real estate investors seldom obtain an option on a property with the express intention of selling the option itself. An exception is the "packager." An entrepreneur who specializes in packaging, e.g., the planning and organizing of the development of a parcel of unimproved land into residential and/or commercial building sites, will usually gain control of the land with an option to purchase. He might well have the intention, from the beginning, of selling his plans and his option on the land to another. Packagers of other planned developments, for example, the conversion of a bakery building into a medical office building, also may have the intention of selling their option along with their plans for development. On the other hand, even though the original intention upon obtaining an option is not to sell it, a creative investor will consider selling as one of the possible ways to make a profit.

CHECKLIST OF POTENTIAL OPTION BUYERS

An entrepreneur seeking investors to join a syndicate needs to look for only two fundamental characteristics. His potential investors need to have an interest in real estate investment and the financial wherewithal. But the option holder seeking to sell his option has a comparatively shorter list of potential buyers. A packager or other option holder who wishes to sell an option without any ongoing participation will most likely sell to an experienced real estate investor. A list of potential buyers or those who would know of a potential buyer includes:

- Accountants
- Active investors in real estate
- Attorneys
- Bankers
- Commercial building owners
- Industrial building owners
- Investment counselors
- Management companies in real estate
- Mortgage brokers
- Real estate brokers
- Savings and loan companies

I don't recall any real estate investor who was holding an option to purchase, asking the question, "Do you want to buy my option?" Certainly no active individual who knows the insider's secrets of real estate investment would pose such a question directly. The most important reason for not making a *direct* offer to sell your option is that any experienced investor in real estate will know that your hold on the property is a temporary one. If he becomes interested in the property, but believes that you most likely will not be successful in selling the option and if his scruples allow it, he may decide to wait until it expires and approach the owner directly. There is also the possibility, again depending upon the scruples of the investor, that he might express an interest in order to stall and let many days pass by. As the end of the option period approaches, your position becomes weaker and may result in your lowering the asking price for the option.

A much better approach in marketing an option is to propose forming a syndicate or a partnership with an individual. You might propose assigning your option to the syndicate or partnership in exchange for a share of the profits and/or income. Further, propose that you continue to be the active one in management of the property.

Once having assumed a position of strength, you may then hint at the possibility of selling the option. It is a much better marketing and bargaining ploy if you can get the other party to make an offer to buy your option. The chances of selling it and of getting a good price for it will be much better than if you had made a direct approach with an offer to sell.

In the first example in Chapter 3, Andrew K.'s original intent was certainly not to sell his option. He was attempting to exchange his option rights for profit sharing, income sharing, and a management agreement for himself when he approached the investment counselor who later bought the option. Even if Mr. K.'s intent had been to sell his option, he probably would have used exactly the same approach which he used in his presentation to the investment counselor and other private investors.

SALE OF PLAN AND $1,000 OPTION NETS $22,000 PLUS 20 PERCENT OF MEDICAL BUILDING

Fourteen years experience as a successful agent for a corporate and industrial insurance company had made Victor V. well acquainted with the commercial/industrial sections of his city. For the last two years, as a spare time activity, he had taught evening courses on industrial insurance at a private school.

He had noticed a corner lot near the school and only one block from a hospital. A tiny house on the property appeared to be at least fifty years old. He checked the zoning at city hall and found that the entire area had been rezoned as a part of a master zoning plan for the city six years earlier. The zoning ordinance permitted an office or medical building on the corner lot but the height limitation was three stories.

Victor V. obtained the owner's name from the city's tax records and contacted him. The disgruntled owner said that he would sell the property and that the "city bosses" had killed a sale two months earlier. He said he had had a signed sales agreement for $65,000 but that it was contingent upon the buyers getting a zoning variance to build an eight story medical building. The owner had to return the buyer's deposit of $3,000 when the variance was denied.

Victor V. returned to city hall and found that two zoning variance applications had been turned down on the property. Both had been for a proposed medical building. The first denial was for a six story building three years ago and the second was as described by the seller. A visit to the hospital's chief administrator confirmed what was already indicated, i.e., that there was a definite need for a nearby physician's and surgeon's office building.

Instead of having another talk with the seller immediately, Victor V. took the more aggressive step of having his attorney prepare an option to purchase, ready for signing by the seller. It called for a 120 day option to purchase the property for $40,000 with a $2,000 initial payment. In their talk before Victor V. presented the option agreement, the seller expressed a willingness to consider an option, but he was

MAKING MONEY ON PROPERTY YOU DON'T OWN

emphatic about no dependency upon rezoning and that any money deposited up front would be non-refundable. He realized that the inability to get a zoning variance reduced the value of his property, but he refused to consider less than $45,000. Victor V. inserted "non-refundable" ahead of the $2,000 payment called for in the option agreement and changed the option purchase price to $45,000. The seller granted the option.

Victor V. toured and took photographs of recently built three to five story medical and office buildings in his metropolitan area. He had an artist make a rendering of a proposed three story medical building. He had decided not to fight city hall as two others had done. It meant, of course, that the site would not be put to its highest and best use if the prior entrepreneur was correct in planning an eight story medical building.

At the same time he made up a list of six well known, prominent physicians and surgeons by talking again with the chief hospital administrator, bankers, and others in the city. The hospital administrator said he might be interested in participating in Victor V.'s planned syndicate. Victor V. also had a preliminary talk with an architect. The estimated cost for the completed project, including the land, was $325,000.

He presented the plan, the rendering, and a proposal that the administrator, the medical doctors, and he share equal ownership in the property. And further, that the resulting syndicate pay Victor V. $25,000 plus the equal ownership position for his plan and option. He further strongly urged that everyone who chose to participate, except the hospital administrator, move his offices to the new building.

Three of the physicians and the administrator made commitments of $40,000 each and ten days later signed the syndication papers prepared by Victor V.'s attorney. The physicians who participated were more than willing to move their offices because of the property's proximity to the hospital. The other three who did not join the syndicate stated they most likely would be interested in moving to the new building if they could sublease their present offices.

Work started on the building as soon as the architect completed the plans. Obtaining the financing was no problem. The completed project cost $350,000 including the $25,000 paid in cash to Victor V.

Victor V. did not ask that his initial $2,000 be returned to him. By investing only $2,000 and by creatively marketing the project, he had sold his option and plan for a clear profit of $22,000 cash and he had a 20 percent equity in the completed building.

HOW TO MAKE AN EFFECTIVE PRESENTATION TO A POSSIBLE OPTION BUYER

The details of preparing for a sales presentation, wherein your primary purpose is to sell your option, depend upon the nature of the optioned property. In many cases it is advisable to present a plan wherein the sale or surrender of your option is merely one of the details. It is preferable to let the idea of simply acquiring your option, without your further involvement in the project, be one which occurs to the buyer without your having directly suggested it.

In Chapter 5, Bill D. had become the optionee of an option on an industrial property because his corporate client had asked him to do so. Then the corporation changed from becoming the automatic buyer of the option to a probable lessee. Bill D. prepared a folder including the latest financial statements of the corporation, a statement of what he (Bill D.) believed would be the terms of a lease to the corporation, a description of the property, and a financial analysis showing the net income, cash flow, and tax benefits to an assumed purchaser or to syndicate members. He made a presentation to two screened, possible buyers and mentioned he was contacting others and also considering forming a syndicate. He had a salesworthy presentation. And he had an alternate plan ready for implementing if the investors he approached were not interested in buying the option.

The second example of this chapter showed how Victor V. approached the intended buyers for his option with a complete plan of which the option was an integral part. His presentation included estimated costs, pro forma financial statements for ten years, tax benefits for investors, exchange terms for his option, and an artist's drawing of the proposed medical building. The effort he put into making a salesworthy presentation paid off handsomely.

Doing your homework by preparing a complete package for presentation to buyers or investors is as important as when you are applying for a loan. A potential buyer may not be able to "read between the lines" to see the advantages of buying your plan and option. The old statement is still valid—put yourself in the "other man's shoes" in preparing your presentation package.

SALES PRESENTATION CHECKLIST

Some items in the following list may not be pertinent to include in a presentation package for your particular optioned property. But don't omit any item if it will help. The items include:

- All financial data on property
- Past financial statements on the property

MAKING MONEY ON PROPERTY YOU DON'T OWN

- Physical description of property
- Legal description of property
- Map
- Photographs or drawings
- Copy of option agreement
- Capital improvements and their costs
- Competition in marketplace
- Description of your plan for property's future
- Pro forma financial statements
- Tax advantages for typical investor

Caution: Maintain contact with your attorney in the preparation of materials for your presentation. He can help keep you out of trouble with the Securities Exchange Commission and your state's laws.

BE CAREFUL—YOUR OPTIONED PROPERTY COULD SLIP AWAY FROM YOU

An option to purchase gives control of the optioned property, but it is a temporary one. It is merely the exclusive right to purchase a specified property for a specified period of time. If you are in the position of needing to sell your option you must act quickly. The closer it gets to the expiration date the less chance you have of selling it. If a potential buyer learns that you have only a few days left and if he believes he could then purchase it, he will be tempted to wait out those few days.

The difficulty of simply selling an option in a direct way is why most experienced entrepreneurs devise and offer a plan including the option. Or they initially propose forming a syndicate and exchanging the option for an interest in the property. Then if someone offers simply to purchase the option the optionee is not in such a disadvantageous position.

Any plan or a proposed syndication including the optioned property must be genuine on the part of the optionee. Deception has no place in any field of real estate investment. The optionee should be prepared to go ahead on any desirable basis which offers him an opportunity for profit. Any sound and mutually profitable real estate transaction sets the stage for future deals.

FIVE KEYS TO MAKING A PROFIT IN REAL ESTATE WITHOUT OWNING IT

1. The most important key to making a profit on real estate without actually owning it is to obtain an option on a property and assign your right-to-purchase for a profit, i.e., sell the option itself.

2. One key to how to market an option profitably is to devise an overall plan for your real estate project and include your option as only a part of the plan; sell the plan including the option.
3. Another approach is to propose a syndication and sell your option to the syndicate for a profit.
4. In selling your option, the consideration does not necessarily have to be cash. You can profit by taking an equity position or a share of profits or income as the consideration for your option.
5. Don't depend solely upon selling your option. Propose and consider other avenues to profits and be prepared to take an alternate course.

REMEMBER THESE POINTS

- It's not necessary to own real estate to make a profit on it. You can obtain and sell an option.
- Have an attorney check your state's laws and Security Exchange Commission's regulations pertaining to selling an option.
- Devise a plan to develop the property or to improve its return on investment and sell the plan, including the option.
- Alternately, propose forming a syndicate and include your option; don't merely ask someone to buy your option.
- You can make a profit by selling your option for cash or by accepting an equity position or a share of profits as your compensation.
- Let the other party be the one to suggest buying your option without ongoing participation by you.
- Do your homework. Make your presentation a salesworthy one.
- Have an alternate route to pursue.
- Put yourself in "the other man's shoes." Ask yourself, "Why should he buy my option?"

7

HIGH LEVERAGE LEASE AND LEASE-PURCHASE CONTRACTS USING OPM

Businessmen in many fields have increasingly leased equipment and space during the past several years. Higher and higher taxes have encouraged this trend because of the tax benefits from leasing rather than owning. The second advantage is that a businessman's capital is not tied up in fixed assets and in equipment such as trucks and computers; his capital can be better used in production and marketing. What is not so widely known is that entrepreneurs, those who know the inside secrets of real estate investment, use leases to gain control of real estate with very little or no money of their own. They get the use of real estate on a long-term lease and the financial benefits of future real estate values.

An owner of unimproved land who gives a long-term lease to someone who erects a building on the property gains an income without selling his property and without paying a capital gains tax. It also means that his property gains improvements without capital outlay by himself.

Similarly, the owner of improved property may find that he can do better financially by giving a long-term lease rather than selling and that he avoids a capital gains tax which would result from a sale with a profit.

In this chapter, you'll see how a creative and innovative man structured a lease on a $650,000 office building with substantial benefits to the owner and an annual income of $37,000 for himself. In a second example, I relate how an investor used an organized, systematic approach in finding candidates for purchase-leaseback deals. The third example illustrates how an enterpreneur combined a lease and a purchase agreement to gain full control of a building without a down payment.

HOW AN INVESTOR LEASED A $650,000 BUILDING AND POCKETS $37,000 PER YEAR

Steven C., a free lance writer, had written several articles for a large real estate management firm during the prior five years. As his interest in real estate grew he learned of an older office building which was owned and managed by a 75 year old man. Because of less than vigorous management after the loss of a major tenant four and one-half years earlier, the percentage of vacancies was very high. One entire floor was rented to a friend of the owner at a warehouse-level rent rate on a month-to-month basis. The owner was averaging barely enough income to cover cash outflow for the building. He was receiving essentially no positive cash flow even though he was spending his time managing the building.

The building itself had not been maintained with respect to cosmetic details. There had been no upgrading to keep it competitive with other office buildings constructed during the past eighteen years. The owner, however, had been conscientious in repair and maintenance of the building's roof, heating system, and air conditioning.

An article, which Steven C. had researched and written for the real estate management firm, covered the subject of subleasing after obtaining a master lease on a group of small industrial buildings. His creativity as a writer and the research he had done for the article naturally led him to consider a similar approach for the office building.

Upon contact, he learned that the owner was considering selling the building and retiring from active management. During their conversation it became evident that the owner was wealthy and not in need of cash. The owner insisted that the building was worth at least $700,000 even though he admitted that it had not produced any net income for the last few years. The owner pointed out the potential for increasing income by renting the vacancies and of the future long range value of the site. The owner finally offered to sell the building for $650,000 cash. He stated that he might be willing to carry part of the purchase price himself at nine percent interest, but that the price would have to be higher. In response to Steven C.'s question, the owner said he had depreciated the building essentially to zero.

Steven C. withdrew, but six days later approached the owner again. He had used the time to obtain estimates on upgrading the building and to check the market for office rentals. He pointed out that an all cash sale would mean the payment by the owner of approximately $125,000 in capital gains tax. He asked what the owner would do with the remaining $525,000. The owner said he would most likely invest in mortgages, probably at eight and one-half percent interest.

Steven C. asked the owner if he would like to, in effect, "sell" his property but retain ownership, invest the money simultaneously without having to seek mortgages for investing, and not pay the capital gains tax which would result from an actual sale. The owner was puzzled and dubious but interested in learning how it could legally be done. Steven C. proposed that the owner lease the property to him for fifty years at an annual rate of eight percent of $650,000 or $52,000 per year to be paid annually in arrears. The lease would be on a net, net, net basis. He pointed out that the owner would be receiving approximately $52,000 more per year than he had been receiving and he would still own the property. Also that the owner would not have the task of looking for mortgages in which to invest. And, further, that since there was not an actual sale, there would be no capital gains tax to pay.

Mr. C. also explained the benefits for himself. He said that he obtained a total estimate of $90,000 to $100,000 for remodeling the lobby, upgrading the elevator and toilet facilities, and refurbishing the floor rented to the owner's friend for storage use. He stated that he could increase the total income by approximately $90,000 by leasing the present vacant offices and by upgrading the building. Thus, he would realize an income of approximately $38,000 per year for his efforts and investment of the costs of upgrading.

The owner agreed after stipulating that the lease agreement specify what leasehold improvements were to be made by Steven C. and that a minimum of $90,000 would be spent within 15 months.

The lease agreement was signed a week later. The existing leases by tenants and rents from the month-to-month renters were assigned to Seven C. These lease and rent payments gave him an immediate cash flow. With the help of local real estate brokers and with a direct mail campaign he rented the vacant suites. He evicted the tenant who was using a floor for storage and refurbished it for offices. With the new tenants and increased income, Steven C. was able to borrow the money necessary to complete the upgrading as agreed. The total cost was $97,000. By the fourteenth month he had increased the annualized net income by $89,000 per year.

Steven C. had used his creativity and his knowledge of only one of the insider's secrets of real estate investing to gain control of a $650,000 office building. He had financed a profitable project using other people's money. In particular, he had used the owner's money in such a way as to yield substantial financial benefits for both the owner and himself. And he had no money of his own invested. After deducting $52,000 per year lease payments from the $89,000 per year increase in income from the building he had $37,000 annual income in his own pocket.

ADVANTAGES OF SALE-LEASEBACK TO USER AND INVESTOR

There are many people and companies who are interested in controlling and using real estate as a tool or means of making money, but who are not necessarily interested in owning it. These users are usually seeking as low a financial investment as possible in real estate itself. Fortunately, there is a large number of complementary people and institutions who have great amounts of money for investing in real estate but who wish to be investors only and not users. These investors are looking for a high return on their investments and many are not interested in a turnover in investment. Once they have located an apparently secure investment with a good return they like it to continue for a long time.

Bringing these two different types of people together is frequently accomplished with the use of a sale-leaseback agreement (also called "purchase-leaseback"). If a company sells a building and site and leases it back, then, from the company's viewpoint the agreement is a sale-leaseback. The buyer (of the same property) has made a purchase and then leased the property back to the former owner. From the buyer's viewpoint it is a purchase-leaseback agreement.

There are, of course, advantages to both the investor and user of property in a sale-leaseback agreement. Evidence that this is so is given by the continued use and popularity of this type of transaction.

Advantages of sale-leaseback to user

In recent years, manufacturers and other types of companies have had increased emphasis on financial liquidity and on decreasing their indebtedness. By selling a property and leasing it back their liquidity is improved. If they had a mortgage on the property they thereby eliminate a long-term liability. They also eliminate a fixed asset, e.g., the value of the property. Bankers find fixed assets difficult to evaluate and also are dubious about the ease of liquidating a fixed asset if the owner found it necessary to do so in order to pay off a loan. Ownership of real estate has many advantages, but liquidity is not one of them. Finally, and most importantly, the balance sheet is improved by the resulting increase in "cash on hand."

Another advantage is that many companies increase their profits by freeing capital via a sale-leaseback. Their profit-equivalent on money tied up in real estate is typically in the six to nine percent range. Many companies, by freeing the money for use as working capital, can make double, or 12 to 18 percent return on the cash.

Many manufacturers and other businessmen have a need for a special purpose building — one which is designed especially for making their particular line of products. By designing and building a plant and selling it on a sale-leaseback contract they get what they need and end up without having their own capital tied up in it.

If a businessman buys a lot and erects a building and then holds it for a long enough period to qualify for capital gains tax, he can turn ordinary income into capital gains income provided he makes a profit on the real estate. By selling the property in a sale-leaseback transaction at a high enough price to make a profit he will have to pay a higher rental (compared with selling it at cost) during the period of the lease. Thus he will make a smaller profit in future years. But he will have traded future ordinary income for immediate capital gains profit.

The most sophisticated businessman — the one familiar with the insider's secrets of real estate investing — will go one step further. If, for example, he constructs the building he wants and then sells only the land in a sale-leaseback deal, he can write off both the depreciation on the building and the lease payments on the land. If he retained ownership of the land he would not receive any write off on the land's value. Furthermore, if he made a profit on the land and had owned it for a long enough period, he would qualify for a capital gains tax under present law.

Companies which have contracts with the U.S. government have another incentive to sell their real estate and lease it back. Odd as it may seem, on most government contracts the contractor cannot list as a cost, for reimbursement by the government, the interest he pays on money borrowed on real estate, but he can sell and leaseback the property and list the rent as a cost.

Advantages to investor

From an investor's point of view an investment in a purchase-leaseback on a triple net basis is one where he can essentially relax and take his return as lease payments are made. The lessee must maintain the property, pay the taxes and insurance, and take care of other matters related to operating the property. It is the type of investment many wealthy individuals and others seek.

A typical problem for owners of commercial or industrial property is finding good tenants. This problem is automatically resolved at the time of investing in a purchase-leaseback deal. If the investor has carefully checked the credit and future earning power of the lessee he should reap the return on investment as provided by the terms of the lease. In most cases the investor has found his future tenant even before choosing the property for investment. He does not have the problem of finding a good, financially solid long-term tenant; this problem can plague the speculative investor who buys land on improved property without having solid tenants committed to leases.

In a purchase-leaseback contract the term of the lease may be quite long, e.g., 40 years, but it is seldom less than 10 years. If you, as the investor, are getting a net, net, net 10 percent on the total cost of the property then you will have collected your full 100 percent of the property cost by the end of the tenth year. Thus your investment is paid back entirely and the property is still yours. A further benefit is that if the value of the property increases during the period of the lease — as has been true in the USA for many years — then you will benefit again. Your property can then be leased based upon the increased value or you can sell and pay a capital gains tax on the profit. Traditionally, real estate has been a good hedge again inflation.

If the seller in a purchase-leaseback were to borrow 50 to 66 2/3 percent on the real estate, his interest rate would be lower than your return on investment as the investor. You would, however, be investing 100 percent (whether it is your own or other people's money) of the cost of the property and consequently have a higher risk than the lender if the seller borrowed from conventional sources; you therefore deserve and can get a higher return. Also, an investor in a purchase-leaseback deal must plan for a higher return because a purchase-leaseback contract is not as saleable as an ordinary mortgage.

HOW PURCHASE-LEASEBACK PROVIDES 278 PERCENT RETURN ON CASH INVESTED BY SMALL INVESTOR

Life insurance companies, pension funds, and other large investors are the most notable users of the advantages of purchase-leaseback transactions. They are, of course, interested only in sizeable deals such as shopping centers or large plants with the very best tenants. The best known user of sale-leaseback contracts in many areas of the USA is Safeway Stores.

Investors familiar with the insider's secrets of real estate investment know that a purchase-leaseback is also a profitable investment for the small investor if he knows how to find and structure it. Because so few small investors are acquainted with this type of transaction, it has not been widely used for small deals.

After relinquishing an option on a 45 year old apartment building (see Chapter 3), Benjamin G. continued his search for a desirable real estate investment. As a former owner-operator of a small shop, he was well acquainted with the needs and desires of smaller businessmen. He contacted a wealthy friend who had made a purchase-leaseback deal with Safeway Stores several years previously. The friend cheerfully answered Benjamin G.'s questions on purchase-leasebacks and agreed that such an investment on a much smaller scale would be a good one provided the lessee had a good credit rating and a good record. The friend mentioned that banks and savings and loan associations, in considering making a loan on such property, would be more interested in the financial soundness and future for the lessee than in Mr. G.'s credit rating. He also asked Mr. G. to contact him if he located an opportunity on a sizeable property and needed a partner.

What to look for in a lessee

Mr. G. first made the following list of criteria for the future lessee in a purchase-leaseback deal.

- A merchant or small manufacturer
- Owner-user of the property
- Long-time user of the property
- Those with a good financial base in the community and well known to the local financial institutions
- Those with a good credit rating

- Those with a good track record
- Those with a long-term future in the community
- Those who could be trusted to honor their obligations.

He prepared a list of selected merchants and manufacturers with the help of the local Chamber of Commerce and his banker. He then checked ownership records at city hall to determine which ones met the requirement of "owner-user." After working his way through the remainder of the requirements, he had a list consisting of two merchants and a small manufacturer. Mr. G. approached all three owners. He suggested that the owner sell the real property to him and lease it back on a triple net basis. He pointed out to each that he, the present owner, would then have additional working capital for use in his business and that he would almost surely make a higher return on the released capital than he was realizing as the owner of the property. He also mentioned that lease payments would be fully deductible as a business expense and that this would be considerably more beneficial, taxwise, than the owner's continued depreciation of the building on the property.

One of the three men was a pharmacist who owned and used improved property in three different locations. He had just purchased another lot for a fourth neighborhood pharmacy and was getting bids for construction. The pharmacies were well known in the community and were popular, in part due to their home delivery service. The pharmacist had been in business for 26 years and was well known in the financial community. One of his buildings was 80 percent and another more than 50 percent depreciated. On each property the land value to improvement value was a high ratio and, of course, land value cannot be depreciated for tax purposes. The pharmacist said that his accountant claimed that the pharmacist was getting an "equivalent return on investment" of approximately eight percent on the three store buildings.

To make a long story short—the pharmacist had the three properties appraised. Mr. G. purchased them for approximately 90 percent of the appraised value and leased them back to the pharmacist for 25 years on a net, net, net lease basis. Their agreement also included a right-of-first-refusal for Mr. G. on the planned fourth pharmacy. The annual lease income yielded a return of 11.4 percent of the total purchase cost of $171,000. Based in large part upon the credit rating and reputation of the pharmacist, Mr. G. borrowed $164,000 at nine percent interest on the three properties.

HIGH LEVERAGE LEASE AND LEASE-PURCHASE

By learning and applying an insider's secret known only to a few small investors, Mr. G. was getting a good yield of 11.4 percent of the cost value of the property. In addition, he had made excellent uses of leverage by borrowing all except $7,000 of the property's cost at a percentage 2.4 percent lower than the yield, i.e., at nine percent interest. This arbitrage meant that he was making 2.4 percent on other people's money. His annual yield in dollars is $19,494. At the beginning of the long term lease he was getting the very high return of 278 percent on the $7,000 cash he had tied up in the property.

HOW TO USE THE LEASE-PURCHASE IN LIEU OF A DOWN PAYMENT

A lease with option of purchase or a lease purchase agreement can sometimes be used to gain control and use of real estate without the necessity for initial cash or a down payment. I say "sometimes" because the agreement must meet the needs and desires of the owner of the property as well as yours.

These two forms of agreement are different. In a lease with option of purchase, the lessee may choose to purchase or not to purchase per the terms of the agreement. In a lease purchase, the lessee is obligated to consummate the purchase per the terms of the agreement.

A lease with option of purchase agreement is similar to an ordinary lease agreement with an added provision for the option. Depending upon the terms of the possible purchase, the option portion of the overall agreement might read as follows:

> Lessee shall have, and Lessor hereby grants to Lessee, the exclusive right at his option, at any time during the term of this lease, to purchase the property for the sum of _____ Dollars ($ _____) to be paid to Lessor upon delivery by Lessor of a good and sufficient deed conveying to Lessee the property, free and clear of all encumbrances, except such as may have been made or suffered by Lessee, and except taxes and assessments, if any, and this lease. In case Lessee shall elect to purchase the property, he shall signify his election by written notice served upon Lessor within the time above limited; and thereafter Lessor shall deliver to Lessee an abstract of title to the property within _____ days from the date of the service of such notice, and Lessee shall have _____ days after the delivery of such abstract in which to examine the title and to complete the purchase; provided, however, that the right of Lessee to exercise his option of purchase is expressly conditioned upon the faithful performance and observance by Lessee of all the

agreements, covenants, and conditions on his part herein contained and the payment to Lessor of all rents accrued up to the date of the completion of said purchase.

Instead of a full cash payment, as called out in the above sample paragraph, the terms of payment can be whatever is mutually agreed.

A lease purchase agreement will have a section similar to the above except that instead of an option, the agreement will contain a firm commitment to purchase. Usually, both types of agreements will contain all details of a purchase; an exception is that sometimes the future purchase price will be linked to some factor which can pinned down at the time of purchase.

The following example shows how a knowledgeable investor used the lease-purchase approach and benefited himself and the seller.

LEASE-PURCHASE GIVES CONTROL OF APARTMENT BUILDING WITH NO DOWN PAYMENT

The owner of four apartment buildings had been urged by his physician to move to Arizona and to "take it easy." He had already sold his 24 unit, 30 unit, and 32 unit buildings. He still had no buyer for his fourth building which had only seven units. He owned it free and clear.

George J., a purchasing agent for a manufacturing company, had read advertisements on residential income property for sale for the past two years and had inspected several two to four unit buildings. He had purchased his home eighteen years before and had only two more years to pay on a 20 year amortized loan.

Mr. J. learned of the seven unit building. The asking price of $135,000 was 7.1 times gross revenue. This "gross multiplier" (7.1X) compared favorably with other apartment buildings in the community. The building was well kept with no apparent deferred maintenance. The rents being charged were perhaps slightly under market. He also learned that the owner was eager to sell and complete his move to Arizona.

George J. proposed a lease-purchase contract with a five year lease and the purchase to be consummated at the end of five years. The lease would be on a triple net basis with monthly payments of $1,250 or $15,000 per year. He proposed that the owner consider $12,150 (nine percent of $135,000) as his annual return on investment and that the monies paid over and above this amount be applied to the purchase price. By the end of the fifth year the total amount to be credited would

HIGH LEVERAGE LEASE AND LEASE-PURCHASE

be $14,250. The seller agreed provided the contract included adequate protection for himself in case of default during the five year lease period. Ten days later they signed the lease-purchase agreement.

Thus, George J. had accomplished his objective of gaining control of an apartment building with eventual ownership scheduled and he had done it with no down payment. He would have a slightly negative cash flow at first but he considered this factor to be more than offset by the no-down-payment feature. He also had, in reserve, the possibility of refinancing his home for additional cash if it became necessary. The seller's needs were satisfied and he retained the protection of not passing title until the buyer had paid in the equivalent of an acceptable down payment.

SIX KEYS TO USE OF PURCHASE-LEASEBACKS AND LEASE-PURCHASE AGREEMENTS

1. If you want to purchase real estate from an owner-user and lease it back to him, itemize and describe all the advantages of the transaction to him. Do your homework thoroughly!
2. Organize your search for an owner-user for a purchase-leaseback deal. An organized, systematic search will help you locate the most advantageous deal. Reread the example of Benjamin G. in this chapter.
3. Keep in mind that the purchase price of property in a purchase-leaseback and the size of the lease payments are interdependent factors. You may be able to purchase property for less than full market value if you accept lower lease payments.
4. It is not necessary to have ownership in order to make profits in real estate. Whether you have a substantial amount of money for investment or none at all, consider obtaining a long-term lease as a possible road to your fortune in real estate.
5. Use other people's money to gain leverage and increase your own profits.
6. Make use of the lessee's credit rating in order to borrow money for a purchase-leaseback deal. Lenders are more interested in the lessee's credit rating than they are in your own.

REMEMBER THESE POINTS

- A sale-leaseback and a purchase-leaseback agreement describe the same document. The term used depends on whether you are the seller or buyer.

- Use an organized, systematic search to find the best property for your investment.
- Some sellers will accept a lease-purchase agreement instead of an immediate sale with a down payment.
- You can profit by subleasing after obtaining a long-term lease. Ownership is not necessary for earning profits in real estate.
- The main advantages of sale-leaseback are:
  - improves liquidity
  - decreases indebtedness
  - improves balance sheet
  - frees tied-up capital for use as working capital
  - can get special purpose building constructed without tying up own capital
  - possible capital-gains profit
  - obtain tax advantage of charging off land value.
- The main advantages of purchase-leaseback to investor are:
  - reap profits with almost no personal attention required
  - get excellent built-in tenant
  - typically, a building has several years life after lease expires and property is usually then owned free and clear
  - investor has a "hedge" against inflation
  - high return on investment
- A small investor can profit from purchase-leaseback deals. A large amount of money is not necessary.
- You can use leverage in a purchase-leaseback and increase your profits.

8

HOW TO GET THE MONEY YOU NEED FOR YOUR REAL ESTATE VENTURES

The best source of financing for a proposed real estate investment depends upon several factors. And because conditions change, an astute entrepreneur who is always seeking the optimum financing to suit his own needs and goals may choose three different types of sources for three successive deals even though the properties in each case are similar. Some factors affecting the choice of a financing source are:

- The type of real estate, i.e., residential income, commercial, industrial, or raw land
- Your needs and goals at the time of structuring the deal
- Who has money at the time, e.g., savings and loan associations may be temporarily short of funds and local syndicate prospects may be fully invested
- The terms of various available loans

- Whether improvements exist or are to be constructed, e.g., savings and loan associations cannot lend money on property which does not exist
- Whether high leverage is needed
- Whether a seller is in a position to extend credit
- Tax considerations, especially if the seller is involved in the financing
- Government regulations, e.g., laws in your state
- Whether government financing or guarantees are available.

A loan application form is a document which should be examined and completed with care. The key points to consider will be discussed in this chapter. Borrowing from savings and loan associations and insurance companies will be covered. An example in this chapter shows how an entrepreneur obtained financing for a $1,500,000 building from his best future tenant. Other examples and discussion cover two-step loans (interim and takeout), finding private investors, and the financing of a special-purpose building.

FINANCING BY SAVINGS AND LOAN ASSOCIATIONS

Savings and loan associations have been under the control of and regulated by our government for so long that many people assume that they are all alike. Differences still exist, however, and it pays to compare. On any given day the interest rate at one savings and loan association may be ⅛ or ¼ percent lower than at another. Also the "points" and other fees charged will vary from one to another.

Avoid the appearance of having a financing need which has been shopped around. A comparision of interest rates and points charged should be done before making it known you are seeking financing for a specific venture. Ask your local Realtor for information. If he is a member of the local realty board, he may even have an up-to-date summary sheet showing current interest rates and points for all of your community's savings and loan associations.

WHAT LENDERS LOOK FOR

Whether your intended source for a loan is a savings and loan association or not, it pays to approach the lender fully prepared. A lender will look at:

- *Integrity*—Your integrity is of prime importance to a lender. The documentation you present to a lender should include both business and personal references. He will check your credit

HOW TO GET THE MONEY YOU NEED

history; be sure to include data on any loans you have or have paid off.

- *Ability to Pay*—Any lender will want to know how you plan to pay your debt obligations, including your proposed new indebtedness to him. Your documentation should include a written plan for payment. Point out your reserve ability to pay in lean times, e.g., a period of unusually high vacancies in an apartment building.
- *Balance Sheet*—Prepare your personal balance sheet before approaching a lender. Tell the lender you have one already prepared and present it to him at the proper time, i.e., perhaps when he indicates he is interested in a loan of the type you're requesting. A form for a personal balance sheet is given in Chapter 19. You may want to review it first with your accountant when you have completed it—or have your accountant prepare it.
- *Personal Data Sheet*—You could, of course, orally convey personal information about yourself to the lender. It is much more professional to take with you a personal data sheet. Use the format presented in Chapter 19 and add to it items you think will be of interest to a lender.
- *Projected Cash Flow*—Your ability to pay and the property's ability to pay for itself should be illustrated by a cash flow sheet. Use the following abbreviated form, but itemize all items, especially those under "operating expenses."

PROJECTED ANNUAL CASH FLOW
FOR PROPERTY AT 1313 MAPLE ST.

Gross Scheduled Cash Income	$ _____
Less Vacancy Allowance	_____
Net Scheduled Cash Income	_____
Less Operating Expenses	_____
Less Allowance for Maintenance/Repair	_____
Less Taxes	_____
Net Cash Income Before Interest	_____
Interest Expense (1st year)	_____
Net Cash Income After Interest	_____
Reduction of Principal (1st year)	_____
Net Cash Flow	_____

The preceding format is similar to a profit and loss statement. The difference is that your P & L statement at the end of your taxable year will have actual (instead of projected) dollars and you will include the non-cash items of depreciation and amortization for tax purposes.

- *Loan-to-Value Ratio*—Lenders are interested in "down-side" protection, i.e., they consider their position in the event you default on your payments. Thus, they are interested in the ratio of your requested loan and the market value of the property. If you are seeking a large loan, you will need to stress your overall ability to make payments. Emphasize your liquid assets and other assets which can readily be converted to cash.
- *Data and Financial Information on the Property:* If the seller of a property has not furnished you with a complete portfolio on the property, one should be assembled before contacting the lender. Professionalism in this area pays off.

PREVIEW ALL LOAN DOCUMENTS BEFORE APPLYING FOR LOAN

In the prior section the emphasis was on what the lender looks for in considering your application for a loan. I have found that it is equally important, as a borrower, to be as critical as the lender in considering all aspects of a loan. Lenders are, of course, seeking (1) the highest return on loans they can get, (2) the greatest security, and (3) high loan fees (points) and charges. Borrowers are typically seeking (1) lowest possible interest rate, (2) lowest available loan fees, (3) longest term possible, and (4) avoidance of personal liability.

Most loan application forms contain only a minimum of details about the proposed terms and conditions of the proposed financing. When a lender approves your loan application, the legal documents (i.e., the note, the trust deed or mortgage, and other documents) are suddenly presented for your signature. Many entrepreneurs have then found themselves in a position of not having time to negotiate another loan with a different source and necessarily accepting provisions in the loan which they would normally have considered unacceptable.

I have found it highly advisable to get samples of all documents to be used *before* signing a loan application. Items which should be checked before signing include the following.

Checklist for use before applying for loan

- All loan documents and the loan application form to be examined by borrower and his attorney before signing loan application
- Cost of obtaining the loan, i.e., loan fees (including points)
- Time allowed for lender to approve loan application
- Prepayment penalties—for possible full prepayment and for partial prepayments of principal

HOW TO GET THE MONEY YOU NEED

- Loan appraisal charge, if any
- Provisions for late payments per terms of loan
- Required insurance—obtainable from any company
- Restrictions on secondary financing
- Guarantees required
- Personal liability by the borrower
- Possible assumption of loan by new owner if property is sold at a later date
- Escalation clause requiring payment of loan in full if property sold at a later date
- Requirement for a new land survey
- Assignment of income from the property to secure payments by borrower
- Restrictions on occupancy of mortgaged property
- Cost and type of title policy required and by what company
- All other costs associated with obtaining the loan.

Whenever it is possible, I suggest that you get a firm loan commitment before signing any documents. If it is not possible, then obtain samples of all documents to be used and review them with your attorney to help ensure that you do not find yourself in a position of accepting a loan with unanticipated and undesirable provisions.

HOW AN ENTREPRENEUR OBTAINED FINANCING FOR A $1,500,000 BUILDING FROM HIS BEST FUTURE TENANT

An attorney, Anthony A., had formed a three-man syndicate nearly two years earlier to purchase a small suburban office building in which he had leased space for seven years. His two partners had recently suggested to Anthony A. that he seek a larger office building and perhaps trade in their small one. The real estate broker who handled Mr. A.'s purchase two years ago mentioned a 24 year old office building located at the corner of a major intersection. He had been trying to sell it and/or to lease the vacant ground floor for nine months. The upper floors were leased as office suites. He mentioned that a bank and another well known businessman had made a brief inspection, but had rejected it quickly because of inadequate off-street parking. One possible buyer had obtained estimates for making selected cosmetic improvements, but had purchased another building instead. After inspecting the property, Anthony A. obtained the name of the bank from the broker and learned that the bank had not yet leased other quarters for their proposed branch office.

In a conference with the bank's regional vice president, Mr. A. described his plans for nearly doubling the parking capacity by constructing a second story parking lot above the existing parking. The new parking level would be sufficient for all tenants above the first floor. He also described his plans for improving the appearance of the building. He asked if the bank, with these changes made, would be interested in leasing the ground floor. With encouragement from the bank Mr. A. and his two partners obtained an option on the building and estimates for building the parking structure and renovating the building. They also found three additional investors who were interested in becoming members of a syndicate if a new one were formed. Mr. A. then asked for and received a construction loan commitment for $1,500,000 from the bank for a period equal to the time needed for construction plus nine months.

Mr. A. formed a six-man syndicate, exercised the option, obtained a long term lease agreement with the bank contingent only upon governmental approval of a new bank branch at that location, and completed the construction within 15 months. The bank occupied the first floor three months later.

Thus, Mr. A. had shown his own creativity by recognizing and overcoming the shortcomings of a property and by satisfying the needs of an A-1 future tenant. And he had obtained the needed financing from that same tenant.

TWO-STEP—INTERIM AND TAKEOUT

Partly because of law or government regulations and partly as a result of voluntary specialization, many lenders do not make loans on properties which do not exist. Savings and loan associations and insurance companies are prohibited by law from doing so. If, for example, you purchase a lot and wish to build an office building, the usual procedure is to obtain a short-term loan (also called an interim, temporary, or construction loan) to finance the construction costs. Depending upon your financial position, the lender may require that you have a long-term loan (also called "takeout" loan or "permanent" loan) commitment valid after construction is completed, before granting you an interim loan. The takeout loan takes the short-term lender out of the project after construction is completed.

It is sometimes possible to deviate from the above procedure somewhat and minimize loan fees and costs. For example, I purchased a house several years ago which had no swimming pool. I had a savings and loan association state what their maximum loan would be if a swimming pool already existed. The final loan papers were drawn for a loan with pool included, but the lender withheld an amount equal to the pool construction costs and gave it to me when I presented evidence that the pool was built and all costs paid.

If Mr. A., in the example in the preceding section, had followed a similar procedure in financing the second level parking structure, he might have saved some loan costs and paid a lower interest rate on the amount borrowed before construction.

MASTER SERGEANT GETS INSURANCE COMPANY TAKEOUT COMMITMENT FOR $850,000

Five years before he retired as a master sergeant, Michael N. had inherited a vacant lot which was zoned for apartments. He owned it free and clear. He and Mrs. N. had talked at length with Mrs. N.'s Realtor-brother about building on the lot. The Realtor advised building, in part because the community had changed from one which had been overbuilt with apartments to one with a shortage of rental units. When Mr. N. applied for a construction loan of $850,000 for a proposed 60 unit building, his banker told him that he would make the loan if Mr. N. obtained a takeout commitment. Mr. N. telephoned the East Coast headquarters of a major insurance company and was referred to the company's local representative for real estate loans. Eventually, he obtained a letter from the insurance company with a takeout commitment of $850,000. Upon presentation of the commitment letter to the bank, he was granted the requested interim loan.

LOCATING PRIVATE INVESTORS FOR YOUR PROJECT

In Chapter 2, in the section "How to Find Syndicate Investors," I described a highly organized, methodical way of building a list of potential investors for your real estate ventures. The emphasis there was on locating and compiling information on private individuals who would be possible investors. I highly recommend that you follow this structured way of preparation ahead of your next project if you plan to include other investors in your real estate projects.

In addition, all of the creativity and innovativeness you can muster should be utilized. A creative real estate entrepreneur tends not to merely accept situations as they are presented or described to him. He is continually thinking of alternatives. He is always interested in the needs, wants, and motivations of sellers and potential investors.

I know from direct experience in teaching at a Los Angeles university that how to teach creativity and innovativeness is a question which continues to plague educators. In the real estate investment area, one approach is to learn all you can about creative and innovative actions by others in your field. Then by asking yourself how those actions could have been more beneficial to those involved you may be able to devise an even more creative course of action.

INVESTMENT REVIEW CHECKLIST

Another approach is to ask yourself the following list of questions, whenever they are pertinent, about any new potential project or potential investor in your project:

- What is the highest and best use for this property?
- Why is the seller selling?
- What will the seller do with the money he receives?
- Is the seller a potential source for funding this venture?
- Should I consider a very long term lease instead of purchasing this property?
- What type of private investor is the best for the financing I need?
- Would I be better off to get maximum financing from a savings and loan association or by forming a syndicate?
- Should I insist upon a long term option and buy it only if I locate additional tenants?
- Is there a major user of office space who might be interested both in investing and in occupying vacant space?
- Should I concentrate in looking only for properties which are being mismanaged?
- Should this apartment building be converted into a condominium complex and would the units sell readily?
- Am I active enough in making sure that people I contact know of my involvement and interest in real estate?
- Are my attorneys and his acquaintances interested in investing?
- What are my strong points in real estate?
- What do I need to learn about this proposed venture?
- Why should private or public sources of funds be interested in funding my project?
- Should I reexamine my own goals, needs, and desires in real estate investing?

- What are the needs, goals, desires, and motivations of each potential investor on my list?
- How can I structure the financing to give tax benefits for possible investors?
- How could I have done things better on my last project? And the one before that?
- Am I missing any real estate needs of my community?
- What are the best types of property for investment now, one year from now, and five years hence?
- What is happening in various geographical areas of my community?

The possible list of such questions is almost endless. Add your own to the list above. Each time you encounter a new situation or read about an interesting transaction, see if another two or three additions can be made to your list.

HOW TO CONVINCE INDIVIDUALS TO COMMIT THEIR MONEY TO FINANCE YOUR PROJECT

Once you have completed the investigation and analysis of your proposed project and prepared the documents described earlier in this chapter, you are ready to approach your selected sources for financing. The most important next step is to preselect and qualify potential investors. They should be known to have an interest in the type of investment represented by your project. If possible, one should also determine whether an investor currently has funds available before approaching him.

The four most important questions to ask yourself before meeting a potential investor face-to-face are:

1. Why should he invest in this particular project?
2. Why should he invest in *me*?
3. What is in it for him?
4. Does the project offer benefits which would satisfy his needs and/or wants?

If some of the above questions are still unanswered when you meet with your selected investors, the initial part of the meeting can be used to fill in the gaps. With a quality project and satisfactory answers to the above questions, your presentation should result in a commitment by the investor. I do not, however, rely on an investor seeing the answers to these key questions himself. I include them as a part of my presentation.

HOW A $2,300,000 SPECIAL-PURPOSE BUILDING WAS FINANCED BY SPECIAL-INTEREST INDIVIDUALS

Roger Z. is a computer analyst turned salesman. He had originally been hired by a small accounting firm to computerize the bookkeeping and billing services they performed for their professional clients. Most of the firm's clients were physicians, surgeons, and dentists. Roger Z. had spent the last three years soliciting new accounts and servicing existing ones.

One of their clients, a physician, happened to mention that he had heard that a proposed new medical building would not be built after all. Mr. Z. learned that the owner of the vacant lot had indefinitely postponed the project when he had suffered a financial setback on another venture. Construction plans for the building were virtually complete. The lot was within easy walking distance from a major hospital.

Roger Z. talked with four of his more affluent clients (all physicians) and found all interested in investing and moving into a new building so near the hospital. He also talked with many of his other clients and found that there was a shortage and a good demand for desirable office space by medical professionals. The developer told Roger Z. that he was thinking of selling the lot and retiring. He had paid $450,000 for it and owed $250,000 to the former owner. Mr. Z. borrowed a copy of the building plans. The building was designed specifically for use by medical professionals. The estimated total cost was $2,300,000 including the land. The developer gave a 60 day option to Mr. Z. for $1,000.

After four more weeks of effort, Mr. Z. presented a complete plan of action to the developer and six prequalified physicians and surgeons. He had been assured by his banker that the venture was financeable. He proposed forming a syndicate in the form of a limited partnership with himself as the general partner. The developer would own 2/9 of the partnership's assets for assigning his $200,000 equity in the land to the partnership. Mr. Z. would have 1/9 for assigning his option and managing the venture. Each of the six medical men would have 1/9 interest upon each furnishing $100,000 capital. The medical professionals agreed, but the developer wanted $100,000 in cash plus 1/9 of the partnership. Mr. Z. located another surgeon who agreed to participate on the same basis as his colleagues. Roger Z.'s attorney prepared the limited partnership agreement and other documents and they all signed.

Roger Z. made a formal application to his banker for a construction loan. The bank said they would make the requested loan, but that they would require either the developer's personal guarantee (the developer had an excellent credit rating and a high net worth) or the signatures of the medical professionals involved. The bank also required a letter of commitment for a takeout loan on the property. At this point Mr. Z. had learned, the hard way, that it is important to check out all points of proposed financing before making a loan application and before forming a syndicate. It was Mr. Z.'s first large venture in real estate. He was not aware of any checklist, as given previously in this chapter, for use early in seeking financing.

At a meeting of all the partners, the developer refused to personally guarantee the entire financing, but said he would sign along with the other partners. They agreed. The limited partnership agreement was redrawn as a general partnership. Mr. Z. obtained a letter of commitment for a takeout loan from an insurance company, and the bank granted the interim (construction) loan. The building was constructed and was fully leased before construction was completed.

The importance of checking all aspects of proposed financing at an early time cannot be overemphasized. In the example above, Mr. Z. was quite fortunate. The venture might have easily fallen apart when he learned of the requirement for personal guarantees beyond his own signature at such a late stage in the project. It is very difficult to return to investors and ask them for their personal guarantees after they have taken a limited partnership position. A primary factor which enabled Mr. Z. to complete the financing on the medical building was a shortage of desirable medical office space and the personal interest by his investors in occupying space in the building themselves. His special-purpose building had been financed by special-interest individuals.

SIX KEYS TO SUCCESS IN OBTAINING FINANCING FROM PRIVATE AND PUBLIC SOURCES

1. Maintain up-to-date knowledge of factors in the real estate financial world. Your optimum type of source for money on a proposed current venture may be different than the type of source you used a year earlier. Conditions change. Up-to-date knowledge is essential to know which type to approach.
2. Make an effort to predict future conditions in the financial world. For example—if savings and loan associations have plenty of money on hand but the federal government plans to borrow heavily a few months later, then an entrepreneur should head toward other types of sources for future projects.

Heavy government borrowing tends to deplete deposits at savings and loan associations.

3. The number of your successes and the financial benefits to you can most likely be increased by checking all aspects of proposed financing *before* signing a loan application. Use the checklist provided in this chapter.
4. The method of financing and the source should be selected only after thorough analysis. The financial results of your venture can vary from mediocre to very good depending upon your expertise in financing.
5. Successful entrepreneurs do their homework first. Whether you are approaching private individuals or an institution, a well prepared presentation will definitely increase the probability of getting funds on terms favorable to you.
6. Deliberately consider every creative or innovative way you can think of in structuring the financing or finding and selecting sources for money.

REMEMBER THESE POINTS

- Analyze various means of financing your project to determine the optimum mode.
- Request a copy of the loan application form and copies of all documents to be used in a loan. Have your attorney examine them with you.
- Use the checklist given in this chapter before applying for a loan.
- Avoid getting in the position of having a financing need which has been shopped around.
- Enlist the aid of your local realtor or other professionals when needed.
- Do your homework. Be fully prepared before approaching any source of funds.
- Before making a construction loan, a lender most likely will require a takeout loan commitment.
- Organize your efforts in locating investors.
- Before approaching a potential investor in your project, ask yourself:
  - Why should he invest in this project?
  - Why should he invest in me?
  - What is in it for him?
  - Does the project offer the benefits he wants?

9

USING THE SELLER'S MONEY TO FINANCE YOUR INVESTMENTS

The owner of property which you want to acquire is one of the best bets for participation in financing your real estate ventures. Experienced and innovative entrepreneurs realize that involving the seller is frequently one of the most powerful and productive approaches in structuring the financing. But, of course, they also deliberately consider various other ways of financing for their own best interest and the interest of others involved with them.

Frequently, one can get a somewhat lower interest rate from the seller but usually the loan is for a shorter term, in comparison with financing by conventional sources. If secondary financing will be required for a project, then the seller should be approached early in negotiations and asked to accept a second mortgage. In all states where it is legal, there is usually a large fee charged along with a high interest rate if a third party, i.e., one not involved in the negotiations, agrees to take a second mortgage. In states with stringent regulations and controls on interest rates, fees, and mortgages, it is difficult to get secondary financing from anyone but the seller.

There are various ways of involving the seller in financing your venture. One is to ask the seller to sell to you on credit, that is, on an installment basis. The security for the credit in this approach is the property he values so highly, i.e., the property he is trying to sell to you. A variation is to ask the seller to borrow money on the property before selling it to you. If he does so, you are then making use of the seller's credit rating to finance your acquisition. This approach provides the seller with cash although he has the primary responsibility for repaying the borrowed money. A check list of the various ways of structuring such deals is given in the following section.

LOOK FOR TAX ADVANTAGES TO THE SELLER—HE MAY FINANCE DEAL HIMSELF

One example in this chapter shows how a tax advantage to the seller enabled an entrepreneur to convince him to finance the transaction. Another example illustrates the use of the seller's credit to finance the acquisition of a property without a down payment. The convincing factor was an appreciable financial advantage for the seller.

A seller is naturally most interested in the number of dollars he will have *after* taxes are paid. If you can show him a way to structure the sale or financing to reduce or postpone the taxes to be paid by the seller, your chance of acquiring the property on terms favorable to you are substantially increased.

CHECKLIST OF TAX ADVANTAGES

Various ways of reducing and/or postponing taxes to be paid by a seller are discussed in this book and case examples are given to show how others have used these ways. Transactions (with tax advantages to the seller) which are most frequently used by those familiar with insider's secrets are listed in the following checklist.

- *Installment Sale*—you must pay less than 30 per cent of the purchase sale to the seller during his tax year which includes the date of the sale.
- *Installment Land Contract*—this approach is similar to an ordinary installment sale except the seller has additional protection by not passing title until a later date (see Chaper 11).
- *Lease with Purchase Option*—a purchase option means, of course, that the lessee may or may not exercise the option within

USING THE SELLER'S MONEY TO FINANCE

the specified time period. No sale has occurred at the outset and no tax liability (because of a sale) is incurred by the lessor. Also, the option may call for less than thirty per cent down and further allow the seller to postpone most of the ultimate capital gains tax to years beyond the date of exercise of the option.

- *Lease Purchase Agreement*—most of the lease purchase agreements I've seen will not qualify for tax benefits. If, however, the future purchase price is not fixed but depends upon factors not predictable at the outset, then the transaction *may* be considered "not a sale" by the IRS until the price is fixed. If you are the seller, this latter point should be checked carefully before signing the agreement.
- *Land Cost*—an owner cannot depreciate the portion of the value of a property which is assigned to the land. It may be to your tax advantage to sell the underlying land and lease it back for a large number of years. Lease payments are deductible as an expense.
- *Corporate Ownership*—if the seller personally owns property you're buying on a lease with option, it *may* be to his advantage to convert to corporate ownership before selling to you. Conversely, it may be to your advantage to change your form of ownership before selling a property.
- *Borrowing*—a seller may accept less than 30 per cent down from you and then borrow money with your note as security if he must have the additional money up front.

Learning about the seller's wants and needs during your negotiations with him may enable you to suggest a way of structuring a deal to provide tax advantages for him.

HOW AN ENTREPRENEUR STRUCTURED FOR FINANCING BY SELLER—SELLER'S ORDINARY INCOME CONVERTED TO CAPITAL GAINS PROFIT

Kenneth E. is an accounting instructor with four years tenure at a junior college. He has a degree in business administration. In his spare time he was handling the bookkeeping and tax returns for an individual who owned apartment and industrial buildings. His part time employer mentioned that the owner of one of the city's oldest office buildings was thinking of selling. The employer was not interested in diversifying his activity by becoming involved in office buildings.

Mr. E. learned that the owner of the office building was 63 years old, a wealthy widower, and had no heirs. Besides his income from the building, the owner had ordinary income in the six-figure range from non-real estate investments. The owner's net income from the building was $82,000 per year. It was, of course, taxed as ordinary income. He had purchased the building 39 years ago and owned it free and clear. He told Kenneth E. that he felt the building was worth at least $750,000 and that he would sell it for 29 percent down. He'd carry the balance himself at 8 ½ percent interest with payments on a 30 year amortization schedule. He expressed a wish to "take it easy" and not be concerned with daily management of real estate.

Kenneth E. admitted frankly that he had very little to pay down. He asked that they meet again three days later to discuss an offer which he said he felt would be of interest to the seller.

In order to increase the chance of the seller accepting an exceptionally low down payment, Kenneth E. decided to offer $50,000 more than the seller had stated as his price. He offered $800,000 with $5,000 down, payments of $5,750 per month ($69,000 per year), and an interest rate of 7 per cent. Thus, assuming that the net income remained the same, Mr. E. would have $13,000 per year ($82,000 − $69,000) cash income plus a buildup of equity with each payment.

The advantages of the deal for Mr. E. were straightforward and obvious. The advantages to the seller were not so obvious. Mr. E. described them in detail to the seller. The seller's after-tax income was $24,600 per year on his before-tax income of $82,000 from the building. Of the first year's payment of $69,000, $55,650 would be interest income (taxable as ordinary income) and $13,350 would qualify for capital gains treatment. Thus the seller would have an after-tax income of approximately $16,695 plus $10,012.50 or $26,707.50 in the first year. His after-tax income would thus be $2,707.50 higher than before the sale and he would not have to devote time to management. Mr. E. also mentioned that if there were no changes in tax laws, the after-tax income would increase each year because the amount of the annual payment attributed to interest income would decrease with a corresponding increase in payment of principal. For example, when interest and principal payments reached $40,000 and $29,000 per year respectively, the seller would have $33,750 per year after-tax income (compared with $26,707.50 the first year) if the seller's other income remained high and the tax laws remained unchanged. The seller re-examined the figures presented by Kenneth E., step by step. Although he would qualify for capital gains tax treatment even if he sold for all cash, he would then have the problem of investing the cash which remained after payment of the tax. Also, as he pointed out to Mr. E., if he sold for $750,000 cash he would have only approximately $600,000 to invest whereas in Mr. E.'s proposal he, the seller, was in effect lending Mr. E. $795,000 and collecting interest on the larger amount. The fact that the seller would be collecting interest on an additional $195,000 (in comparison with selling for cash and lending the after-tax cash proceeds on other real estate) was an important point Mr. E. had overlooked. Fortuitously, he had added another advantageous factor to his knowledge for possible use on future real estate deals. The seller accepted the offer.

Thus, Mr. E. had made use of one of the least known insider's secrets of real estate investing. He had structured a deal whereby a seller could convert a portion of ordinary income into capital gains. He had found a seller and a property with the right characteristics. The seller was actively wanting to retire, he had no heirs, he had bought the property many years before, the property had a very low cost base, and he owned it free and clear. Mr. E. had the knowledge of this insider's secret of real investing and the ability to show the seller how it was in his own best interest. With only $5,000 invested, Mr. E. controlled an $800,000 building. He was on his way to a fortune in real estate and was receiving $13,000 cash per year!

USE SELLER'S CREDIT TO FINANCE REAL ESTATE VENTURE

Even an experienced, successful entrepreneur in real estate investing will sometimes find that he is fully extended in borrowing funds and is not in a position to finance another venture by using conventional sources of money. For example, he may have fully used his line of credit in financing his last investment. In several examples given in this book, the entrepreneur is one who is involved in his first or second project in real estate investment. In many cases, such investors do not yet have balance sheets built up sufficiently to qualify for financing any but the smallest projects.

Whether you are fully extended or not, using a seller's credit to finance your next venture may be the best approach for you. In any event, use of this insider's technique for financing a venture should be considered along with all of the other possible ways of financing.

Most properties which are for sale stipulate "cash to existing loan" (C/EL) or "cash to new loan" (C/NL) as the terms offered to a buyer. A buyer is, of course, free to make an offer stipulating the terms he desires. In fact, an experienced entrepreneur will regard terms offered or specified by a seller or real estate broker as merely one input.

He will consistently use all the creativity and innovativeness he can to determine the optimum possible way to structure a purchase contract and the desired financing.

Almost all real estate brokers make an effort to avoid the buyer and seller meeting face-to-face before a transaction is finalized. I believe that brokers are perfectly justified in this effort. There have been many deals which have fallen apart because of some triviality or a personality conflict between buyer and seller. With a broker as a middle man, acting as a buffer between buyer and seller, many of these stumbling blocks can be much more easily resolved or prevented if they do not occur during a face-to-face discussion between the two principals. Emotions or ego-bruising situations in the real investment area are not as frequently encountered, in comparison with sales of personal residences, but they do sometimes occur.

On the other hand, if I plan to ask a seller to use his credit in financing a project for me, I will hold bringing up the subject until I am face-to-face with the seller. Then I discuss other aspects of the transaction before asking or suggesting a plan with liberal credit given by the seller or wherein the seller would use his credit to borrow funds before transferring the property to me. If a broker is involved one must first convince the broker that an in-person conference between principals is desirable.

Use of the seller's credit in financing a real estate investment may be just the factor needed to enable you to take the next step along your way to a fortune in real estate. If it is the best way for you, do your homework and then present your offer to the seller, including the use of his credit rating.

HOW ANDREW K. USED SELLER'S CREDIT TO FINANCE APARTMENT BUILDING AND POCKETED $20,000

Andrew K. is the U.S. mail carrier who attempted to acquire a 60 unit apartment building as described in an example in Chapter 3. After selling his option on the large building for a profit of $50,000, he abandoned his search for another apartment complex until the credit crunch among lending institutions was much less severe. He had paid income tax on the $50,000 profit as ordinary income. During the interim he had attempted to make money in commodity futures, but had lost $15,000. Although he personally knew investors who spoke of very good profits in commodity trading (and probably truthfully so) he resolved to confine his efforts to residential income real estate.

He learned that a 20 unit apartment building was possibly

available, although it had not been placed on the market. Each unit had two bedrooms and one and one-half baths. The building was U-shaped and built around a swimming pool. It was seven years old. The rent of $190 per unit had remained constant for two years. The actual vacancy factor for the last one and one-half years was a very low 1.3 percent. The scheduled gross income was $45,600 per year.

In answer to the question of why the owner was selling, he learned that the owner had taken the building in trade on a $2,100,000 industrial building which he had sold sixteen months earlier. The trade-in value was $310,000. The seller's occupation for the past twenty-five years was the development of and investment in industrial property. He was interested in selling the apartment building and staying in the area of real estate he knew best. He said he had devoted very little time to the apartment building and felt that the rents were overdue for an increase. He asked $310,000 for the property with $79,000 down and buyer to assume the $231,000 existing mortgage with an eight percent interest rate. Andrew K. verified that there was no payoff penalty clause in the mortgage.

A few days later Andrew K. offered $310,000 for the property with an initial payment of $20,000, a one year note for $59,000 at nine percent interest, and assumption of the existing mortgage. The offer also stated that Andrew planned to refinance the property within less than one year and stipulated that the seller would either (1) cosign with Andrew K. on the new loan or (2) lend an equivalent amount to Andrew K. himself. After the seller added the limitation that the said loan would not exceed eighty percent of an amount equal to 7½ times the annualized gross income at the time of the loan, he accepted the offer.

Andrew K. immediately repainted portions of the building, improved the appearance of the front of the building, the lobby, and the yard. He then increased the rents to yield an annualized scheduled gross income of $57,600. At the end of eight months he obtained a loan of $340,000 at nine percent interest and 30 year amortization. The combination of increased income and the seller's signature on the loan made it easily possible.

After paying the note to the seller, paying off the old mortgage, and deducting the costs of improvements, Andrew K. had recovered the $20,000 down payment he had made and pocketed an additional $20,000! By using the seller's credit, he obtained a loan of a size which he would most likely not have been able to get alone, even though he had substantially increased the income from the apartments.

BUYER-SELLER RAPPORT HELPS IN USING SELLER'S CREDIT

In the first example given in this chapter the emphasis was on tax benefits. In effect, the seller was using the buyer to convert ordinary income to income qualifying for capital gains treatment. The seller further benefitted by deferring taxes (by use of an installment sales contract) in that he was collecting interest income on a larger amount than he would have by selling for all cash and lending the after-tax proceeds. Making use of tax benefits is indeed an important factor in structuring deals in real estate.

Another factor just as important is the rapport which you, as the entrepreneur, establish with the seller during negotiations. For this reason, it is desirable to cover all of the financial and information data aspects of a deal before bringing up the subject of involving the seller in financing the property. The seller will be looking at your integrity—if he is not convinced that you are an honest, forthright, and capable individual he is much less likely to respond favorably to your request to extend liberal terms or to use his credit rating.

Experienced entrepreneurs never forget that they are selling themselves as well as the merits of an investment in talking with possible financial investors in a proposed venture or in negotiating with an owner to purchase his property. This people consciousness becomes even more important if you are thinking of involving the seller in financing the property you want to acquire.

SEVEN KEYS TO FINANCIAL SUCCESS BY USING SELLER'S MONEY OR CREDIT RATING

1. A seller can sometimes be the best source of all for financing your proposed real estate acquisition. A seller should automatically be considered as a source for money along with all other possibilities.

2. Your tax adviser may be able to help you determine tax advantages for the seller of property you're interested in. A tax advantage is one of the most powerful and attractive features you can present to a seller.

3. If the property you're intending to buy has an existing low loan-to-value ratio, consider asking the seller to refinance the property before selling it to you. Your tax adviser can help you determine advantages to the seller in this approach. In any event, it is a way for a seller to get the cash he wants and it

enables you to use the seller's credit rating to finance the project for you.

4. You, as the buyer, are free to propose terms which are much different from those offered by the seller. Many real estate brokers simply stipulate terms of cash to existing loan or cash to new loan. Your analysis may show that it is to your and the seller's advantage for the seller to give you liberal terms and carry the financing himself. Make your offer and back it up with a description of advantages.

5. You can frequently get a lower interest rate from a seller who carries the financing. Try for it on either a first or second mortgage basis. Also, you may be able to save the points or loan fees charged by conventional loan sources if you can persuade the seller to carry the financing.

6. If it is to your advantage, you may go so far as to offer more than the asking price (or at least equal it) if you can get extraordinarily liberal terms on other aspects of financing by the seller.

7. The amount of money one can borrow from conventional sources is naturally influenced by the cash flow from the property being financed. Give yourself time to increase income and/or decrease expenses by asking the seller to carry short-term financing. Then refinance when cash flow is improved.

REMEMBER THESE POINTS

- Consider financing by seller as one possible way to finance your venture.
- Ask seller to give financing terms to suit your need.
- Seller's proffered terms are just a starting point. Make your own offer.
- You may be able to use the seller's credit rating to get desired loan from a conventional source.
- Some sellers will accept lower interest rate than conventional source.
- You may be able to avoid loan fees charged by conventional sources by getting seller to carry financing.
- A seller is a potential candidate for joining your syndicate on property he's selling to you or on future projects.
- The best time to try for terms you want is while negotiating the purchase.

- Showing the seller how he can gain a **tax** benefit is a powerful and attractive factor.
- If the income of a property can be improved, ask the seller to carry a short-term note until you can refinance for a higher amount.
- Real estate brokers justifiably try to preclude buyer and seller meeting until deal is finalized. As a buyer, you may get better terms by overcoming broker's objection and presenting the offer in person.
- Try to establish rapport with seller.
- Remember **you're** also selling buyer on your integrity and capability. To get ultraliberal terms, seller must be convinced you will and can perform per the requested terms.

10

MORE KEY SOURCES OF OPM TO FINANCE YOUR WAY TO WEALTH

Sometimes an entrepreneur who has had one or more noteworthy successes in real estate ventures tends to use over and over again the techniques and the mode of financing which he used in his successes. But the ones who will achieve their ambition of making a fortune in real estate are those who view each new potential project as an entirely new situation and challenge. They enter into an analysis and evaluation with an open mind with respect to structuring the financing. If it has been a few months since they last evaluated the best way to finance a project, they will first make sure they have *up-to-date* knowledge of the financial community as it pertains to real estate. They know that conditions and circumstances change with time. They know that the type of source they chose for their prior venture is not necessarily the best type of source for the next one. They do their homework first and then determine which type of financing and which source is best for their proposed new project and for themselves.

The first example in this chapter shows how an entrepreneur used the limited partner approach in talking with sources for financing. The second example describes how an innovative and creative buyer used a contract-to-purchase in a no-money-down transaction. A third example illustrates the use of a lease-purchase contract and use of other people's money.

HOW TO USE LIMITED PARTNER APPROACH WITH NO MONEY OF YOUR OWN

Most private individuals with enough money to be considered a source for involvement in financing your real estate venture are familiar with what it means to be a partner. Some, however, may not be familiar with the differences and advantages of being a limited partner rather than a general partner. If you are asking private individuals to invest money and become limited partners in your prosped venture it is advisable to review the advantages (and restrictions) as a part of your presentation. The presentation is a selling effort and it may be the best chance you have of convincing them to join with you.

The most important advantage of a limited partner status is that the investor is financially liable only to the extent of his investment. On the other hand, if all partners in a general partnership except one goes bankrupt then that one is liable for all the debts relating to the partnership's property. In certain states, any remaining, non-bankrupt partner may even be held responsible for the personal debts of the bankrupt partners.

Forming a limited partnership is simple (compared with forming a corporation) and is inexpensive to organize in most states. But have your attorney, one familiar with real estate, prepare the limited partnership agreement. It is risky to use a so-called "standard" agreement. Also, for your further protection, urge each of the limited partners to have his own attorney review the agreement before he signs.

Another advantage is that all partners can share in depreciation as well as profits. Profits can be disbursed to the partners with each being taxed only once on the profit. Most corporations are taxed on the corporation's profits and then investors are taxed again on the same profits if the profits are distributed.

The major disadvantage is that no limited partner can have any voice in the management of the partnership's property. Any limited partner who violates this restriction is in danger of losing the protection of his liability being limited to the amount he invested.

Each partnership must have at least one general partner. The general partner has the responsibility of managing the property and is liable for all acts on behalf of the partnership. He does not enjoy the protection or limits on liability conferred upon the limited partners.

Many entrepreneurs have used the limited partner approach to acquire real estate without having any of their own money involved. If you have located a desirable property, evaluated it, formulated plans, and made financial projections, then you should be in a position to approach investors on the basis of their putting up the necessary money and sharing profits with you. If you have determined that your past and planned future efforts merit your having 50 percent of profits generated even though you are putting up no money, then this point should be made clear at the beginning of talks with potential investors. If, say, you are proposing that three investors each put up one-third of the required money and that you will manage the property, there is a strong "people" tendency for someone to suggest that the four of you share profits equally. This tendency is why it is important to take a stand early in the negotiations with respect to the percentage of profits you require.

LIMITED PARTNER APPROACH FINANCES APARTMENT BUILDING

James G. is a 34 year old mechanical engineer. He had worked at an aerospace company since he obtained an engineering degree eleven years ago. He joined an investment club one year after starting with the company. The club had specialized in investments in common stock. Adverse results in the market the past 18 months had reduced their club membership from 34 to 6 engineers. At a monthly meeting one member suggested that they sell their stock and distribute the proceeds or consider investing in income property. James G. mentioned that he had already made such a decision himself. He told the others that he had just obtained an option on a 16 unit apartment building and had asked his banker and a real estate broker to recommend potential investors for a limited partnership.

Upon being urged by the other members and impressed by their expressions of interest, James G. made a spontaneous verbal presentation to them. The two story apartment building had twelve one-bedroom apartments and four bachelor units. There was parking for 24 automobiles. The building was four blocks from the beach in an area where rents had been low for the last 15 or 20 years. He stated that the building was sound structurally, but had received minimum maintenance for the past ten years. It was showing a net income of only

6.5 percent of the asking price. James G. said that his analysis indicated that with cosmetic improvements the net income could be increased to eight or nine percent of the asking price. He said that the real profit potential was in the upgrading already taking place within a five block wide strip along the beach. He felt that remodeling the building three to five years later would result in a sale with a very good capital-gains profit.

James G. said that he was seeking an investor or investors to furnish the required capital and form a limited partnership on a fifty-fifty basis with himself, i.e., whether it was one or more investors, fifty percent of the net income and of any future profit from selling the property would go to those furnishing the capital and fifty percent to himself. He took pains to explain that each of the limited partners would be financially liable only to the extent of the capital they invested. Mr. G. would be the general partner and would have full authority along with complete responsibility for managing the property. He would also be liable for all acts or omissions connected with the apartment building. He mentioned that, unfortunately, they could not be active in management if they wished to be limited partners. He said he planned to submit monthly statements of operations (i.e., profit and loss statements) and a semiannual balance sheet. He also covered the tax benefits of depreciation to each one. The property was priced at $260,000 with 25 percent down. Mr. G. said that approximately $70,000 cash would be needed.

Four days later the group called Mr. G. and all five engineers agreed to invest $14,000 each on the terms as outlined. James G. had his attorney prepare papers for forming a limited partnership and recommended that each of them have his own attorney check the documents before signing. Three days later all had signed. James G.'s offer of $240,000 for the sixteen units was accepted.

This venture was Mr. G.'s first in real estate other than his own home. He had zeroed in on one highly effective way of financing a real estate venture with other people's money, i.e., by forming a limited partnership. By working closely with his attorney he had insured compliance with the state's laws and he had covered points ethically required before any investor put money in the project. He had also been careful to establish that he would get fifty percent of profits and he had already started looking for investors on that basis before the subject could come up in their investment club meeting. He has taken an important step toward building a fortune in real estate.

HOW TO USE CONTRACT-TO-PURCHASE WITH NO MONEY DOWN — TAX ADVANTAGES TO SELLER

In the area of residential sales, wherein the buyer is purchasing a house for his personal residence, the purchase contract used has become highly standardized. On the other hand, in the areas of raw land, commercial buildings, industrial property, and residential income real estate, the purchase contracts vary from one transaction to another. A purchase contract in these areas should be tailored to meet the needs of the buyer and seller and the property itself. An attorney with experience in real estate should be used — his fee can be more than offset by added dollars and profits in your pockets.

One type of purchase contract which has enabled thousands of entrepreneurs to build their fortunes in real estate is one which provides for gaining possession of property without any initial payment by the entrepreneur. An important factor in persuading a seller to sign such a contract is to structure it to provide tax advantages for the seller. For example, if a seller accepts a first mortgage as payment for 70 percent or less of the purchase price and if he has sold at a profit, then he must pay taxes on the entire amount. The tax he pays is the same as it would be if you had paid all cash for the property. On the other hand if a seller accepts less than 30 percent as a down payment then he would defer payment of taxes on profits on a proportionate basis until he actually receives payment. For instance, if in the second year you pay an amount on the principal equal to seven percent of the purchase price, then he would owe a tax for that same year on seven percent of his profit.

Sellers who are most likely to accept a purchase contract with no initial cash payment are those who have a good income from other sources and who have a personal (non-economic) reason for wanting to sell. If your goal is to negotiate a no-down-payment purchase contract, it is important that you tactfully learn why the seller wants to sell.

HOW A SHOP OWNER USED A CONTRACT-TO-PURCHASE TO GAIN CONTROL OF COMMERCIAL BUILDING WITH NO INITIAL CASH

Ever since the death of their landlord three years earlier the three tenants of a small, one story, 46 year old, commercial building had wondered if they would be able to renew their leases the next time around. One tenant, Harry C., had operated a radio and television shop in one of the stores for more than 20 years. His lease was due to expire within seven months. The other two tenants were also well established in the community with 12 and 14 years tenancy. Even though under the terms of the leases their rents could have been increased, the rates had remained the same for four years. All three had heard rumors that someone was going to buy the 90 foot by 100 foot property plus the remainder of the one-half block facing the major boulevard and build a multi-story office building.

Mr. C. called upon the widow-owner to see if the property was for sale. He learned she was thinking about selling it and other real estate and moving to another state to be near her married daughter and grandchildren. The price her financial adviser had set was $95,000 with 29 percent down and the balance amortized over ten years. She owned the property free and clear and would carry the balance herself. The building was old and outmoded but in good serviceable condition.

Harry C. talked with local bankers, savings and loan officials, and chamber of commerce executives and became convinced that the land alone was worth the asking price. The existing building added very little to the value of the property. He also found support for the belief that the block would eventually be occupied by multi-storied new buildings.

Mr. C. presented an offer in the form of a contract to purchase. The contract called for a price of $95,000 with zero down payment, nine percent interest rate, quarterly payments of $2,396.85, and a lump sum payment of $10,000 to be made not later than five years from the date of acceptance. Taxes, insurance, and all other costs associated with owning real estate were to be paid by Harry C. He mentioned that since their two children were almost grown, he and his wife planned to sell their four bedroom home within two or three years.

The seller reviewed the offer with her financial adviser. He recommended acceptance after he noted the provision that a trust deed would not be given until the lump sum payment was made. And, of course, the seller would be liable for taxes on her profit from the sale only as she received payments on the principal. If she had sold for cash or if she had extended credit for less than seventy percent of the purchase price, she would have incurred tax liability on the entire amount.

Thus, Mr. C. had become a landlord and an investor in income-producing real estate without using any of his cash, by using the contract-to-purchase approach. Time will tell the validity of his projection of a sale with a substantial profit within five to seven years. In the meantime, he is looking for another real estate venture.

USE OF LEASE AND LEASE-PURCHASE APPROACH TO PROFITS USING OTHER PEOPLE'S MONEY

Usually when an entrepreneur uses a straightforward lease to gain control of a property the lease is for a long term, say forty years or sometimes much longer. Steven C.'s use of a fifty year lease (described in Chapter 7) is an example of this approach. It gave him full control of the property for a fifty year period. It provided tax advantages for the owner (compared with selling the property) and annual profits for Mr. C. without Mr. C. owning the property.

A lease-purchase agreement goes one step further. If an owner does not need immediate cash and prefers to reap the profits from a sale at some future date then the entrepreneur without initial investment capital may be able to negotiate a lease-purchase. The contractual arrangement between the principals is on a lease basis, usually a triple net lease for the first few years, then a purchase is consummated per the terms of the original contract.

The following example describes how an entrepreneur tailored a lease-purchase agreement to take into account the seller's wants and needs. It shows how he gained control of a property with high promise for future capital gains profit and without any initial investment or down payment on his part.

HOW AN ENTREPRENEUR USED LEASE-PURCHASE CONTRACT TO GAIN CONTROL OF AN INDUSTRIAL COMPLEX

After making a profit of $60,000 by selling his option on a $1,100,000 office building (see Chapter 6) Elliott U. resumed his search for another real estate project. The buyer of his option had no need for further participation by Elliott U. after he increased the occupancy to 96 percent. As before, Mr. U. was searching for commercial or industrial property.

In driving through a small, three year old industrial building development he noticed that the percent occupancy seemed to be rather low. He went to the hall of records, obtained the names of the four owners of record and called upon one of them. The owner said that he had set up a limited partnership with the other three owners as limited partners and himself as the general partner. Based on statements made, Elliott U. inferred that the general partner was under heavy pressure by his partners to "do something." The records showed a negative cash flow. The complex consisted of 15 foot and 20 foot wide modular units offered for lease in one or more units. The typical tenant was a small manufacturer or specialized service company. One tenant was building a "Formula" racing car.

After he thoroughly checked the market and completed his analysis, Elliott U. presented a proposal for a lease-purchase agreement to the general partner. He proposed leasing the entire building complex on a triple net basis for six years at a rate equal to the monthly payments on their 30 year loan plus $4,000 per year. The contract provided for purchase of the property on or before the end of six years from date of acceptance, at a specified price and all cash (i.e., the sellers would receive the full purchase price in cash). The sellers made a counter offer accepting Elliott U.'s offer provided the agrement was amended to include either (1) splitting any profit realized upon resale of the property with 50 percent to Elliott U. and 50 percent to the sellers or (2) increase the purchase price by $40,000. They also required clarification that they would be paid all cash if Elliott U. completed the purchase before the end of the six year lease period.

Mr. U. agreed to alternate number two and had his attorney revise the lease-purchase agreement. After each of the others reviewed the agreement with his own attorney they signed.

The first month, Elliott U. had the same negative cash flow (after allowance for taxes) as the owners had been experiencing. At last contact, Elliot U. had substantially increased the occupancy and was pocketing a profit "in the lower four-figure range" monthly. He had not yet made any effort to find a buyer and complete his own purchase, but was planning to do so within a year or two.

Thus, Elliott U. had gained control of an industrial property without the use of any of his money to enter into the control position. For six years he will reap the benefits of profits from the property although he did have to cover the initial negative cash flow for the first three months. It appears he will also benefit from a future profit upon sale of the property. He had chosen to accept a higher purchase price rather than to share profits from a future sale. He still has the $60,000 profit (minus taxes) from a prior venture for use if needed in buying or gaining control of another property. Elliott U. maximized the use of other people's money to make money for himself. He had refrained from tying up his own capital when his analysis of the industrial property and his knowledge of why the sellers were interested in selling led him to believe he could gain control with no money down.

SHARING YOUR PROFIT

In proceeding in time from one real estate project to another an entrepreneur building his fortune must recognize changes and differences. The financial world relative to real estate is not static; it changes. The sellers in your last project and a new proposed project are different; most likely their reasons for selling will be different. A limited partnership may have been the best way to structure financing the last project, but perhaps the seller is a candidate for involvement in financing your new proposed project.

There are no cookbook rules on "How to Share Profits," but there are a few general comments on how the most successful entrepreneurs operate. If possible, they will try to structure financing without provisions for sharing future profits. In the prior example, Elliott U. preferred to increase the purchase price rather than to share profits with the sellers. If, however, you must enter into a profit sharing arrangement with investors furnishing the capital, do not underestimate the value of your finding, acquiring, and managing the investment. In typical times in the financial community, it is usually easier to find investors than to find and gain control of desirable real estate.

FIVE KEY CONSIDERATIONS ON SOURCES FOR MONEY TO ENABLE YOU TO PROFIT USING OTHER PEOPLE'S MONEY

1. Determine what type of source of money is best for you before contacting any source. The most successful entrepreneurs treat each proposed project as a new situation and challenge. They analyze financial structuring without pre-formed opinions with respect to money sources.
2. Frequently the best source for financing your venture with no money down is the seller. Find out his tax situation and consult with your tax advisor on structuring a proposal with tax advantages for the seller.
3. Find out the reason a property owner wishes to sell. Perhaps the seller has had a recent change in his or her financial status or personal life. Anything you learn about the seller's motivation may help you involve the seller in financing the property.
4. A limited partnership position will appeal to many investors. He or his financial advisers will look at the risk and for downside protection. Limiting an investor's risk to the capital he in-

vests may be the key to your success in using other people's money to make your furtune in real estate.

5. Many entrepreneurs have made very good profits in real estate by gaining control of profitable properties using a lease or lease-purchase agreement. Both ways can result in gaining control without any initial cash investment. Many times you can get the owner to accept lease payments in arrears. Again, you're using other people's money to increase your own wealth.

REMEMBER THESE POINTS

- Analyze the financing of a new project without pre-formed opinions.
- The way you financed your last project may not be the optimum way for your new project.
- The financial world is in constant flux. The most successful entrepreneurs stay abreast of changes.
- A limited partnership allows an investor to be financially liable only to the extent of his investment.
- Knowledge of a potential investor's needs and wants helps in structuring a venture; a limited partner position may fit.
- Take a position on your share of profits early in negotiations with intended limited partners.
- A contract-to-purchase agreement can be used to gain control of a property without a down payment.
- Ask your tax adviser what tax advantages you can present to your intended investors.
- Leasing a property or a lease-purchase agreement can put profits in your pocket.
- A lease-purchase agreement can relieve the seller of management problems and defer his tax liability until a future year.

11

HOW TO GET HIGH PROFITS USING INSTALLMENT LAND CONTRACTS

An installment land contract is a purchase agreement which contains a commitment by the seller to deliver the title to a property to the buyer when the buyer has paid the required installment payments and has complied with all other terms of the agreement. The seller (vendor) retains legal title to the property during the initial period specified in the agreement. The buyer (vendee) typically acquires all features of ownership including possession, use, profits (or losses), taxes, and insurance. The agreement may be a two-party one or there may be a third party involved, e.g., a trustee, an escrow company, or a holder. A land contract is usually used when a sale involves little or no money down. It is a purchase-money secured transaction. The retained legal title is the seller's security for the debt owed to him by the buyer.

An installment land contract in some parts of the U.S.A. is referred to as contract for deed, or simply as sales contract or land contract. There is no difference in terms of economic consequences between the installment land contract and a mortgage or deed of trust; the difference is in the retaining of the legal title by the seller until the specified installments have been paid by the buyer.

Knowledgeable and repeated use of the installment land contract has enabled thousands of entrepreneurs to build their fortunes at a rapid rate with other people's money. It is one of the most powerful and effective insider's secrets for those with very little capital. A detailed understanding of how others have used it and of your state's laws will help you make deal after deal with none (or very little) of your own money tied up.

The first example in this chapter describes an entrepreneur's use of an installment land contract to gain control of an apartment building with no down payment. The seller almost surely would have refused to agree to the sale if he had had to convey title to the buyer. The second example shows how another entrepreneur's detailed knowledge of this powerful insider's technique helped him convince the seller to agree to sell on terms very favorable to the buyer.

LAND CONTRACT YIELDS NO DOWN PAYMENT DEAL FOR APARTMENT BUILDING

John P. is an automobile mechanic who quit his job after forming a syndicate to purchase a shopping center (see second example in Chapter 2). Subsequently, he bought an 18 unit apartment building (see first example in Chapter 12); he was fully extended financially. In fact, he had refinanced his home in order to buy the apartment building without the necessity of involving other investors in an equity or profit-sharing position. While working on and managing his newly acquired properties, he became acquainted with other owners in the vicinity of the apartment building. The owners of a six unit building next door were a retired husband and wife who occupied one unit and managed the property themselves.

Approximately seven months after John P. took possession of the 18 units, the husband next door died. The widow subsequently decided to sell the property and move into a large complex designed specifically for people such as herself. Two of her widowed friends were living in the complex. She asked John P. if he was interested in buying.

All six units had two bedrooms and one bath. The lot was the same size as John P.'s lot. Zoning provided for as many as 18 units. The original building plans showed the existing, thirteen year old six units with a layout for six additional units plus garages. The additional units were intended to be built toward the front of the lot. The seller's asking price was $140,000 with 15 percent down. She would carry the balance herself on a 30 year amortization payment schedule with balance due and payable at the end of twelve years.

The ability to build an additional six units in the future was particularly appealing to John P. The fact that the building was next door to his 18 units meant that he could extend use of the swimming pool and laundry facilities to the tenants of the six units. The owners had not raised rents when their taxes went up substantially ten months earlier. The rents were slightly lower than in John P.'s building.

The only way John P. could buy was if she would sell on a no-down-payment basis. His analysis showed that the cash flow, with 100 percent financing, would be essentially zero even after increasing rents to the market level. He showed the figures to the seller and presented a full price offer with no money down. He also pointed out that her price was appreciably higher on a per-unit basis than he had paid for the 18 units only nine months previously.

The widow's attorney had been her husband's lifelong attorney and friend, but he was not a specialist in real estate. At a meeting with the seller and her attorney, they accepted John P.'s offer provided he paid at least ten percent down. In the discussion, John P. realized that the attorney was not experienced in real estate. When he explained that the intent in his offer was that the seller would retain the legal title until she had received payments reducing the principal by $15,000, the seller accepted his offer with her attorney's assent. The attorney amplified the wording relating to passsing of title and they signed.

The seller's wants and needs were satisfied by the transaction. She had gained a more than comfortable monthly income; she did not have a need for tax benefits.

John P. had taken another step toward his fortune in real estate. His future plans are to build another six units on the property and refinance it well ahead of the twelve year due date in the contract with the seller. Even though he had recently purchased an 18 unit building, he was able to acquire the property next door by using his knowledge of installment land contracts. And he had leveraged to infinity. With all three of his properties he was building his wealth with other people's money almost entirely.

FINANCE DEALS WITH LITTLE OR NO MONEY DOWN BY USING INSTALLMENT LAND CONTRACTS

Entrepreneurs who have intimate, detailed, up-to-date knowledge of the insider's secrets of installment land contracts (or contracts for deed) have a definite competitive advantage over other investors without such knowledge. With this knowledge, deals can be made which otherwise would fade away. An entrepreneur who wants exceptionally high leverage is actually handicapped without knowledge of this powerful and effective approach.

Years ago, investors who used the contract for deed approach typically did not record the transaction. In many cases they used either double or holding escrows. But, as is known to those familiar with the insider's secrets of real estate investing, one needs better protection from the risks and uncertainities listed below:

- Lack of title insurance protection for the seller, in his position as the junior secured lender if there is a senior lender.
- Lack of title insurance protection for the buyer.
- Omission of recording of documents in many cases.
- Uncertainty of future receipt of title by the buyer by reason of seller's death or disability.
- Costly and time consuming remedy for seller upon default by buyer.

Refined and improved procedures for land contracts are now available and they cover all of the above points. In most large cities there are one or more title companies which will provide title insurance for land contract transactions for both the buyer and seller. If you don't know of a title company offering this specialized service, a good attorney who is experienced in land contracts, can recommend one best suited for your circumstances and location.

LAND CONTRACT REVIEW CHECKLIST

I recommend that you personally review land contract documents to insure that:

- The documents accomplish what you and the seller want.
- Both you and the seller have title insurance.
- The documents provide for delivery of the title to you when you have met the contractual requirements and that delivery is independent of any disability on the seller's part.
- The documents to be recorded show your and the seller's interests.
- Provision is made for remedy in the event of default by either buyer or seller.

USING INSTALLMENT LAND CONTRACTS

- The interest of the senior lender is protected.
- The income tax consequences and other taxes are upon the appropriate party.

In negotiating the terms of payments per a land contract the goals of a knowledgeable buyer and an experienced seller are different. If you are the buyer, you will want:

1. To make payments on the senior loan directly to the senior lender.
2. To avoid payment of interest on the principal of the senior loan at a rate higher than the existing one.
3. To negotiate a low interest rate for the amount owed above the principal balance of the senior loan.

An experienced seller will want:

1. A note for the entire amount owed with full payments made to himself (with his making the payments on the senior loan).
2. An interest rate higher than that of the senior loan (so that he will also make money on the loan made by the senior lender).

A transaction incorporating these latter two points is sometimes called a "wrap-around." The wrap around approach will be discussed in detail in Chapter 15.

Many entrepreneurs have built fortunes by becoming intimately familiar with the *advantages* in an installment land contract *for the seller*. During negotiations they emphasize these advantages in *selling the seller* on using the land contract approach. As a result, the buyer gets very high leverage on any cash (if any) which he puts into the deal at the beginning. Advantages to the seller include:

- Seller may be able to sell for a higher price than if he sold for a normal down payment and/or all cash to an existing or new loan.
- Seller postpones all or nearly all income taxes on profits to future years.
- Seller may be able to get a higher rate of interest on amount buyer owes above first lender's loan balance.
- Seller may even be able to structure a wrap-around (see Chapter 15) and collect interest income on the amount owed to the first lender.

- Seller has a large number of potential buyers, i.e., a bigger market and increased opportunities of selling his property expeditiously and at a favorable price.

The installment land contract approach is a powerful one for building a fortune in real estate. Many sellers can be persuaded to use it and give you, as the buyer, the high leverage needed to speed your progress toward wealth.

HOW ENTREPRENEUR USED LAND CONTRACT TO ACQUIRE A 21 UNIT BUILDING WITH NO DOWN PAYMENT; TAX AND INCOME BENEFITS TO SELLER HELPED CLOSE THE DEAL

After closing of escrow on an $800,000 office building acquisition (see first example in Chapter 9), Kenneth E.'s attorney happened to mention that a partner in his law firm had recently handled an installment land contract (or contract for deed) on a small shopping center. Mr. E. had heard of such contracts but was not familiar with them. His attorney gave him a briefiing and reprint of an article on the subject. Kenneth E. expanded his knowledge on land contracts at the library of the college where he was teaching. He soon realized that the land contract approach would be an invaluable technique for himself, especially in view of the fact that he did not have funds for a normal down payment on properties of interest.

Six weeks after acquiring the office building, he quit his job as a part time accountant for the owner of several apartment and industrial buildings. He devoted his spare time to his recent acquisition and to a search for a property which might be purchased for no money down. He let his attorney, banker, real estate broker, and others know what type deal he was seeking. Four months later, his attorney put him in contact with the owner of a 21 unit apartment building.

The building comprised 20 one-bedroom units plus one two-bedroom unit. It was near an older, well established shopping center, restaurants, and 1 1/2 blocks from a bus stop. The building was 26 years old. The owner had acquired it while it was under construction. He now owned it free and clear. His cost basis was quite low compared with the current market value after many years of inflation. Because of thie high demand for apartments in a highly desirable neighborhood, the actual vacancy factor was less than one percent; currently there was a waiting list of three potential tenants.

Mr. E. asked why he was selling. The owner said that he had decided to hold only commercial income property as investments, even though he had made good profits in the apartment area. The seller requested all cash to a new loan. The asking price of $400,000 was 6.93X gross scheduled income. When Mr. E. pointed out that the seller would have a large capital gains tax to pay, the seller said he realized that but that Uncle Sam has his expenses to pay also. He said he would probably buy first or second mortgages on income property with the after tax proceeds. The seller gave Kenneth E. a schedule of current rents and financial statements on the property for the past five years; they scheduled another meeting for one week later.

Mr. E. immediately contacted his attorney to prepare a complete installment land contract. The attorney had his partner in the law firm (the one with recent experience in such contracts) work directly with Mr. E. Kenneth E. prepared a complete list of points to be covered in his next meeting with the seller and they met at their scheduled time. Point-by-point, Mr. E. discussed the following in his presentation.

- *Price:* Mr. E. said he believed that the asking price was somewhat above the market — especially in view of the fact that the building was 26 years old. But he said that he would be willing to pay the price if the seller agreed to the terms of the offer. He said he was confident that the seller would have to accept a lower offer by someone else if he insisted on all cash to a new loan.

- *Taxes and Seller's Interest Income:* Mr. E. pointed out that if the seller sold for all cash he (seller) would pay a tax of approximately $60,000. He suggested an installment land contract wherein the seller would retain legal title until Mr. E. reduced the amount owed to the seller by an amount equal to a 12 1/2 percent down payment. He pointed out that the seller would initially receive income on $400,000 rather than on $340,000 after tax proceeds on an all cash sale. This last feature was one which the seller of the office building had pointed out to Kenneth E. (See first example in Chapter 9.) He also mentioned that the seller would not have the problem of locating good, secure mortgages or trust deeds and the temporary partial loss of income while looking. Seller would also defer all income tax due to profits on the sale and pay them only on a pro rata basis each succeeding year.

- *Installment Land Contract:* Kenneth E. said that if the seller had not recently been involved in an installment land contract, he might not be aware of refinements and improvements in recent years which resulted in much increased usage of the contract. He pointed out that the proposed contract provided for:
    - title insurance protection for both seller and buyer

- retention of legal title by seller until principal is reduced by $50,000
- no down payment; buyer to pay legal and other initial costs of the transaction
- third party to be authorized to convey title to buyer per contract and independent of any disability of seller
- remedy for seller in case of default by buyer
- buyer to have *all* consequences of ownership except possession of legal title until satisfaction of terms of contract
- use of specified title company.

Kenneth E. suggested that seller review the overall proposal with an attorney who had had experience with installment land contracts and to check with his adviser regarding tax benefits and consequences to the seller.

They met again a few days later and consummated the deal as presented by Mr. E. The seller complimented Mr. E. on his thoroughness. He said that his initial reaction was negative, but that he particularly liked Mr. E.'s emphasizing that he check with an attorney and tax adviser.

Kenneth E.'s self-education on installment land contracts had paid off by making possible his second acquisition in income property. His newly acquired knowledge of this insider's secret in real estate investing plus his thorough preparation for the critical session with the seller plus his salesmanship in presenting his proposal added up to closing the deal. Furthermore, he had extremely high leverage. The only cash he had invested was for legal and miscellaneous expenses. He planned not to seek another investment for awhile and to retain his teaching position while consolidating his new acquisition.

SENIOR LENDERS VERSUS INSTALLMENT LOAN CONTRACTS

Mr. E.'s experience in the last example lacked one feature which is usually present in installment land contract deals. Usually, there is a sizeable loan in existence; it is rare for a seller to own the property free and clear. In many such loans the loan papers call for the loan to be paid off in the event the property is sold.

If current interest rates are higher than they were when the loan was made the lender will, of course, want to exercise the acceleration clause (the "due on sale" clause). In the case of an increased rate of interest, paying off the loan is not in the best interest of the principals — they would like the loan to remain as is. The resulting conflict has been the subject of court cases. In California, the State Supreme Court decision in *Tucker v. Lassen Savings and Loan Association* held that an acceleration clause may not automatically be exercised where the property is being sold by an installment land contract which secures a significant part of the purchase price (above the senior loan).

No matter which of the fifty states you're in, if retaining the senior loan as is makes a difference to you, check with your attorney very carefully. Also, become acquainted with the senior loan aspect of installment land contracts; ask your attorney for up-to-date material to study.

SIX KEYS TO BUILDING YOUR FORTUNE WITH INSTALLMENT LAND CONTRACTS

1. Use of the installment land contract is an effective way to acquire property with little or no money down. It can enable you to close a deal which otherwise might fade away. And the leverage is very high.
2. Master all of the details of an installment land contract and how to use it to benefit yourself and the seller. Work closely with an attorney experienced in such contracts but depend upon yourself for its use and application.
3. From the seller's viewpoint, the most appealing point of the land contract is that he retains legal title until you, the buyer, have paid the installment payments per the contract. In case of your default, remedy for the seller usually takes less than 90 days! Explain this point to the seller during your presentation; don't assume he already knows it.
4. Find out the laws in your state concerning acceleration clauses used by many lenders. If current interest rates are higher than when the loan was made, knowledge of the law may be to your benefit. Ask your attorney.
5. Check the land contract carefully to be sure it fulfills your intent and protects your interest. Check particularly for title insurance protection and whether it provides for you to receive the title per the terms of the contract and independent of death, bankruptcy, or other disability of the seller.

REMEMBER THESE POINTS ON INSTALLMENT LAND CONTRACTS

- Title insurance protection is available for both the buyer and seller in an installment land contract.

- Remedy for a seller in the event buyer defaults usually takes less than ninety days.
- A seller can sometimes get a higher price if he accepts little or nothing down, compared with selling for all cash or with a normal down payment.
- The interests of a senior lender can be protected.
- The senior lender gains an additional responsible party (yourself) to make payments on the existing loan.
- If interest rates are currently higher, the senior lender may want his loan paid off and may attempt to exercise an acceleration clause.
- Learn your state's laws on land contracts. Use your attorney but still learn the facts for yourself.
- Record all appropriate documents.
- The fact that the seller retains legal title is an attractive feature to emphasize when you make a presentation.
- Seller can defer payment of income taxes to future years and pay pro rata taxes on principal payments he receives each year.

12

LEVERAGING YOUR WAY TO HIGHER PROFITS AND INCOME

When long-term amortized loans replaced "straight mortgage financing" the stage was set for building fortunes in real estate. The willingness of so many people to defer spending (and lend their accumulating capital on notes secured by real estate) made money available for long term loans. Approximately ten years after the end of World War II, the techniques of leveraging were being refined by innovators in real estate investment. Within the following years and ever since then, many entrepreneurs have become millionaires by using *leverage* on one investment after another.

An entrepreneur is using leverage whenever he uses other people's money to multiply results he would get by using his own money alone. For example, an entrepreneur may have enough captial to buy a small apartment building and pay all cash. If, instead, he finds an apartment complex with five times as many units owned by a seller who is willing to sell for twenty percent down, then he has a leverage of four-to-one. In other words, for every $1 the entrepreneur puts into a property, the seller, in effect, puts in $4. Then, if the percentage profit on the total value of the property exceeds the cost (rate of interest) of the other people's money in the property, the entrepreneur is using leverage sucessfully and is on his way to achieving financial security.

Net profit on a leveraged investment and cash flow are both important and both affect the market value of the property. An entrepreneur using leverage is seeking to control the largest property possibe with the smallest amount of invested cash—consistent with sound business principles. His goal is to get the largest cash flow possible with little or even no capital of his own in the project.

The first example in this chapter illustrates how an entrepreneur used leverage and accelerated depreciation to get a tax sheltered income of $15,000 per year. No down payment on a 40 unit apartment building was the result of a retired Army man's use of leverage achieved by syndication (see the second example in this chapter). The third example describes an investment opportunity which looked good at first, but would have resulted in *negative* leverage.

HOW TO USE LEVERAGE AND GET TAX PROTECTED INCOME OF $15,000 PER YEAR

After John P. quit his job as an automobile mechanic to devote full time to real estate investments, he began an aggressive search for another venture. He had successfully used leverage to generate sufficient income to cover his personal expenses by syndicating and purchasing a shopping center (see second example in Chapter 2). In fact, he had leveraged to infinity for the other two members of the syndicate as well as for himself. He had, however, found it necessary to agree to take only one-third of any profits resulting from a sale of the property in order to get the other two members to sign for a large loan obtained from a conventional source.

Mr. P. located an eighteen unit apartment building available for $349,000. Seventeen units had two bedrooms and one and one-half baths. The remaining "owner's unit" had three bedrooms and two baths. The building was six years old and had been well maintained. There was no apparent deferred maintenance. The books showed a net profit (sometimes called "net operating income") of 13 percent of the asking price, but there had been a recent large increase in property taxes of 75 percent. There was also no management fee included in the expenses. The cash flow for the prior year was approximately $15,000. The stated terms were all cash to a new loan. The seller mentioned that he was selling all of his investments which required in-person attention and returning to Puerto Rico.

John P. considered various ways of structuring the financing, including another syndication, perhaps with the same two investors he obtained for the shopping center. He wanted to handle it himself if possible, but he had only a few thousand dollars in his savings account. John P.'s personal residence had appreciated substantially since he purchased it. The savings and loan association which held his mortgage said they would refinance the house based upon the current market value. He estimated he would net $32,500 cash from the refinancing.

Mr. P. told the seller he would pay the full asking price if the seller would accept a ten percent down payment and carry the balance at 8 ½ percent interest rate. He requested that the payments be based on a thirty year amortization schedule with all due and payable at the end of ten years. Two days later, the seller called Mr. P. and countered with an interest rate of nine percent and all due and payable at the end of seven years. Mr. P. agreed. He refinanced his house, withdrew some of his savings, and made the ten percent down payment.

The rents were competitive and in line with other apartments in the area. In general, rents were increasing slightly because of the recent large increase in taxes in the community. John P. increased rents a similar amount and maintained the profitability enjoyed by the previous owner. His accountant valued the land at $45,000 and the improvements at $304,000. John P. managed the apartments himself. After servicing the new debt he had a cash flow of $1,250 per month ($15,000 per year). He decided to use an accelerated depreciation of 125 percent of straight line. The amount of depreciation was just above $15,000 the first year.

Thus, John P. again used leverage successfully. By getting the seller to finance ninety percent of the purchase price, Mr. P. had a leverage of 9:1! A further and very important benefit was that he had a tax-protected income of $15,000 per year. His tax protection will, of course, decline each year because he is using accelerated depreciation, but he is reaping the benefits at a time most important to him, i.e., early in his new career of building a fortune in real estate.

WHY USE LEVERAGE—ITS ADVANTAGES

If your goal is to make a fortune in real estate you will achieve it much faster if you apply the principle of leverage. In other words, you need to achieve the maximum profit or income on any cash of your own which you tie up in a deal. The answer to "Why use leverage?" is given in the two prior sentences! In order to build a fortune it is necessary to use other people's money. The fortune builder makes money on their money as well as his own.

Leverage is gained in real estate whenever an entrepreneur pays only a portion of the purchase price in cash of his own. The balance is "paid" either (1) with funds borrowed from a conventional or private source, (2) by a mortgage given to the seller (sometimes called a "purchase money mortgage"), (3) by a note calling for future installment payments, (4) by funds furnished by partners brought into the deal, or (5) assuming obligation for an existing debt or mortgage on the property. During the lifetime of an entrepreneur who is knowledgeable in the inside secrets of real estate investments, he may well use all five of the above alternatives in building his fortune.

The way in which an entrepreneur benefits from leverage, whether it is from selling a property for a profit or from income each year, is shown in the following two *simplified* examples.

Example 1: Assume a buyer purchases a property for $50,000 and it doubles in value. If he uses $10,000 of his own cash and borrows $40,000, the results are:

	At Purchase	At Sale
Property Value	$50,000	$100,000
Borrowed Money	40,000	40,000
Owner's Equity	10,000	60,000

His original $10,000 has been increased by $50,000; he now has $60,000 for a larger deal. Compare this result with his position if he had purchased a $10,000 property for all cash and it doubled in value. Instead of a $50,000 profit he would have a profit of only $10,000. In both cases, it is assumed that the property doubled in value.

Example 2: Yield on cash which an entrepreneur puts into a deal can also be substantially increased by leveraging. Assume a buyer purchases property for $100,000 by using $20,000 of his own money and borrowing $80,000 at eight percent interest. Assume the property yields a net operating income of $10,000 per year, or ten percent of its full value.

Property Cost	$100,000
Net Operating Income (per year)	10,000
Interest Cost (First year)	6,400
Net Income After Interest (First year)	3,600

On the other hand, if he used his $20,000 cash to purchase a $20,000 property which yields a net operating income of ten percent the results would be:

Property Cost	$20,000
Net Operating Income (per year)	2,000

LEVERAGING TO HIGHER PROFITS AND INCOME

Interest Cost	zero
Net Income After Interest (per year)	2,000

By leveraging his $20,000 cash, the entrepreneur gets an income after interest of $3,600 instead of $2,000, a multiplying factor of 1.8! The leveraged return on $20,000 is 18 percent instead of ten percent without leveraging.

These two simplified examples illustrate why every successful entrepreneur I've known has mastered the prinicple of leveraging and used this insider's technique over and over again.

HOW A FORTY UNIT APARTMENT BUILDING WAS LEVERAGED WITH NO DOWN PAYMENT

Alexander P., a retired Army non-com and John P.'s older brother, had watched John P.'s progress (see second example in Chapter 2 and first example in this chapter) from an eight-to-five job as a mechanic to a man who had just completed two deals in real estate. Alex P. located a 40 unit apartment building which was available. He learned that the owner was in poor health and had been advised by his physician to give up active, daily participation in business matters. Because of the owner's other income, his accountant had advised him to sell the property for not more than 29 percent down and thus defer taxes on profits to future years on a prorata basis. The building was 23 years old. The owner had virtually paid off the original 25 year loan. He owned it almost free and clear. His asking price was 6.1X scheduled gross income.

Upon checking the area, Alex P. learned that the rents were perhaps slightly below competition but not significantly so. More importantly, he learned that two companies were planning to build new manufacturing plants near the building and that a hospital was planned. He reviewed the overall venture with his brother and asked for suggestions on structuring the deal. His brother suggested a talk with the two investors who had joined him on the suburban shopping center purchase. The investors were interested and suggested that Alex P. try for a no money down deal with all three of them signing with personal responsibility. Alex P. stated he would "give" the two investors fifty percent of any profits from a future sale and fifty percent of net income generated. The two investors were just as forthright in saying that they were simply not interested in ordinary income and that the split would have be as it was on John P.'s deal, i.e., each would get one-third of any future sale profit and Alex P. could have two-thirds of net income generated for managing the property. They provided Alex P. with their personal financial statements.

Mr. P. had his attorney prepare a purchase contract offering the full asking price, with nothing down, nine percent interest rate, with payments on a thirty year fully amortized basis. Alex P. asked the seller what he would do with the cash from a 29 percent down payment. The seller said he would pay the pro rata captial gains tax and most likely use the remaining amount to make first or second mortgage loans on real estate at nine or ten percent, respectively. Mr. P. suggested that the seller consider lending (in effect) him and his partners not only the 71 percent of the purchase price but also lending (in effect) them the other 29 percent by accepting no down payment. As he pointed out, the seller would be collecting interest on the full 29 percent in this way, whereas if he accepted 29 percent cash he would have only the after tax amount to lend on real estate. He emphasized that his two partners were exceptionally strong financially and presented their personal financial statements along with the purchase agreement.

Four days later, after checking with his attorney and financial adviser, the seller accepted the offer, provided the full balance owed at the end of 20 years would be due and payable at that time. He told Mr. P. he had not even considered the possibility of no down payment originally. Mr. P. and his partners agreed to the altered terms and they all signed.

Alex P. had equalled his brother's accomplishment in the sense that both had leveraged to infinity! He had a one-third interest in a 40 unit apartment building with no money down. He and his partners had, in effect, used the seller's money to finance the purchase. Both Alex P. and his brother have taken important steps on their way to a fortune.

Most of the examples on leveraging in this book are about successful entrepreneurs who are acquainted with the insider's secrets of real estate investing. The next section describes some of the dangers and risks in leveraging. Unfortunately, experienced investors, as well as beginners, can lose in attempting to leverage their invested captial.

DISADVANTAGES OF LEVERAGING—CAUTIONS

High leverage, properly used on financially sound real estate ventures, is a fortune builder. A successful, highly leveraged project benefits lenders, builders, construction workers, and many others as well as the entrepreneur who uses leverage in his activities.

Maximum leverage is all too often linked with maximum risk. For example, if an owner owns an office building free and clear, he can endure a high vacancy rate or last through a recession in the economy. On the other hand, if the building were highly leveraged, the owner would have to be able to come up with cash out of his pocket to service the debt

LEVERAGING TO HIGHER PROFITS AND INCOME

during a high vacancy period or in a recession. As in the section, "Why Use Leverage—Its Advantages," the following two simplified examples illustrate what happens to an investor if the market value of his property declines or if the income is reduced.

Example 1: Assume a buyer purchases a property for $50,000 and that its market value drops by fifteen percent ($7,500). If he used 4:1 leverage by investing $10,000 of his own cash and borrowing $40,000, the results are:

	At Purchase	At Sale
Property Value	$50,000	$42,500
Borrowed Money	40,000	40,000
Owner's Equity	10,000	2,500

Thus, with a drop in market value of only fifteen percent the owner's equity drops from $10,000 to $2,500 (a drop in equity of 75 percent)! A leverage of 4:1 means that for every one percent drop in market value, the owner's equity falls by five percent! A drop in market value of more than twenty percent would, of course, mean that the owner would owe more on the property than he would get by selling it; he would have a negative equity!

Example 2: Assume a buyer purchases a small shopping center for $100,000 by using $20,000 of his own cash and borrowing $80,000 at eight percent interest. Assume a net operating income of $10,000 per year. If a tenant moves out and the net operating income is reduced by $3,500 the result is:

	At Purchase	Later Date
Property Cost	$100,000	
Net Operating Income (per year)	10,000	$6,500
Interest Cost (First year)	6,400	6,400
Net Income After Interest (First year)	3,600	100

The buyer's interest expense remains unchanged. In this example, a drop in net operating income from $10,000 to $6,500 per year (a reduction of 35 percent) reduces his net operating income after interest from $3,600 to $100 per year!

These two simplified examples show what can happen to an entrepreneur on the down-side. And the results can be much worse than described in these examples. For instance, a prolonged recession which causes several vacancies in a commercial or office building can bankrupt the entrepreneur. Treading the fine line of heavy leverage with a net profit which barely covers the debt service is not for the faint-hearted. Heavy leverage and a correct forecast as to the future can enable the building of a fortune at a rapid rate. But a drop in income or in market value of property can wipe out an entrepreneur who is heavily leveraged.

Negative Leverage: I have seen deals put together by over-eager and over-optimistic investors wherein the interest rate on the borrowed money was higher than the percentage figure for return on total investment. Many investors refer to this situation as one with "negative leverage." In one instance, the net operating income was approximately 7¾ percent of the total purchase price and the purchaser borrowed 75 percent of the purchase price at 8¾ percent interest rate (a leverage of 3:1). Thus, the return on the cash he invested was reduced by three percent; he was getting only 4¾ percent return on his invested cash!

ANALYSIS OF APARTMENT BUILDING SHOWED NEGATIVE LEVERAGE; DEAL IS REJECTED

The last example in Chapter 3 described Benjamin G.'s analysis of a 30 unit apartment with high leverage available. He rejected it when his investigation indicated that creeping blight would cause a drop in income within a very few years. Then he acquired commercial property (see second example in Chapter 7) and achieved very high leverage. His search for either an apartment complex or more commercial property turned-up a 12 unit apartment building for $315,000. It was 22 years old and located only two blocks from a major university. The occupancy rate, even in summer months, had been virtually 100 percent for several years. The building had been well maintained with no apparent deferred maintenance. The owner was willing to sell for 25 percent down and carry the balance himself for twenty-five years at the prevailing interest rate of nine percent. Mr. G. reasoned that the occupancy rate would "always" be high; demand for rentals was high and there was no more land on which to build apartments.

He obtained financial records on the building for the last five years. The asking price of $315,000 was 12.2X the gross scheduled income (GSI) of $25,650 per year. Stated another way, the GSI was 8.2 percent of the asking price. Operating expenses (including taxes) and a vacancy allowance of only 1 percent added up to approximately 34 percent of the GSI. Thus, the return (net operating income) was 8.2 minus 2.8 percent (34 percent ÷ 12.2) or 5.4 percent of the asking price. The 3.6 percent difference between the interest rate of 9 percent and the 5.4 percent return on the total asking price meant that with 75 percent being financed by the seller, Mr. G. would receive a negative

LEVERAGING TO HIGHER PROFITS AND INCOME

return on cash invested by himself or fellow investors. They would have had to put in additional cash each year. The negative leverage ruled out the purchase. Mr. G. checked four other apartment buildings, all located within two to six blocks from the campus and found they were priced from 11.5X to 14X gross scheduled income. He abandoned his search in the community. What had apparently happened during the last few years was that supply and demand, coupled with higher interest rates, had resulted in such high prices that positive leverage was no longer possible in that community.

When he heard, four weeks later, that a newcomer to the state had paid $295,000 (all cash) for the property he felt no regret. The new owner would have a yield of only 5.73 percent on his investment—well below the prevailing interest rate of 9 percent.

SIX KEYS FOR BUILDING YOUR FORTUNE WITH LEVERAGE

1. Use leverage to increase substantially the rate at which you build your fortune in real estate. Leverage is a powerful technique for making money with other people's money.
2. Be sure that the return on the total investment is greater than the interest rate you pay on borrowed money. If it is, then leverage is working to your benefit.
3. Get a margin of safety in your leveraged investment for protection against an unexpected reduction of income or an economic recession.
4. Analyze a proposed investment thoroughly. It is easy to let enthusiasm, or a presumed need to move fast, carry you into a deal with negative leverage.
5. The seller may be an excellent source from whom to get a low interest rate on the money you need to finance the venture. The greater the excess of the return on the total investment over the interest rate you pay, the greater the safety margin you have.
6. *Caution*—Heavy leverage will work against you if the project is an unsound one. Prediction of the future market for users of your real estate project is of paramount importance; research it carefully.

REMEMBER THESE POINTS

- Successful leverage can multiply results you could get by using your own money alone.
- Buy the largest, most profitable property possible and use leverage to finance it.

- Successful use of leverage for income-producing property requires that your percentage return on the total investment exceed the cost (interest rate) of borrowed money.
- Leverage is the use of other people's money to make money.
- Leverage is achieved either by borrowing money or by others investing their capital to finance a project partially owned by you.
- Your net profit and cash flow are both important in a leveraged deal.
- Leveraged investments can sometimes also provide tax sheltered income for you, the entrepreneur, and for investors in your project.
- If the seller is the one financing your project, try to structure it so the seller has return on more money than if he sold for a substantial down payment.
- You can sometimes pay a larger price for property if terms are exceptionally liberal.
- The five major ways of financing with leverage are:
  - borrow from conventional or private source
  - give mortgage to seller ("purchase-money mortgage")
  - purchase from seller on installment plan
  - bring partners into deal as investors
  - assume debt or existing mortgage on property.
- Very high leverage means high risk. The value of your real estate or income from it can drop heavily in a recession.
- Allow a safety margin. If a major tenant vacates, you could find yourself in a negative-leverage position.
- Use leverage wisely and you will make your fortune much faster.

13

USE SECOND MORTGAGES TO CLOSE MORE DEALS AND PUT MORE MONEY IN YOUR POCKET

Of the broad field of second mortgages the emphasis in this book is on how an entrepreneur can use them to speed his way to wealth. The discussion and examples here zero-in on second mortgages as a source of money—and how to use them as another tool in the entrepreneur's kit for using other people's money to make money.

There are many people with excess cash who more or less actively look for opportunities to lend on real estate. They are not interested in managing or acquiring property but instead seek the "trouble-free" opportunity of lending on "safe and sound" properties. Individuals who accept first mortgages are competing directly with banks and savings and loan associations. Individuals interested in carefully selected second mortgages have the marketplace much more to themselves—

although there are real estate agents, "mortgage bankers," corporations, and institutions which are active in the second mortgage market.

Entrepreneurs who are building their fortune in real estate typically will use one of the following approaches in the second mortgage area:

1. give the seller a second mortgage as part payment for the property being sold
2. give a third party (not the seller) a second mortgage for money to be used as part payment for property
3. give a second mortgage on his own home or other real estate he owns to obtain money for purchase of additional property or to pay for an option on a chosen property.

The first example in this chapter describes how a buyer started out to "trade-up," i.e., trade his equity in a small income property as the down payment for a larger property. A purchase money second mortgage made the deal close; he used his equity in the smaller property as additional security for the second mortgage.

The second example shows that sometimes a 12 percent interest rate is better than 8¾ percent! It describes how an entrepreneur's analysis caused him to change his mind about refinancing at 8¾ percent and instead getting second mortgage financing at 12 percent.

HOW A SECOND MORTGAGE HELPED BUY A TWENTY-EIGHT UNIT APARTMENT BUILDING WITH NOTHING DOWN

Edward H., a 44 year old baker, was seeking a larger apartment building with the intent of trading in a three unit building. He and his wife had sold their home and purchased the triplex when their younger daughter had married five years earlier. The three units had a market value of approximately $39,000; the balance owed on the first mortgage was $18,900. They occupied one of the units.

Mr. H. learned of a 28 unit, two story, garden apartment complex which was for sale. The building was 38 years old. It had twenty-seven one-bedroom units and one two-bedroom owner's apartment. The asking price was $310,000 which was approximately 5.9X gross scheduled income.

Before contacting the owner, Edward H. canvassed the neighborhood thoroughly. The area was an older one which had been fully built up for many years. Some of the buildings were showing signs of deterioration due to lack of upkeep and maintenance. In general, the area was not suffering from neighborhood blight, but the question of which way it would go in the future was a serious one. Mr. H. noticed particularly that the average age of tenants in the district was quite high. Inquiry revealed that some had lived in the same apartment for more than thirty years. Department stores, restaurants, and churches were plentiful and within walking distance.

On the other hand, some of the apartment buildings had been remodeled and upgraded. Two buildings had been extensively renovated and were renting for approximately twice the monthly rate of the units Mr. H. was considering. The managers of two other apartment complexes said that they were planning to start substantial remodeling programs in the near future. Edward H. concluded that the area was upgrading—that the likelihood of increasing blight was very low.

Furthermore, it appeared likely that the building he was evaluating could be remodelled at a future time and resold for a good profit provided the area experienced a continuation of the upgrading already in progress.

He prepared an offer of $290,000 for the property contingent upon (1) obtaining a 70% loan ($203,000), (2) seller accepting a second mortgage for $67,000 at nine percent interest, payable on a 30 year amortization schedule with the balance due and payable at the end of 10 years, and (3) seller accepting Mr. H.'s triplex in trade with the equity valued at $20,000.

When Mr. H. presented the offer, the seller said that he had suffered a loss on a venture capital investment earlier in the year, and that he was interested in reporting, for tax purposes, a full profit during the current year on the sale of the apartment building. But he was not interested in owning a triplex. He also said that any second mortgage he took would have to be at 9½ percent interest.

Edward H. was about to terminate the discussion when the seller said he would accept Mr. H.'s offer if he changed the price to $300,000 and accepted a 9½ percent interest on the purchase money second mortgage. He said he would make the second for $90,000 if Mr. H. also pledged the equity in the triplex as additional security. He repeated his lack of interest in owning the triplex. Mr. H. agreed to the counter offer.

Thus, with the help of a purchase money second mortgage Mr. H. took a big step in building his fortune in real estate. He had also learned a valuable lesson for future dealing. He had been less than aggressive and innovative in that he had not been the one to propose the larger second mortgage to make the deal go. He had not even thought of pledging his equity in the triplex as an alternate to assigning the equity to the seller as part payment. In any future negotiations on other real property he resolved to keep the overall picture in mind instead of fixing upon an approach and not deviating from it.

A more experienced entrepreneur would have considered all possible ways of structuring the financing ahead of the negotiations. An innovative man would have immediately proposed pledging the equity in the triplex upon learning the seller's aversion to taking a trade-in.

USE SECONDARY FINANCING TO HELP BUILD YOUR FORTUNE

An experienced entrepreneur in real estate investing will consider all possible ways of financing a new purchase. As time passes, he will have increasing equity in the various properties he owns. In recent years, many have found that their equity has increased, because of appreciation in value and/or inflation, even faster than the building up of equity by the payments applied to their mortgage balances. Whenever they need to raise cash they will automatically consider refinancing selected properties in comparison with giving a second mortgage for cash they wish to raise. Conversion of a passive asset (i.e., increased equity in real property) into cash for use in a dynamic way becomes a way of life for an aggressive entrepreneur. And, of course, experienced entrepreneurs simultaneously consider all other feasible approaches for financing a deal other than the second mortgage route.

Frequently, those who are relatively new in real estate investing have only one property (their home) which is a logical candidate for refinancing or for use as security for a second mortgage. They may have become interested in real estate investing only after owning their home for several years.

No matter what your past experience in real estate, it will pay to analyze the costs and comparative advantages of refinancing a property—versus the second mortgage approach—if you need cash for buying property.

The example given in the next section is that of a newcomer in real estate investing. It describes his comparative analysis of refinancing or giving a second mortgage on his home to raise investment capital for a real estate venture. Even though it is for a newcomer, the principles apply as well for an experienced entrepreneur who owns several properties. The difference is that Randolph Q. had only his home, while the seasoned entrepreneur may have several properties which are logical candidates.

WHY A 12 PERCENT SECOND MORTGAGE IS BETTER THAN REFINANCING AT 8¾ PERCENT

After several months of looking, Randolph Q., a senior supervisor in electronic assembly for a manufacturer, had located a small income property he wanted to buy. The required down payment was $29,000. Mr. Q.'s cash on hand was low, but he had a considerable equity in his home. He talked with a friend in the assembly department who had recently refinanced his home to raise several thousand dollars because of an emergency. He checked with the savings and loan association which carried the first mortgage on his home and decided to apply for refinancing. That evening, his brother-in-law suggested that Mr. Q. calculate the costs and benefits of refinancing and compare with obtaining a second mortgage from a private party.

Mr. and Mrs. Q. had purchased their home when it was new approximately eleven years ago at a price of $37,500. Landscaping and fencing cost approximately $2,500. They had obtained a first loan of $32,000 at 5¾ percent interest, amortized over 25 years. The balance owed was $23,500. Based upon the original cost of $40,000, Mr. Q.'s equity was now $40,000 − $23,500 or $16,500. Actual equity is, however, based upon market value. During the eleven years, the U.S.A. had experienced considerable inflation; real estate market price increases had more than kept pace. Also, land in the subdivision had appreciated in true value (as opposed to inflated value) due to the city's growth beyond what had then been the outskirts. As shown by recent sales of comparable homes in Mr. Q.'s neighborhood, his house had a current market value of approximately $71,500. Thus, based upon market value, Mr. Q.'s equity was $48,000.

The savings and loan association had given a preliminary estimate of a 30 year loan of 80 percent of an appraised value of approximately $70,000 at 8¾ percent interest. The loan officer said he thought the loan approval committee would waive the pay-off penalty on Mr. Q.'s existing loan.

Randolph Q.'s brother-in-law, a public accountant, described Mr. Q.'s house and financial position to his financial contacts and asked about borrowing $31,500 on a second mortgage and what the interest rate would be. He was assured that it was feasible at an interest rate of 12 percent. When Mr. Q. heard the 12 percent figure he was very doubtful about it being a sensible approach.

He and his brother-in-law made the following comparison of refinancing versus obtaining cash via a second mortgage. The proceeds and costs of the two approaches are given below.

Refinance—Proceeds

S & L new mortgage	$56,000
Loan fee (1½% + $100)	940
	$55,060
Closing costs	350
	$54,710
Existing mortgage balance	23,500
Cash Proceeds	$31,210

Refinance—Costs

A. New loan of $56,000; 8¾ percent interest; 30 year amortization; payments of $440.56/month.

Payment per month	$440.56/month
Number of months	360 months
Total Payment (30 years)	$158,601.60

B. Original loan of $32,000; 5¾ percent interest; 25 year amortization; payments of $201.91/month.

Payment per month	$201.91/month
Number of remaining months	168 months
Total payments (remaining)	$33,920.88

C. Costs and proceeds

Cost of new loan	$158,601.60
Cost of original loan (remaining)	33,920.88
Additional cost of new loan	$124,680.72
Cash proceeds	31,210.00
Cost of cash proceeds	$93,470.72

Private Party Second Mortgage Loan—Proceeds

Loan of $31,500 on a second mortgage; 12 percent interest; 8 year amortization; payments of $511.97 per month.

Loan	$31,500
Closing costs	300
Cash Proceeds	$31,200

Private Party Second Mortgage Loan—Costs

Payment per month	$511.97/month
Number of months	96 months
Total payment	$49,149.12
Cash proceeds	31,200.00
Cost of cash proceeds	$17,949.12

Thus, in order to receive $31,200 in cash, the cost of refinancing would be $93,470.72 and the cost of a second mortgage loan would be $17,949.12. The ratio of the two numbers is 93,470.72:17,949.12 or 5.2:1! The cost of obtaining $31,200 cash by Mr. Q. would be 5 ½ times the cost of obtaining the same amount with a second mortgage even though the two interest rates are 8¾ and 12 percent respectively.

Special Note: The simplified example given above does not include consideration of the present (time) value of payments to be made in the future. It also does not include allowance for inflation during the time periods involved. The effect of these two factors would be a ratio somewhat lower than 5.2:1 but the advantage of the second mortgage approach would still be substantial.

Mr. Q., of course, negotiated a second mortgage loan and obtained the necessary cash for a down payment on the income property he wanted. He had learned not to make snap judgments in analyzing various alternate ways of financing.

When to refinance to raise cash

As exemplified by the prior example, it can be less costly to borrow on a second mortgage rate at 12 percent than to refinance at 8¾ percent. If, however, you have a property with an existing mortgage which could produce the cash you're seeking by refinancing and if the interest rate on the new loan would be the same or nearly the same as on the old mortgage, then calculations as in the prior example may show that you should refinance rather than obtain a second mortgage loan at a higher interest rate. Again, as has been emphasized in other chapters, it is important to compare the advantages and disadvantages of all various possible ways of financing rather than considering (almost with blinders on) one or two possible ways. The success of many entrepreneurs in using second mortgages means that this approach should be included as one of the possible approaches in your analysis.

WATCH FOR PITFALLS—DON'T STRETCH TOO FAR

One common characteristic of a second mortgage is that the terms of payment are frequently not on a fully amortized basis. At the end of the term of the loan there is thus a lump sum payment to be made. This payment is usually referred to as a "balloon payment." For example, if you borrow $10,000 for a five year term at 10 percent interest and pay $132.16 per month (which would fully amortize the borrowed amount in ten years) then at the end of the five years a lump sum or balloon payment of $6,220 must be paid. A relatively new investor in real estate may well not go ahead with an investment because of dread of having to make a large lump sum payment on a fixed date. Such loan arrangements are, however, frequently signed by the most successful real estate entrepreneurs. The important thing is to plan ahead with respect to making the payment. For example, if your intent is to refinance a first mortgage in order to make the balloon payment it is wise not to wait until near the end of the term of the second mortgage loan. Money availability is in constant flux; if a credit crunch occurred just a short time ahead of the due date you might not be able to refinance and make the required payoff.

Making payments on two mortgages frequently places stress on cash flow. It is wise to have a safety factor in the cash flow you require in a specific investment. A recession or an unexpected vacancy in income property could plunge you into a dangerous position with respect to cash flow and profits.

As with all loan applications, all documents to be used in a second mortgage and all charges in connection with it should be checked carefully before you sign any papers. I have heard of "placement fees" or points being charged which were nearly as much as the cash proceeds from the loan. If an entrepreneur allows himself to get into the position where he absolutely must close a loan quickly, he may have to accept highly undesirable terms and costs of a second mortgage loan.

WHY THE SELLER IS THE BEST SOURCE FOR SECOND MORTGAGES

The gap between the purchase price of a property and the amount of money available from a first mortgage must be filled one way or another. If the buyer has sufficient cash to fill the gap then the transaction is a simple one. The practice of a seller accepting a note secured by the property being sold to fill all or a part of the gap is so widespread it has been given a name—it is called "purchase money mortgage."

USE SECOND MORTGAGES

In your role as buyer the possibility of using the second mortgage approach is merely one of the alternatives you will consider in structuring the financing of a venture. If a second mortgage is to be used then the seller is likely to be the best possible source. Once an owner has decided to sell his property he may be willing to accept a second mortgage to partially fill the gap between the sale price of the property and the cash the buyer obtains from a first mortgage loan and the buyer's own cash. Furthermore, if the seller is somewhat eager to make the sale you may be able to negotiate an interest rate on the second mortgage no higher than the interest rate on the first. Many entrepreneurs do exactly this; they take the aggressive and propose the entire financial terms including a favorable interest rate on the proposed purchase money mortgage. In fact, I have even seen purchase money (second) mortgages with an interest rate lower than the interest rate on the first. A lower rate means, of course, that the seller was exceptionally eager to sell and wanted to sell quickly.

The experienced entrepreneur automatically looks at the seller as a possible financial source for helping to finance a deal. In many deals, analysis shows that he can get better terms and more financial benefit by persuading the seller to accept a purchase money mortgage.

SIX KEYS TO INCREASED PROFITS AND MORE DEALS WITH SELLER OR OTHER PRIVATE PARTY HELPING TO FINANCE THE PURCHASE

1. Successful entrepreneurs have second mortgages on their list of financial approaches and techniques. They consistently consider the possible use of a second mortgage loan as they are analyzing how to structure the financing of a proposed new venture.

2. Second mortgages can speed your progress toward building a fortune. A proposed deal may be dropped because of a gap between the purchase price and the amount of money obtainable from a first mortgage plus the owner's cash. An aggressive entrepreneur will try to fill this gap with a second mortgage if his analysis shows it to be feasible and profitable for himself.

3. An entrepreneur who owns property in which he has a considerable equity is not using his assets to the fullest extent possible. The "excess" equity is a "semi-passive" investment. By turning this so-called excess equity into cash and investing in another property he can increase his total annual profit. He will again be making increased use of other people's money to make money. A seasoned investor may have more than one

property suitable for raising cash via a second mortgage. A beginner may have only his personal residence with this potential.

4. To be successful, objectively carry all analyses through to completion. It is indeed true that raising cash with a 12 percent second mortgage can be more beneficial profitwise, than refinancing the first mortgage at a lower interest rate. A snap judgment that 12 percent is out of the question may cause a missed opportunity.

5. In most cases, the seller of a property is the best source for second mortgage financing. This purchase money mortgage can frequently be negotiated at an interest rate equal to the current market interest rate on first mortgages. If the seller is particularly anxious to sell, you may be able to get an interest rate even below the current first mortgage rate. If conditions appear right, try for the below market rate.

REMEMBER THESE POINTS

- Always consider second mortgage financing as a part of your overall analysis of financially structuring a venture.
- A large or excess equity in property you own can be converted to cash for another investment. Consider a second mortgage.
- Review your portfolio periodically. See if you can raise investment cash via the second mortgage route.
- Consider the equity in your own home. Potentially available cash tied up in your equity is not making money for you.
- Avoid snap judgments in your analysis. A high interest second can be more advantageous than refinancing to gain cash.
- The seller of property you want to buy is potentially the best source for secondary financing. Try the purchase money approach.
- In negotiating the interest rate on purchase money mortgages try for a rate equal to or even lower than current rates on first mortgages.
- Second mortgages with balloon payments have worked well for many entrepreneurs, but use caution in obligating yourself.

14

HOW TO LOCATE THE BEST SOURCES OF SECONDARY FINANCING

The best known (and most easily used) avenues to private individuals with money available for second mortgages are real estate agents and mortgage investment companies. There are, however, several other avenues to people with available money and a predilection toward second mortgages. In this chapter, some of these avenues will be discussed along with suggestions on how to find second mortgage financing with desirable terms.

As examples in this chapter illustrate, it pays to become knowledgeable with respect to the second mortgage market in your geographical area. The terms and costs of second mortgage money vary widely from one investor to another. Shopping around pays off in the form of increased profits and the ability to make deals which could not be made without a second mortgage. Use of second mortgages also increases the leverage gained with respect to any of your own cash involved.

The first example in this chapter describes the use of a second mortgage to purchase property intended to be held for retirement income. A profit of $14,500 changed the buyer from an ultraconservative investor into a full fledged entrepreneur. The second example describes a relatively inexperienced entrepreneur who used all of his cash on hand to obtain income property at a lower price. He used funds from a new second mortgage loan on the acquired property to pay for an unexpected emergency.

SECONDARY FINANCING—DOES IT COST MORE?

If one looks only at the usually higher interest rate and the points or loan fees on most second mortgages and compares these two factors with the same aspects of a first mortgage, then, indeed, second mortgages are more costly. As shown in Chapter 13, however, analysis of how to structure financing of each individual proposed venture may well show either that (1) giving a second mortgage will put you in a better potential profit position than refinancing a first, or (2) a second mortgage will enable you to close a desirable deal when no other approach will.

In the absence of controls by government (e.g., your state's laws) the marketplace determines the costs of second mortgages. Generalizations about costs of second mortgages throughout the U.S.A. by no means determine what you may be able to negotiate with respect to interest rate, other costs, and terms in a specific case. The interest rates on first mortgages in effect at the time you are seeking second mortgage financing influence the rates and costs of second mortgages. Generally speaking, the second mortgage interest rate will be 1 ½ percent to 6 percent higher than for a first. My personal experience includes paying 1 ½ percent more than the first mortgage rate although I know of second mortgages with interest rates 2 percent to 9 percent(!) above first mortgage rates.

Many times, in addition to charges by an attorney and a recording fee, a "loan fee" or "placement fee" will be paid by the borrower. In most cases wherein a fee is charged, it is in the range of 2 percent to 7 percent of the amount borrowed via a second mortgage. Again, unless your state's laws set a limit, the fee can be whatever the borrower is willing to pay.

Whenever a third party, i.e., not one of the principals in a real estate transaction, is the lender on a second mortgage to enable closing a deal, it is called a "hard money" second. Or it is referred to in the same way when an owner obtains second mortgage money on property he already owns. In such second mortgages, there is almost always a fee charged to the borrower. In general, the fee for a hard money second is usually on the high side. In many cases, I have seen fees of 10 to 20 percent (and one of 33 ⅓ percent) charged.

The term of a second mortgage can be whatever the two parties agree upon, subject to conformance with law. Most frequently, the term is somewhere between three and ten years.

Payment schedules also vary over a wide range. For example, periodic payment of interest only, with the principal being paid at the end of the term is one possibility. A fully amortized payment schedule is another.

Even though a second mortgage generally costs more than a first mortgage the important factors in the analysis of any transaction are the profit you predict and how much of your own capital you will have to commit in order to realize the profit. An investor is, of course, always desirous of getting low interest money and low costs of financing. But if the proposed venture has a large enough profit potential and if a second mortgage proves to be the best way (or perhaps the only way) to finance it and get the leverage you're seeking, then the fact a proposed second has a high interest rate is not of primary importance. It is the profit potential, the risk, and the leverage which determine the advisability of proceeding and not the fact that a portion of your financing carries a high interest rate.

THE BEST SOURCES FOR SECONDS

The degree of effort that an entrepreneur puts into becoming and remaining well informed in financing real estate ventures depends in part upon his own nature and drive. For example, many investors have a good accountant or a financial adviser and depend heavily upon him for analysis and advice in structuring and obtaining financing for a new venture. I much prefer to have the personal knowledge and personally to maintain up-to-date knowledge of the current market in the financial realm, including tax aspects as well as data on borrowing money. Many entrepreneurs have a similar attitude; they use their adviser primarily to cross check their analyses and decisions.

An important part of successful investing in real estate is knowing where to get the financing you want—and at the time you want it. An entrepreneur who does his homework ahead of time will be prepared to close a deal more expeditiously and perhaps to his additional advantage. Accumulating information on potential investors in second mortgages as well as on investors in other forms of investing in real estate will pay off. In the second mortgage area, first find out the interest rates, costs, and other terms being offered by institutions. Contact those listed under "Loans" or "Real Estate Loans" in the yellow pages of your telephone directory. Then check with real estate agents to find out the details of any second mortgages they have placed recently and what fee they charged. Make a 4 by 6 file card record for each of these sources.

The list of occupations of potential investors given under "How to Find Syndicate Investors" in Chapter 2 is applicable in your search for candidates for investing in second mortgages as well as other forms of real estate investing. If you already have a card file as described in Chapter 2, it will be easy to add to it for additional forms of investing. If not, start with your friends and relatives. Get from them and your banker, attorney, and savings and loan officials, the names of people who are active in second mortgages. Then review the list of sources in Chapter 2 to help determine others to contact.

Make a file card on every potential investor even though a particular one may be currently fully committed in real estate investments. The sample file card given in Chapter 2 was for a dentist with an aggressive interest in real estate. He was interested in taking an equity position (perhaps in a high risk venture). The file card for another dentist with different goals and interests (one with an interest in second mortgages) might appear as shown in the card prepared for Robert Roe.

ROE, ROBERT R.　　　　　　　Born Approx. 1928
2000 Maple Street　　　　　　　Dentist
XXXXXXXX, XXXXX　　　　　Married 24 yr. (Janet)
Orig. Card Date_____　　　Children: Grown,
　　　　　　　　　　　　　　　　　　　　Living elsewhere.

(orig.)	Has approximately $250,000 for real estate investments.
(date)	Approx. $100,000 presently uncommitted.
"	Has 1 outstanding sec. mort. on apt. bldg. for $45,000 @ 10% interest; due _?_
"	Makes sec. mort. loans directly; usually through personal contact; sometimes through real estate agent.
"	No loan fees charged unless through real estate agent.
"	Wants payoff penalty for early payment in full.
"	Might make loan with ballon payment feature; prefers fully amortized.
"	Prefers "longer" term for loans; 7 to 12 yrs.
"	Accountant is Roger Doakes.
"	Attorney is Paul Stokes.
"	Has accountant analyze proposed loans.

THE BEST SOURCES OF SECONDARY FINANCING

The action steps in locating potential investors in syndications were described in detail in Chapter 2. An abbreviated description of a similar procedure was given above for candidates for second mortgage financing. Actually, the card file is usable for potential investors in any of the various ways of financing a venture. A particular individual may be a potential investor in more than one type of investment. Also, an individual who is interested in syndicates only, this year, may become a candidate for first or second mortgages a few years later. Updating the card file anytime you learn of a new investment or a change in needs and desires of an individual is easily done and will pay off.

HOW SECOND MORTGAGE YIELDS $14,500 PROFIT ON COMMERCIAL BUILDING

Donald J., a 41 year old printer, and his wife had recently sold their home in a Northeastern state and moved to the Southwest because of his wife's health. He found a job in a print shop and paid $5,000 down on a townhouse under construction. The owner of the print shop mentioned that the owner of the building he occupied was in need of cash and had offered to sell the building to him at a good price, but that he could not buy it. The building owner then listed it with a commercial real estate broker for $85,250. Mr. J. learned from the broker that the owner of the print shop and another tenant each occupied one-half of the building and each had nine years remaining of a ten year lease on a triple net basis. The broker gave Mr. J. a copy of financial statements on the building for the last five years. Upon questioning, the broker was unusually insistent that the asking price was firm and that the seller must have all cash to a new loan. He had a preliminary loan commitment from a savings and loan association for a 20 year, 75 percent loan at nine percent interest.

Mr. J. had $12,000 of the proceeds from the sale of his home in a savings and loan association earning 5 ¾ percent interest. Mr. and Mrs. J. were primarily planning ahead for income when they reached retirement age. Mr. J. found that $11,500 deposited in a savings and loan association at 5 ¾ percent, compounded, would increase to $36,230 by the end of twenty years and that the interest, if withdrawn monthly beginning then, would be $173.50 per month. Analysis of the financial statements on the building showed that the return (net profit) on an investment of $85,250 would be approximately 11 percent. Thus, when the loan was paid off at the end of twenty years, they would have an annual income of $9,337.50 or $781.46 per month. Comparison of the two monthly income streams twenty years hence made the decision to invest an easy one.

Furthermore, by borrowing at 9 percent he would be making 2 percent on the borrowed money plus 11 percent on the cash he invested, from the very beginning.

He told the broker he had insufficient cash and asked him to submit an offer of $83,000 with $11,500 down, with the owner to carry a ten year second mortgage at 10 percent interest and contingent upon obtaining a 20 year, 75 percent first loan at nine percent interest. The owner countered at $85,000 and all cash to a new loan. Mr. J. declined the offer.

Fortunately, the broker was an aggressive salesman. He was motivated toward getting a willing buyer and seller together rather than seeking a new buyer. He returned to Mr. J. the following day to tell him that an old client was willing to consider making a second mortgage loan to fill the gap; the terms would be ten years at ten percent interest rate with a payoff penalty if paid off during the first five years. He added that he would arrange it and charge a commission of only three percent of the borrowed amount. Mr. J. said that he felt the six percent commission the broker was getting on the sales price was sufficient without a commission on the second mortgage. He had the broker submit a counter-counter offer contingent upon getting the second mortgage as stated, but without loan fees or commission. The seller accepted.

Mr. and Mrs. J.'s entire original purpose for buying the commercial property was to keep it indefinitely to provide for a better retirement income than they could get by depositing their cash in a savings and loan association (and get some tax advantage along the way). Eighteen months later, however, when the print shop owner wanted to buy the building, they sold for a negotiated price of $99,500. They decided to become aggressively active in real estate; they now had nearly $30,000 cash with which to gain control of a larger property. If the broker had been less motivated eighteen months earlier, they might never have taken their first step. A second mortgage worked to their advantage and started them on a spare time career of real estate investing.

SHOP AROUND—IT PAYS

No matter what type financing is being sought, it usually pays to shop; even first mortgage terms vary among savings and loan associations. The interest rate quoted depends, in part, upon the quantity of available money in the individual association. Interest rates quoted by various associations are usually within a ⅛ percent spread but the spread is sometimes ¼ percent. Hence, it pays to check rates being offered by various associations.

THE BEST SOURCES OF SECONDARY FINANCING

Check with a local title company; you may find one or more who can furnish you with a list of interest rates and loan fees currently being charged by various savings and loan associations. Some publish weekly summaries of such information.

An entrepreneur who needs hard money second mortgage financing will usually find it much to his advantage to shop. As stated previously the spread in interest rates is from two percent to nine percent above first mortgage interest rates. Any borrower who takes the first loan offered may unnecessarily have settled for a higher rate than he could have obtained by shopping.

Shopping should be done ahead of need for two reasons. First and foremost is that when the need for second mortgage financing comes up, it is frequently in the middle of negotiations to acquire a property. By knowing various sources and current terms you will be in a position to move promptly to close the deal. Secondly, by making it known that you are contacting various sources but only in anticipation of a future deal, you will be likely to be quoted comparatively favorable terms and you avoid being labelled as a man in need who's shopping. Your reputation in your community will affect your success; it should be carefully guarded.

The following example is all too typical of what sometimes happens when an entrepreneur strips himself of cash on hand. A second mortgage saved the day and eventually led to a handsome profit.

A HARD MONEY SECOND MORTGAGE SAVES THE DAY FOR ENTREPRENEUR

Ronald W., a 32 year old automobile salesman, had recently purchased a six unit apartment building. He had the cash on hand to pay all cash to the existing loan of approximately 68 percent of the purchase price. As a result, he had negotiated a very favorable purchase price with a seller who was eager to "cash out."

As a commission salesman, he had decided not to carry major medical insurance for himself and his wife. Unexpectedly, his wife had to be scheduled for major surgery.

Mr. W. had had a second mortgage with the seller on his first home which he purchased at age 22 and sold five years later. He decided to raise money for his wife's surgery via a second mortgage on the six units. He quickly found that hard money second mortgage financing was being quoted on much less favorable terms than the second he had with the man from whom he purchased his home. He started with the yellow pages and called three firms advertising second mortgage loans. He was shocked to hear interest rates quoted at 14 to 18 percent. He then went in person to talk with his banker, savings and loan officer, and attorney. The banker had two customers of the bank who had asked him to let them know of opportunies to lend money on first or second mortgages on local real estate. The banker introduced Ronald W. to them and five days later, Mr. W. had the needed money in hand. The loan was at ten percent interest amortized over seven years.

By moving aggressively, Ronald W. was able to pull a "save" by getting a hard money second mortgage loan. He met the emergency need for cash and was able to retain his recently purchased income units. Shopping had paid off for him. Instead of paying a 14 percent or more interest rate he located the needed second mortgage loan at 10 percent.

LOW COST SECONDS—PURCHASE MONEY MORTGAGES

Statistically speaking, the most favorable terms for second mortgages financing are obtainable from the seller of property you are buying. Generally, these purchase money mortgages are written with comparatively low interest rates, with the longest payback period, and with payments arranged for the buyer's convenience. Also, they are most frequently written without the mortgagee requiring the borrower to pledge assets other than the asset he is buying. An experienced entrepreneur in need of additional financing (beyond that obtainable by a first mortgage) to make a purchase will try for a second mortgage to be held by the seller. In some parts of the country a purchase money second is called a "soft money" second.

Next in order, with respect to favorable terms, is second mortgage financing obtained from a private party. A direct approach to the lender (i.e., not through a middle man) is most likely to yield the best obtainable terms. Bankers and real estate attorneys are good sources for recommending private individuals who are interested in second mortgages.

A somewhat higher cost, because of a charge for a loan fee or commission, is encountered when one uses a real estate broker or mortgage investment broker. The loan fee charged varies over a broad range. If you use this approach, shopping should be of substantial benefit to you.

The highest costs and least favorable terms are usually met when one turns to the institutions as Ronald W. did in the prior example. They are, however, easily located and generally react more promptly than the sources mentioned above. They also have funds on hand, in contrast with individuals or small mortgage investment firms who may

THE BEST SOURCES OF SECONDARY FINANCING

be fully committed and out of available funds when you approach them.

Again, it is desirable to know of sources for low cost secondary financing ahead of your need. Otherwise, time pressure may mean settling for one of the higher cost sources.

SIX KEYS TO PROFITABLE USE OF SECONDARY FINANCING

1. As a part of his overall professional activity in keeping up to date in the financing of real estate, the successful entrepreneur will be prepared, ahead of his need, to obtain second mortgage financing. Even though he does not currently foresee a need, he will automatically update his information and add cards on new possible sources for such financing.
2. The needs and goals of private financiers of real estate change as time passes. It may well be to your advantage to approach those who have not been previously active in secondary financing.
3. Secondary financing can be used to increase your leverage in a new (or existing) investment. If the property is a wise investment it will intensify your use of other people's money to make money.
4. It is, of course, desirable to get the lowest possible interest rate and the best terms on any financing you obtain. The sophisticated entrepreneur also will try for the lowest costs and terms, but his primary attention is on the profit potential. If the profit is high enough, then he will not let the greater interest on a second mortgage stop him from making a deal.
5. It is important to know where to get the lowest cost second mortgage money, to try these sources first, and to negotiate a higher cost second only if necessary and if the profit potential justifies it.
6. Shopping pays off in the second mortgage area. Shopping ahead of time is a mark of a true professional in real estate investing.

REMEMBER THESE POINTS

- Increase your leverage by using second mortgage financing.
- Shopping sources will pay off in lower interest rates and better terms.
- Locating sources ahead of your need will help close more deals (and with lower costs).

- In ascending order, with respect to cost of secondary financing, the types of sources are:
  - the seller of property you're buying (i.e., a purchase money second)
  - private individuals
  - real estate brokers and mortgage investment companies (if you shop)
  - institutions.
- Maintain a position wherein you are not *forced* to get secondary financing.

15

WRAP AROUND MORTGAGES: A HIGH LEVERAGE, OPM TECHNIQUE

A straightforward, ordinary second mortgage is a well known instrument in real estate financing. The interest rates and other terms are similar, at least in principle, to a first mortgage. The principal difference is that the second mortgage is junior or subordinate to the first; a consequence is that in the event of bankruptcy or other default by the mortgagor, the holder of the first mortgage must be satisfied in full before remaining proceeds (if any) are paid to the holder of the junior mortgage.

One of the insider's secrets of real estate investing is a little known technique which may be regarded as a more sophisticated version of second mortgage financing; it is called a "wrap around mortgage." It will be examined in detail in this chapter.

The first example is a straightforward, relatively uncomplicated instance of how one entrepreneur used a wrap around mortgage to enable the purchase of a $240,000 commercial property with no initial cash payment. The second example describes an unusual case of a tenant who makes a wrap around mortgage loan to his landlord. It also illustrates the importance of an entrepreneur thoroughly analyzing a proposed loan from all angles.

WHY THE LITTLE KNOWN TECHNIQUE OF WRAP AROUND MORTGAGES IS A POWERHOUSE

If someone agrees to accept an "all inclusive" mortgage for an amount larger than an existing or new first mortgage on real property and if the amount of the first mortgage is included within the all inclusive mortgage, then the latter is a wrap around mortgage. This insider's secret is a little known technique principally used in structuring the financing of deals which otherwise might never be consummated. It is a powerhouse technique used by the most sophisticated entrepreneurs in real estate.

The use of purchase money second mortgages in sales transactions was described in Chapter 13. In most cases wherein such a mortgage is used, the seller simply takes an ordinary second mortgage on whatever terms are agreed upon by him and the buyer. It is used to fill the gap between the sales price and the sum of a new or existing first mortgage and the buyer's cash. In some transactions the amount of buyer's cash in the deal is zero. The usual reason for using a purchase money second mortgage is to bring a deal to a closing. In some sales transactions, a variation of this approach is used. The buyer gives a mortgage for the entire amount of indebtedness on the property. The mortgage includes the amount owed by the seller on the first mortgage plus the amount which otherwise would have been covered by a simple purchase money (second) mortgage. The mortgage given by the buyer is called a wrap around mortgage. In most cases, the buyer pays the seller the full mortgage payment and the seller makes the payments on the first mortgage.

A wrap around mortgage has a substantial financial benefit for the seller. In the typical instance, the pre-existing first mortgage has an interest at or below current prevailing interest rates for new first mortgages. The wrap around mortgage is written at an interest rate higher than the first mortgage interest rate. If the seller takes a simple purchase money second mortgage at an interest rate of, say, 1 ½ percent above the first mortgage interest rate, then his total interest income is a percentage of the amount owed on the purchase money mortgage only. If, however, he negotiates a wrap around mortgage at an interest rate, say, 1 ½ percent above the first mortgage rate, then his interest income would be the same as above on the amount above the first mortgage plus 1 ½ percent of the amount owed on the first mortgage. He would, of course, be making money on other people's money—in this case, on money originally furnished by the holder of the first mortgage. From the seller's viewpoint, the insider's use of wrap around mortgages is indeed a powerhouse.

BUYERS USE WRAP AROUND MORTGAGES FOR THEIR BENEFIT

The terms and conditions of a wrap around mortgage can be whatever is agreed between the lender and borrower subject, of course, to law. The services of a knowledgeable attorney are especially important in preparing the mortgage documents; in some states there have been legislative acts and judicial decisions in recent years which affect wrap around mortgages. Choose your attorney based upon his experience in real estate contracts and laws.

Once the financial results of a wrap around mortgage are examined, the financial benefit to the holder (e.g., the seller in the sales transaction discussed in the previous section) becomes evident. If a seller is at all inclined to remain involved in the financing of the property, then he will most likely be interested in a wrap around mortgage. On the other hand, why should a buyer agree to a wrap around mortgage?

A borrower who gives a wrap around mortgage will, of course, pay more interest than he would if he were paying directly on a first and second mortgage separately.

Analysis of a property which an entrepreneur wishes to buy depends upon whether the interest rate on the existing first mortgage is (1) at or (2) below the current prevailing rate for new first mortgages. In both cases, the buyer increases the leverage on the cash he invests by giving a wrap around mortgage for an amount in excess of the amount owed on the first mortgage. He will, of course, try to get the seller to accept an ordinary purchase money mortgage and let him (the buyer) take over on the first. If the seller will not do so but is willing to use the wrap around mortgage approach, then the important question is whether the profit potential makes payment of a higher interest rate advisable.

In the second case, wherein the existing first mortgage has an interest rate lower than is available for new first mortgages, the buyer's analysis is more complicated. He does, however, then have an incentive in the form of a future benefit for favorably considering a wrap around mortgage. If the terms and conditions are written properly and if projections of his future actions in real estate and his overall cash flow indicate that he will be able to pay off all of the amount owed on the wrap around mortgage which is above the balance owed on the first mortgage at that time, then the buyer will have the advantage of a first mortgage rate which is below the market. The buyer should be careful to double check with his attorney to be sure that the mortgage documents will let him reap this benefit when he pays off the stated amount.

Caution: Be sure to have an attorney check a "due on sale" provision, if one exists, in the first mortgage.

An innovative entrepreneur who is buying will sometimes be the one who suggests that a wrap around mortgage be used, provided that his financial analysis shows a sufficient profit potential and if he cannot get the seller to accept the more ordinary purchase money second mortgage.

The insider's secret of wrap around mortgages is another tool in the kit of an ambitious entrepreneur building his fortune in real estate. He will use it whenever it promises to enable him to make a good profit and simultaneously increase the leverage on any cash he invests.

HOW A WRAP AROUND MORTGAGE ALLOWED PURCHASE OF $240,000 SUBURBAN OFFICE BUILDING WITH ZERO INITIAL PAYMENT

At a time when Samuel M., a semi-retired jeweler, was fully committed in real estate investments, he heard of a suburban office building available at what seemed to be a reasonable price. He had liquid assets and some cash on hand, but he made it a practice to keep it that way. His personal balance sheet showed a net worth of more than $750,000.

The suburban office building was a small, two story structure built seven years previously by the present owner/builder. There was ample parking. The principal tenant was a well known insurance company on a long term, triple net lease. The property was priced at $240,000. The owner was moving to live in and manage a lake marina he owned in another state. The existing, seven year old mortgage had a balance of $131,000; the interest rate was only 7¼ percent. The current prevailing interest rate for first mortgages on similar property was 9¼ percent.

Mr. M. obtained financial statements on the property for the full seven years and copies of all leases. His analysis showed that he could expect a return on investment (net profit) before debt service of approximately 10.5 percent of the asking price. Investigation of the five block long commercial strip showed that the property should appreciate in value. There were still a few vacant commercial lots on the well known, heavily traveled boulevard.

He and his attorney prepared an offer which he presented to the seller along with a copy of his personal balance sheet. He offered

$225,000 with the buyer to assume the first mortgage and the owner to accept a purchase money mortgage for $95,000 at 10 percent interest with quarterly payments based on a 25 year amortization schedule and with all due and payable at the end of seven years. The seller said he had not been involved in a no down payment transaction since he bought a G.I. home as a young man. He said he was not in need of cash; that even if he sold for all cash to a new or existing loan, he would probably lend the money on well secured second mortgages. He requested three days to think it over. Samuel M. said he would most likely sell a property he was renovating within approximately three years, but that he would need seven years on a second mortgage. He hinted at possibly increasing the purchase price offer in view of the requested no down payment.

When they met again the seller complimented Mr. M. on his balance sheet and presented the following counter offer. Purchase price to be $240,000. Seller to accept a wrap around mortgage at 10 percent interest rate for $240,000. Payments to be made monthly on a fully amortized schedule to coincide with the first mortgage (approximately 18 years remaining). No lump sum payment would be required at any time but the mortgage would be payable whenever the buyer wished, with no payoff penalty. Samuel M. said that acceptance of the counter offer would mean a negative cash flow for him which had to be considered even though he was not in need of a positive cash flow if other aspects of an investment were desirable. He asked that they meet again two days later.

Mr. M. had his attorney add an explicit, carefully worded paragraph to insure that, if the wrap around mortgage principal was paid down to a balance equal to the then remaining balance on the first mortgage, the seller would no longer be involved and Mr. M. would have the advantage of the 7 ¼ percent interest rate. The seller signed this counter-counter offer and they closed the deal.

Thus, Mr. M. purchased a $240,000 property with no initial payment by the use of a wrap around mortgage. He had, of course, made an attempt to buy it and get the advantage of a 7 ¼ percent interest rate from the start on more than one-half of the purchase price. Without the advantage of the wrap around mortgage to the seller, Mr. M. believes they would never have closed the deal.

HOW TO FIND INVESTORS TO FINANCE WRAP AROUND MORTGAGES

Most frequently, the use of a wrap around mortgage occurs in a sales transaction wherein the buyer gives the mortgage to the seller. It may, of course, be used by investors in other situations. For example, a buyer may be the one who initiates a proposal to use a wrap around mortgage if the seller has refused to accept an ordinary purchase money mortgage. If the seller still insists on all cash to the existing loan then the buyer may negotiate a wrap around mortgage from an independent lender. Or, an entrepreneur who has owned a property for some time may seek to raise cash via a wrap around mortgage from an individual. In these latter two cases the entrepreneur then has the problem of finding an investor with money to lend. From the borrower's point of view the wrap around mortgage has the disadvantage of a higher interest rate. He will, of course, first try to give a second mortgage to take care of his need. If unsuccessful, then a wrap around mortgage approach is a logical next consideration.

A discussion on finding lenders for second mortgages was given in Chapter 14. The same approach is suggested in seeking lenders on wrap around mortgages. In fact, if you have prepared a card file on potential investors in second mortgages, you have a running start. But, again, because of the interest you will pay, an effort should be made for an ordinary second before bringing up the subject of a wrap around mortgage. Any lender who makes second mortgage loans should be favorably inclined toward a wrap around mortgage loan. If all other aspects of two proposed loans are equal, then the risk of one with a wrap around mortgage is only slightly greater (compared with an ordinary second mortgage), but the interest income is usually substantially greater. The only difference in risk on the part of the lender is that he assumes responsibility for payment of the first loan if he accepts a wrap around mortgage.

ADVANTAGES OF WRAP AROUNDS FOR LENDERS—LEVERAGE!

Leverage is one of the magic words in real estate investing. An entrepreneur who knows the variations of leverage and uses these inside secrets of real estate investing will build a fortune at a faster pace and will minimize the amount of cash he has in each venture.

The maker of a loan or a seller who takes a mortgage as part payment for his property can also get leverage. The technique is to use the insider's secret of wrap around mortgage.

The following example is a typical one for a seller who takes a wrap around mortgage for $180,000 at 10 percent interest. The property had a balance of $110,000 on the first mortgage at 8 ½ percent interest. The sales price was $210,000 with $30,000 down payment.

Sale price	$210,000
Cash down payment	30,000
Wrap around mortgage	$180,000

WRAP AROUND MORTGAGES

Seller's initial interest income rate (10%)	18,000 per year
Seller pays interest on $110,000 first mortgage (8½%)	9,350 per year

Seller's net initial interest income rate ... $8,650 per year.

The seller has, in effect, lent $70,000 of his assets to the buyer. He is, of course, receiving 10 percent ($7,000) on the $70,000 and $11,000 interest income on the $110,000 owed on the first mortgage. He pays interest of 8½ percent ($9,350) on the first mortgage. Thus, his initial net interest income is at the rate of $8,650 per year. He is making money on money furnished by the first mortgage holder in addition to the interest income on his $70,000. His total net interest income is 12.36 percent ($8,650 ÷ $70,000) of his "investment" in the property. In other words, he has leveraged his investment by making money on other people's money!

HOW AN ENTREPRENEUR'S TENANT FINANCED A $40,000 WRAP AROUND MORTGAGE

Jerry T., a mid-level manager in the local Federal Building, had purchased a small quadruplex apartment building approximately eight years ago. He and his family occupied one of the four units. Mrs. T.'s uncle was retiring and offered to sell his duplex to them at a reasonable price. He knew that Mr. and Mrs. T. were looking for a larger income property and planned to trade in their quadruplex. Mr. and Mrs. T. were interested in the duplex, but did not have $11,500 to make the required down payment to her uncle.

Two or three days later, one of Mr. T.'s tenants mentioned that a mortgage he held on commercial property he had sold had been paid off. He asked Mr. T. if he knew of any investment opportunity requiring $12,000.

The first mortgage on Mr. T.'s quadruplex had a balance of $29,000 at an interest rate of 8¼ percent. Its market value was approximately $50,000. The first mortgage interest rate on the duplex was 8½ percent. The current prevailing first mortgage interest rate for new loans was 9½ percent for income property.

Mr. T. told the tenant that he was in need of a loan. He gave the financial information on the quadruplex to the tenant and said he would give a second mortgage for $12,000 at the state's legal limit of 10 percent interest. He suggested a ten year, fully amortized payment schedule.

The tenant pointed out that the current first mortgage interest rate of 9½ percent was almost equal to the state's limit of 10 percent on second mortgages. He mentioned that Mr. T.'s total moneys borrowed would amount to 82 percent of Mr. T.'s asserted market value of the property, whereas most savings and loan associations would lend only 70 to 75 percent of their appraised value. He also said that he had obtained a return (legally) of approximately 12 percent on the loan which had just been paid off. He offered to take a wrap around mortgage for 20 years at a 10 percent interest rate. Mr. T. had never heard of such a mortgage.

The lender explained that the $41,000 mortgage would wrap around, i.e., include the $29,000 owed on the first. Mr. T. would make payments on the 20 year, $41,000 mortgage of $395.66 per month. The lender would make all scheduled payments on the first mortgage and give Mr. T. proof of payment. When and if Mr. T. paid the wrap around mortgage down to the then existing balance of the first, then Mr. T. would make no more payments on the wrap around and would again have the advantage of an 8 ¼ percent loan. Mr. T. would have the right to pay a lump sum at any time without penalty.

Mr. and Mrs. T. estimated that they could pay off the lender and revert to the first mortgage within four years if they made no other transactions in real estate. They also verified that they could assume the first mortgage on Mrs. T.'s uncle's property. They considered trying to refinance their quadruplex for 80 percent of the market value. But at the current prevailing interest of 9 ½ percent they estimated that the slight savings (compared with the 10 percent wrap around rate) would not be enough to offset the advantage of returning to an 8 ¼ percent rate in the future. They made the deal with the tenant on his terms and purchased the duplex.

In this case, the lender was experienced in wrap around mortgages but the borrower was not. Apparently, Mr. T. did not compute the return which his tenant would initially get from the $12,000 cash furnished. The initial interest return would be:

Cash furnished by lender	$12,000
Total amount of wrap around mortgage	41,000
Lender's initial interest income rate (@ 10%)	4,100 per year
Lender pays interest on $29,000 first mortgage (@ 8 ¼ %)	$2,392.50 per year
Lender's initial net interest income rate ...	$1,707.50 per year
Lender's initial rate of return on $12,000 is $1,707.50 ÷ $12,000 or 14.23 percent!	

If the interest rate on the wrap around mortgage had been 9.5 percent the following computation shows that the lender's initial net interest income would have been $1,502.50 or 12.48 percent of $12,000.

Lender's initial interest income rate (@9.5%) ..	$3,895.00 per year
Lender pays interest of $29,000 first mortgage (@ 8¼%)	2,392.50 per year
Lender's initial net interest income rate	$1,502.50 per year
Lender's initial rate of return on $12,000 would be $1,502.50 ÷ $12,000 or 12.48 percent.	

The lender had mentioned early in their negotiations that he received a return of approximately 12 percent on a prior wrap around mortgage. If Mr. T. had calculated the lender's initial rate of return on the $12,000 for the wrap around mortgage interest rates of 9.5 and 10 percent (as shown above), then he might have offered 9.5 percent and showed the lender that the return to him would be as good as or better than on the lender's prior loan. What the lender's response would have been is not known, but it would have been a good negotiating ploy and might have been accepted.

Mr. and Mrs. T. had deviated temporarily from their plan to trade in their equity in their quadruplex as a down payment on a larger building. With their two properties to trade in they continued to search for a larger property. Purchasing the duplex was a worthwhile small step for them. The wrap around mortgage approach made it possible. The needed additional incentive for the tenant to lend cash of an amount which increased the total mortgage to 82 percent of the claimed market value was the leverage obtained by the tenant on the first mortgage loan. He was again making money on other people's money.

USE OF WRAP AROUND MORTGAGE APPROACH GIVES IMPORTANT EDGE IN REAL ESTATE INVESTMENT FIELD

An entrepreneur who has learned the insider's secrets of wrap around mortgages has another powerful tool to use when it is to his advantage. Whenever an entrepreneur is in the buyer's role he will, of course first try other means of filling a gap in financing. He most likely will try for a purchase money second mortgage first. If it is unobtainable, he will then try for second mortgage financing by a third party if he is trying to close a deal without bringing other investors into an equity or profit sharing position.

If the buyer is competing with other possible buyers, a knowledge of when and how to use the wrap around mortgage approach may furnish the additional factor needed to close a deal for himself. It can be just the competitive edge to allow him to get the property rather than his competitor.

Even if there is no competitor involved, use of a wrap around mortgage with its advantage thoroughly described to the mortgage taker may well mean that an entrepreneur would have a sufficient edge to close more deals than he would otherwise. It is another tool which can speed your progress toward building a fortune in real estate.

EIGHT KEYS—BUILDING A FORTUNE WITH WRAP AROUND MORTGAGES

1. One important key technique in building a fortune in real estate investment is use of a wrap around mortgage. Detailed knowledge of this technique will help speed your progress toward financial independence and security.

2. Use of a wrap around mortgage can mean closing a deal for yourself instead of bringing in partners on an equity or profit sharing basis.

3. An experienced entrepreneur who is in the buyer's position will try first for a purchase money second mortgage and, if unsuccessful, then for an ordinary second. Depending upon circumstances and time pressure, he may then turn to the wrap around approach as the clincher.

4. Knowledge of the advantages of a wrap around mortgage for the lender and the capability to illustrate the advantages will help insure your success. The advantages are there, but this insider's secret is not well understood by many lenders.

5. Rather than deplete cash on hand or dispose of liquid assets, it is frequently better to make use of a wrap around mortgage.

6. The two way advantage of a wrap around mortgage makes it a powerhouse in real estate investment. The buyer increases the leverage on any cash he puts into a deal by increasing the total amount he borrows. The lender also gets leverage on the money he furnishes by making additional interest income on money which was furnished by the maker of the first mortgage loan.

7. An attorney with experience in real estate contracts should check all documents. He should pay particular attention to any due on sale provision in the first mortgage loan. The wrap around mortgage technique must not be used in an illegal way to circumvent any such provision.

WRAP AROUND MORTGAGES

8. In seeking investors for a wrap around mortgage loan, try those who have advanced money on ordinary second mortgages. They are logical candidates. Be sure that they know the advantage of a wrap around mortgage for them before you ask for a yes or no answer.

REMEMBER THESE POINTS

- A wrap around mortgage can be used to increase a buyer's leverage and his potential profit per dollar invested.
- A wrap around mortgage also yields leverage for the lender by enabling him to collect interest on money furnished by others on a first mortgage.
- If a seller refuses to agree to a purchase money mortgage and if it is in your best interest, offer a wrap around mortgage.
- From a borrower's point of view, the order of preference in the broad second mortgage area is (a) purchase money mortgage, (b) ordinary second mortgage with a third party, and (c) wrap around mortgage.
- During negotiations, you may decide to use a wrap around approach as a clincher to close the deal.
- A wrap around can sometimes close a deal for you without bringing co-investors in on an equity or profit sharing basis.
- Use of a wrap around can avoid depleting your cash or liquid assets.
- Double leverage, for buyer and lender, makes the wrap around a powerhouse.
- Have an attorney check all documents, particularly any due on sale provision in a first mortgage.

16

HOW TO SELL SECOND MORTGAGES AND GET TOP DOLLAR FOR YOUR REAL ESTATE

Any active entrepreneur in real estate investment is necessarily interested in both sides of financing a transaction. In prior chapters of this book the emphasis is on structuring and obtaining financing with you, the real estate investor, usually in the buyer's position. When an investor decides to sell one of his properties, an intimate knowledge of arranging financing for the potential buyer can mean the difference between closing or not closing the deal. Optimizing financing for the buyer can also mean the difference between the seller getting top dollar versus a mediocre sales price for the property.

In selling a property, an entrepreneur may be able to maximize the price for the property by accepting a purchase money second mortgage or a wrap around mortgage. If possible, he will negotiate a wrap around mortgage both for the additional interest income while he holds it and because of its better marketability. An aggressive entrepreneur is not interested in having his assets tied up in mortgages given by others. He is not in the business of financing property which he does not own or wherein there is no possibility of gain other than interest income. Even though his reasons for accepting a purchase money second or wrap around mortgage may have been entirely sound in selling a property, he will want to sell or otherwise convert the mortgage for his own best advantage for future real estate deals.

The first example in this chapter describes an entrepreneur's first effort at selling a second mortgage. He accepted a discount upon selling, but he converted a second mortgage into cash for use in another venture. The second example reveals how another entrepreneur converted a second mortgage to cash with a discount of only 6 percent. An alternate way of converting a passive asset, i.e., a second mortgage, into active ownership of real estate is illustrated in the third example.

SELLING A SECOND MORTGAGE—THOSE DISCOUNTS HURT

The first time anyone is in the position of selling a second mortgage the realities of the marketplace may come as a surprise if not a shock. In addition to any commission which may be paid to a mortgage broker as a middleman, buyers of second mortgages expect a discount. Depending upon the current market and upon the terms of the second mortgage note the discount can range from zero to 4 percent or more. The discount does, indeed, hurt.

The logic of discounting a second mortgage is straightforward. If the current market calls for a return of 12 percent on seconds, then selling your second calls for a discount which allows the buyer to earn 12 percent on the actual amount he pays for the mortgage. The amount of the discount depends upon the terms of the second mortgage.

An experienced entrepreneur will anticipate the size of the discount and take it into account before taking a second mortgage in selling a property he owns. Entrepreneurs who are familiar with the inside secrets of real estate investing will price a property high enough to allow for the possibility of taking a second mortgage and selling it at a discount. If, during negotiations with a potential buyer, it appears the seller will have to take a purchase money second in order to close the deal, then the seller is more likely to insist upon a higher sales price than if the buyer were offering all cash to a new or existing loan.

HOW TO SELL SECOND MORTGAGES

LOW INTEREST SECOND DISCOUNTED HEAVILY

Gary H., an aerospace engineer, had bought and upgraded several houses, but had always sold them for all cash to a new or existing loan. When he was offered full asking price for his most recent project, he decided to accept the offer even though it meant taking a purchase money second mortgage. The mortgage was for $30,000 with an interest rate of only nine per cent with monthly payments of interest only and with the full principal due and payable at the end of three years. The interest rate was even lower than the current first mortgage interest rate of 9½ percent for individual residences. He soon learned that the marketplace's prevailing return was 12 percent per year on second mortgages purchased by individuals.

Mr. H.'s interest income was $225.00 per month or $2,700 per year. A buyer of the second mortgage would have to buy it for $22,500 ($22,500 = $2,700 per year ÷ 12 percent per year) in order to realize an annual return of 12 percent: 12% per year × $22,500 = $2,700 per year.

Mr. H. called a private individual who had financed a second mortgage on one of his projects three years previously. The price they agreed upon was $22,500 with Gary H. agreeing to be responsible for payments in the event of default by the mortgagor.

Thus, for this specific mortgage with its terms and for a market demanding a 12 percent return on the purchase price of a second mortgage the discount was 25 percent (($30,000 − $22,500) ÷ $30,000 = 0.25)! But Mr. H. then had the $22,500 cash to use in a new venture. Based upon his past experience, he was confident he could make much more than $2,700 per year with the cash and that he would more than recoup the $7,500 discount on his next venture.

HOW TO SELL A SECOND MORTGAGE

Most entrepreneurs in real estate investment consider a second mortgage they hold as a passive asset. It does, of course, provide interest income for the holder, but that is its only good feature. Interest income also is classified by the Internal Revenue Service as ordinary income and it receives no preferred tax treatment. In contrast, ownership or control of real property is an "active" asset in that the owner can improve it, refinance it, and manage it to provide a better (and higher) return on his personal investment and later sell or trade it for a profit with the possibility of being taxed at capital gains rates.

Searching for a buyer for a second mortgage should be done while there is no time pressure on the holder. The fastest, and usually most expensive way to convert a second mortgage into cash, is to call a mortgage broker. There are many listed in the classified telephone directory of any sizeable city. Their commission typically will be in the range of 6 to 15 percent. The size of the commission will vary depending upon the current market and competition between mortgage brokers. Some large banks have subsidiaries which specialize in second mortgages. An experienced entrepreneur familiar with the inside secrets and techniques of making money in real estate will try to use a less costly approach. He will also try to avoid getting into a position wherein he must convert a second mortgage within a very short time.

Finding a buyer for an existing second mortgage you hold is very similar to finding a lender to lend money on a second mortgage which you create and give to him. The way to locate such individuals with money and an interest in second mortgages was described in Chapter 14. Lenders active in furnishing money for second mortgage loans will usually prefer to buy an existing second mortgage rather than to lend money on a new second.

There are two small differences in attempting to sell a pre-existing second mortgage (compared with creating a new second mortgage) which you may possibly use to your advantage. One is that if the mortgage is a seasoned one (i.e., if it has existed long enough for several payments to have been made) and if the payment record shows promptness by the mortgagor in making payments, then you may be able to negotiate a somewhat higher price for the mortgage. The second is that if you are also responsible for payments to the buyer in the event of default by the mortgagor then, again, you should be able to negotiate a higher selling price because of the additional security for the buyer of your second.

ENTREPRENEUR ENLISTS REAL ESTATE BROKER'S AID FOR COMMISSION OF ONLY 2-1/2 PERCENT

When he was in his early thirties, Earl Y. had inherited a 31 unit aparment building in a city approximately sixty miles from the coast. Two years before taking an early retirement at age fifty-five, he and his wife had purchased a 16 unit apartment building within four blocks of the beach. He had retired as the manager of the radio, television, and appliance department of a large retail store chain and had a comfortable pension. They moved to their beach property and were managing their inland property with the help of a part-time manager.

They advertised their inland property and received an offer for $40,000 less than asking price with all cash to a new loan. They countered at full price. The buyer responded that he did not have sufficient funds to accept the counter offer, but that he would pay full price if Earl Y. would accept a seven year purchase money mortgage at ten percent interest. The proffered interest rate was ¾ percent above the prevailing interest rate for first mortgages on apartment buildings. Mr. Y. agreed and they closed the deal.

Taking the second mortgage meant that Earl Y. received top dollar for his property, but he was looking for another apartment building near his beach apartments and wanted cash on hand. He had never had the problem of selling "mortgage paper." He called a mortgage brokerage firm and was told that their fee was fifteen percent and that their lender-clients might want to discount the $40,000 mortgage note. After checking two or three more sources with similar fee structures, a friend suggested that Mr. Y. contact his banker and local real estate brokers. A real estate broker who had shown Mr. Y. two or three apartment buildings said he would be pleased to contact lender-clients for a fee of 2½ percent if he succeeded in placing the mortgage. One client offered to take it at a discount of six percent. The broker told Mr. Y. that the current market discount on existing second mortgages was 6 to 30 percent or more and recommended that Mr. Y. accept the offer. Mr. Y. closed the deal. He received $37,600 and paid the broker 2½ percent or $940.

Thus, the total discount (including the broker's fee) was $2,400 plus $940 or $3,340. Percentage wise, the total discount was ($3,340 ÷ $40,000) × 100% or 8.35 percent. The buyer's annual return would be 10.64 percent. In view of the fact that other approaches to selling a second mortgage were more costly and that the current market called for a return of 12 percent or more on second mortgages, Mr. Y. was fortunate to receive a net of $36,660 for his $40,000 second mortgage paper.

HOW TO DISPOSE OF A SECOND MORTGAGE WITHOUT DISCOUNTING

There are a number of approaches which an entrepreneur can try with the goal of converting a second mortgage into cash without discounting it. In general, these approaches require time and are usually not productive if the mortgage holder is under time pressure. The four approaches most frequently used by entrepreneurs acquainted with the inside secrets of real estate investing are given below.

Real Estate Brokers

Professional mortgage brokerage firms are usually fast and efficient, but they command a high percentage commission or fee for their services. But it is their business and they're in it to make money. On the other hand, small real estate brokerage firms are in the business of selling real estate for a commission. When a broker can sell a house for $200,000 and collect a $12,000 commission, he's really not very interested in placing a $20,000 second mortgage. Frequently, however, a real estate broker will have knowledge of individuals with money and an interest in second mortgages. I know of many such loans which were made on the basis of an individual taking funds out of savings and loan associations where he was receiving the current interest rate being paid to depositors and buying or taking a second mortgage at an interest rate nearly double what he was earning. I've also seen real estate brokers charge from zero to 3 to 6 percent for getting the two parties together. The zero charge was linked to the broker's expectation of cementing a relationship, hopefully leading to a future purchase of income property by the entrepreneur selling the second mortgage.

Bankers, Attorneys, and Others

In addition to contacting individual real estate brokers as discussed in the preceding paragraph, you can sometimes get an equally advantageous sale of a second mortgage by contacting bank officers, savings and loans, attorneys, and even fellow club members. It is important for you not to be in a hurry and for you to locate interested individuals who make second mortgage loans or buy seconds only occasionally. The professional organizations or individuals who are aggressively in the "second mortgage business" will hold out for a high return on their money and a high fee. There are no fixed ratios, but an occasional investor in second mortgages may accept an interest rate nearly double that paid to demand depositors by a savings and loan association; others, in the business in a more aggressive way, will charge an effective interest (including fees) of 2½ to 3 times.

Newspaper Advertising

The old saw, "advertising pays," is applicable in selling a second mortgage. A few minutes in a library will be well spent reviewing advertisements on real estate financing for the last few weeks in local newspapers. If you are not already familiar with the market, add to your knowledge by calling some of the advertisers and asking questions. The

HOW TO SELL SECOND MORTGAGES

best text for your ad depends upon the current market and the competition from other advertisers. In general, it will pay to be specific. Again, if the second mortgage you're selling is a seasoned one, you have a strong advertising point. Emphasize it in your advertisement.

Trade-in

An aggressively active entrepreneur is usually planning or seeking another real estate venture. Whether he is simply buying or is trading in a small property for a larger one, he looks upon a second mortgage he holds as an asset to be used in making a new deal. For example, suppose a property he wants is priced at $100,000 and has an existing first mortgage on it of $73,000 at a desirable rate of interest. Also suppose the entrepreneur holds a seasoned second mortgage with a balance of $18,000. Then the entrepreneur might offer to assume the first, pay $9,000 cash, and transfer the second to the seller. If he succeeds in closing the deal on that basis, then he would have turned a passive asset, the second mortgage, into an active asset, i.e., an equity position in purchased property—and without discounting the second mortgage! Also, he will have the benefit of a desirable interest rate on the first mortgage.

The next example describes how a thinking entrepreneur disposed of a second mortgage and benefited himself and the seller.

HOW TRADING IN A SECOND MORTGAGE FILLED GAP IN FINANCING

Dale R. is an experienced entrepreneur in real estate. He had quit his job as a production worker thirteen years previously and, at the age of twenty-six, entered real estate as a salesman dealing in income property. At thirty, he owned enough income property to leave the realty firm and devote full time to real estate investments of his own. The longest period he had owned any single property was twenty-six months. He bought property only if he could do something to it so he could turn it over for a profit. He had never taken a purchase money second mortgage until he sold a nine unit apartment building to a retiring couple. The second mortgage he held was for $20,000 originally, with 10 percent interest and a fully amortized, eight year payment schedule.

A 16 unit apartment building, a twin to the 16 units Mr. R. had purchased next door only six months earlier, became available. He was interested because the price was reasonable and because he had found that a 32 unit complex was almost ideal for resale to someone who had an eight or ten unit building and wanted to trade up to a larger number of units. There was a loan commitment for a 75 percent loan. Mr. R. had the cash to pay 25 percent down, but he offered a smaller amount down with the offer stipulating that the seller was to accept a purchase money second for $20,000 at 8 ¾ percent interest.

The seller said he would have to have 10 percent interest on the requested second mortgage. He rejected Mr. R.'s offer to increase the interest rate to 9 percent. Mr. R. then offered to transfer the second mortgage he held to the seller. He pointed out that the interest rate was 10 percent and that the mortgagor had promptly paid each of the seven months payments due to date. The seller agreed and they closed the deal. The balance owed on the second was approximately $18,900, which meant that Mr. R. had to increase the cash to be paid down by $1,100.

Thus, Mr. R. converted a passive asset (the second mortgage he held) into an active asset (equity in an apartment building). If he had sold the second he held, he would most likely have had to discount it by approximately $3,000. By bartering with the seller of the 16 units, he had disposed of the second mortgage for the full amount of the principal balance; he had discounted it by zero percent! And he had no fee to pay to a broker!

HOW TO BARGAIN WITH A SECOND MORTGAGE

If the old-fashioned terms, "Yankee Trader" or "Horse Trader" were to be applied to any American today it would surely fit most successful entrepreneurs in real estate investment. In the prior example, Dale R. showed the instincts of a genuine barterer. One of his objectives in buying the 16 unit building was to dispose of the second mortgage he held by trading it for an equity position in the apartment building. Note that his initial step was to include in his offer the condition that the seller accept a purchase money second carrying an interest rate *lower* than the interest rate on the mortgage he was holding. Note also that even if the seller had taken a purchase money second at the proffered interest rate of 9 percent, Mr. R. would have been paying 9 percent on one note and receiving 10 percent on another note approximately of equal dollar amount. When the seller said he would have to have 10 percent, Dale R. was in a perfect position to offer transfer of the 10 percent mortgage he held in lieu of the purchase money second.

If you are selling an existing mortgage note, look at it as if you were

HOW TO SELL SECOND MORTGAGES

a potential buyer. Again, if the mortgagor has made every payment on time, then you have an important point to emphasize. Hopefully, you will have obtained personal financial statements from the mortgagor. Show them to the potential buyer. Point out the mortgagor's net worth and use his income statement as supporting evidence of his ability to pay. If you do not have a cash flow sheet for the mortgagor, make one if there is sufficient information on hand. A cash flow sheet showing debt service on the second mortgage can be quite convincing. Note also that copies of IRS tax returns are highly desirable to support figures given in the mortgagor's income statement.

The above approach is a professional one; it is the mark of successful entrepreneurs in real estate. If you are competing with others for the potential buyer's money, use it. Your chances of a successful sale on terms acceptable to you will improve if you can cover each point listed and if the mortgage note itself has marketable terms and conditions.

Ideally, you will have the objective of selling your second mortgage without having any responsibility for ongoing payments by the mortgagor. As a last resort, you may decide to guarantee payments on the mortgage note.

Finally, with respect to an existing mortgage, don't overlook the mortgagor as a potential "buyer." If the best you can do in the open marketplace is a discount of, say, 10 percent, have a talk with the mortgagor. Tell him you are seeking to raise cash. Offer him a discount of somewhat less than 10 percent if he will pay off the balance by a specified time. The chances are that the interest he is paying to you is higher than on any other debt obligation he has. Your offer of a discount may be just the incentive needed for him to pay off the mortgage balance.

I have learned that the most advantageous way of disposing of an existing second mortgage is by offering it as part payment in the purchase of real estate. The selling approach listed above is also pertinent in this case. Even though you are the buyer of the real estate being offered, the seller will have to be sold on accepting a second mortgage note instead of the cash he would like. The additional ingredient (compared with selling the note for cash) is that the seller wants to sell his real estate to you. Dale R.'s bargaining technique described in the prior section, was excellent. Reread it, but devise your own strategy; your bargaining approach must be tailored to fit the situation and the people involved.

NINE KEYS TO BETTER DEALING IN SELLING SECOND MORTGAGE

1. An aggressive entrepreneur doesn't permit his assets to be tied up in a second mortgage note. If he has taken a second mortgage, he will quickly try to sell it or trade it for an equity position.
2. Plan ahead—if you think you may take a purchase money mortgage in selling a property, set the price high enough so that you can sell it at a discount if necessary. Planning ahead is as important as knowing the techniques for maximizing the benefits you get from selling or converting a second mortgage.
3. Try for a wrap around mortgage instead of a purchase money second mortgage. A wrap around is easier to sell and it provides you with higher interest income until you can convert it to cash or trade it for equity in another real estate venture.
4. Start your effort to sell or convert a second mortgage while you are not under time pressure. Potential buyers of a second mortgage are the same people who are willing to make a loan secured by a new second mortgage. In fact, it is usually easier to sell a seasoned second than to find someone to make a new second mortgage loan.
5. Try to sell your second mortgage without being obligated to guarantee that the mortgagor will make payments as scheduled. Check with your attorney on this point. On the other hand, you may be able to sell for a higher price if you guarantee payments. The decision on guaranteeing is a trade-off between risk and the price you get. A higher selling price may be well worth the risk.
6. Usually, it will cost you more to use the services of a professional mortgage brokerage firm. First try to locate a buyer through your own contacts, e.g., attorneys, bankers, and small real estate firms.
7. Newspaper advertisements are effective in contacting potential buyers for your second mortgage. Give details in the ad. A very good point to emphasize is that the second for sale is a seasoned one if several timely payments have been made.
8. Try to give your second mortgage note in exchange for equity in purchasing another property. Selling a note for cash frequently means discounting the face value, but giving it as part payment for equity during a purchase seldom results in a discount.

9. In selling or trading a second mortgage, it is highly desirable to have the mortgagor's financial statements, IRS tax returns, and cash flow sheet to show to a potential buyer. Also, a credit report on the mortgagor should be included as a supporting document. A buyer will usually pay more for a second if you can show him these backup documents.

REMEMBER THESE POINTS

- In taking a second, try for high interest and a fully amortized payment schedule.
- In selling a property involving the taking of a second mortgage, try to get a wrap around mortgage. They're easier to sell and are seldom discounted.
- In disposing of a second the descending order of preference is:
  - Give the second as part payment for equity in a new purchase.
  - Contact bankers, attorneys, and others to recommend possible buyers.
  - Contact new potential buyers by advertising.
  - Contact small real estate sales firms and pay a small fee.
  - Contact professional second mortgage brokerage firms.
- Your money tied up in a mortgage note earns interest only.
- Converting a second to cash or trading it for a new equity position is a step toward building a fortune in real estate.
- Dispose of your second mortgage paper while not under time pressure.
- Put your best foot forward in advertising your second for sale.
- Emphasize that your second is seasoned, if possible.
- Discounting a second is a step backward. Try to trade it for new equity without discounting.
- Before attempting to sell your second, assemble pertinent information on the mortgagor to show to potential buyers.

17

BUYING AND REZONING FOR HIGH PROFIT

Some entrepreneurs spend a lifetime in buying, selling, and building their fortunes in real estate without once becoming involved in situations wherein rezoning is a factor. Most entrepreneurs, however, eventually become interested in or involved in a venture wherein existing zoning precludes their putting a parcel of land to its highest and best use. Still other aggressive investors actively seek properties which are being underutilized because of zoning; they build their fortunes by correcting the situation.

I have found that the principal reasons some entrepreneurs avoid getting involved in zoning or rezoning are (1) the whole area of zoning seems to them to be mysterious and elusive, or (2) by their nature, they prefer to avoid hassles. One consequence of their avoiding zoning complications is that there is less competition for aggressive entrepreneurs who tackle the problems. Actually, the best attitude is that the possibility of rezoning a property for more intensive use is an opportunity for profits; and the potential profits are frequently large ones.

To be effective in taking advantage of rezoning for profit, an entrepreneur needs to have personal knowledge of all aspects of zoning and rezoning. He needs to understand the philosophy and the logic (or the lack thereof) of zoning. The fundamental points and examples given in this chapter serve as a start in this complicated area.

I highly recommend that you attend hearings or meetings of whatever governmental body in your community has assumed control of the use of private property. Also, when you become involved in zoning matters in property you own, or want to buy, there is no substitute for an attorney who specializes in zoning and who has a record of success in getting properties rezoned. Rezoning has been and will be a major key to building fortunes measured in the millions of dollars.

The first example in this chapter tells how the market value of a property was more than doubled merely by rezoning. The second example describes how a $40,000 profit was made with one dollar down by an aggressive entrepreneur who combined the option approach, syndication approach (two people), and rezoning to increase the market value of a property with essentially no risk on his part.

ZONING — WHAT IT IS AND HOW IT CONTROLS

Those communities which have zoning get the authority for exercising control of privately owned property from state laws. The power behind zoning is the police power of the state or local government.

Zoning: Zoning is the specification by ordinance or limitations on the purposes for which designated parcels may be used.

Zoning Ordinance: Zoning ordinances are the controlling documents which state what you may or may not do with the property you own. Interpretation and administration is by designated individuals who form the membership of a zoning board, zoning commission, or other designated body of individuals. They have the power to "allow" you to make a fortune or to prevent you from doing so.

Zoning ordinances are usually established to conform with a master plan for a community.

Zoning Variance: A zoning variance may be requested to use your property for a different purpose than specified by the zoning ordinance covering your property. For example, you might request a variance to permit building a duplex on your vacant lot which is zoned for a single family residence. Even though a duplex might be the highest and best use for your lot, there is no obligation by the zoning commission to ap-

BUYING AND REZONING FOR HIGH PROFIT

prove your request. Their decision may be appealed, but appeals are seldom filed and rarely result in overruling the commission.

Requests for variance are usually made only for single parcels of property.

Rezoning: Zoning commissions have also assumed the power to rezone properties. Rezoning is the changing of the zoning for a specified area. Rezoning may be initiated by the zoning board or in response to a request. They may rezone a single parcel or an entire community. The new zone designation may be for either more intensive or less intensive use. Usually, rezoning is done for several or many parcels; if only a single parcel is involved in a request by an owner, the zoning variance approach is usually used.

Master Development Plan: Most larger cities and many smaller ones have adopted a master development plan. Many have a separate group called "Planning Commission" or "Planning Board." Typically, a planning commission acts in an advisory capacity to a City Council or Zoning Board. Original or revised master plans recommend controlling the purposes for which designated properties may be used, such as residential, multiple residential, commercial, light manufacturing, and other uses.

Why Zoning Exists: Developers of very large acreages quite naturally set up zoning in their planning. An area in the vicinity of railroads and highways may become an industrial area. A commercial area on major streets will be for shopping centers, gas stations, and other stores. Next to the commercial area will be an area for apartments, townhouses, and condominiums. The balance may be for schools, churches, parks, and single family residences. Parcels which are sold contain a restriction within the deed which limits or specifies the use options for the purchased land.

In most states and cities, lawmakers have decided that control of private property is a desired function of government. A frequently heard statement, supposed to be sufficient justification for zoning control by government, is "You wouldn't want a gas station on the vacant lot next to your $250,000 house, would you?"! Proponents assert that zoning is necessary and is for the public good. Based upon this unprovable assertion, most cities with a population of more than a few thousand now have zoning by government, i.e., governmental control of private property.

Houston — an Unzoned City: The largest US city without zoning by government officials is Houston, Texas. Surprisingly, at least to proponents of zoning by government, the city has flourished and is among the most prosperous in the nation. It appears that oil companies preferred to build gasoline stations on heavily travelled thoroughfares rather than on quiet streets among expensive homes.

A Midwestern city, with a population of less than 40,000 had a zoning scandal involving bribery and favoritism. As a result of action by an aroused citizenry, zoning ordinances were revoked and zoning by government was eliminated.

Most of us, including myself, live in cities wherein zoning by government was established long ago and is firmly entrenched. Until and unless zoning is eliminated, we must operate within the existing web of laws and ordinances.

REZONE FOR PROFIT?

Zoning itself does not create an opportunity or potential for profit. If, however, you own or are interested in a property which is not being utilized to its highest and best use because of zoning, then you might have a beautiful opportunity for profit. Communities change with time. For example, a single family residence may have been the highest and best use for a given parcel of land thirty years ago. It may still be zoned "Single Family Residential" today even though its highest and best use now may be as a site for an apartment building or even a gasoline station.

Many entrepreneurs have taken very big steps toward becoming millionaires by recognizing that present zoning of a certain parcel is keeping it from being utilized to its greatest potential. By taking the time and spending the necessary money to change the zoning obstruction they have made large profits.

The following example describes how a simple zoning change doubled the realizable market value of a property.

HOW REZONING DOUBLED MARKET VALUE OF $50,000 PROPERTY

Ralph D., a chemist for a local cosmetics manufacturing plant, inherited a triplex on a large lot facing a heavily traveled north-south street. It was a key lot adjacent to an alley. The triplex was thirty-three years old; lack of maintenance and upkeep was evident. On the other side of the alley was a large corner lot which was vacant. Mr. D.'s lot was zoned "Multiple Residential" with a maximum of four units allowed. The corner lot was in a commercial zone. He called two real

BUYING AND REZONING FOR HIGH PROFIT

estate brokers who independently appraised the property in its as-is state (existing zoning and the condition of the triplex) at $49,000 and $50,000. The second broker mentioned that there was a shortage of commercially zoned property in the community and suggested that Mr. D. talk with an attorney about getting it rezoned to "Commercial."

Mr. D. located an attorney who specialized in real estate and had successfully handled several applications for zoning variances and rezoning. After Mr. D. engaged him to file for a zone change, the attorney mentioned that the City Council had instructed the Planning Commission to review current zoning for several blocks in an area including Mr. D.'s lot. The attorney later learned that the review report was scheduled to be finished within "three to six months."

In the cover later accompanying Mr. D.'s application for a zone change the attorney suggested that the City Council ask the Planning Commission for a recommendation before the date of the hearing.

The hearing itself was brief. Mr. D.'s attorney made the presentation. Only one neighbor showed up to oppose the proposed zone change. The Planning Commission had recommended approval based upon their review up to the date of the hearing. The City Council approved the application.

The broker who had suggested that Mr. D. try for rezoning had maintained contact with Mr. D. Within a few days the broker presented an offer of $95,000 to Mr. D. The offer was by a large drug store chain which had made a simultaneous offer for the corner lot. Each of their offers was contingent upon signing a contract for purchase for the other property. Their interest in Mr. D.'s lot was to use it for parking. The final negotiated sales price was for $105,000 with Mr. D. to pay a 5 percent commission to the broker.

Thus, by obtaining new zoning for his property, Mr. D. was enabled to sell the property for its true market value. If he had merely placed the property on the market with its multiple residential zoning he would most likely have sold it for $47,000 or $48,000. The only factor not typical about this example is the ease with which the zone change was obtained. In this case, the attorney's intimate and up-to-date knowledge about zoning matters and the activity of the Planning Commission worked to Mr. D.'s financial benefit.

ZONING IN YOUR COMMUNITY

I have learned that one of the most important attidues to take, whenever zoning or rezoning is a factor, is "Don't assume anything."

Even though most owners and real estate brokers act with integrity, every aspect of a property should be checked carefully. Misinformation or wrong information concerning zoning can cause a drastic error in evaluation of a property. For example, if a buyer had purchased the property owned by Ralph D. (see prior example in this chapter) for $75,000 based upon the assumption that he could get it rezoned, then his risk would have been high. If he subsequently failed in trying to get it rezoned, he would most likely lose $25,000 if he resold the property.

As a community grows and develops over a period of years many changes occur. For example, the highest and best use years ago of a given parcel of land may have been "Single Family Residential." As time passed, a series of MAI appraisals might have shown that its highest and best use progressed from "Single Family Residential" to "Duplex" to "Apartment" to "Commercial." In many communities, a master development plan and subsequent zoning may have become obsolete. In some communities, dozens of variances, exceptions, and spot rezoning cases have created a "crazy quilt" pattern to the extent that an original master development plan is no longer discernible. If zoning in your community is "behind the times" there should be several opportunities for a wide-awake entrepreneur to make excellent profits. An entrepreneur who has become acquainted with the what and why of zoning and how it works is in an excellent position to use his knowledge for profits by rezoning and variances.

An attorney who specializes in real estate and particularly in zoning is a must any time you are thinking of becoming involved in rezoning opportunities. Such an attorney will most likely know most or all members of the controlling group in zoning.

The same attorney can also be instrumental in another way as you build your fortune in real estate. He may be a source for more deals. Let him know that you expect to use his services on any zoning matter and ask him if he knows of any parcel which is ripe for rezoning and if it may be purchasable. Also, find out if he may be eligible for inclusion in a syndication if one develops. What you would be doing is making use of synergism by using the multiple capabilities and interests of an individual for his profit as well as yours.

The more knowledge an entrepreneur has regarding the mode of operation of the zoning body and planning commission in his community the better his chances are of making profits by rezoning. An excellent way to increase one's knowledge is to attend meetings and hearings by the zoning board or city council in the community. By attending, you can get an understanding of the attitudes of the various members regarding various reasons for rezoning. Also, as is true of

BUYING AND REZONING FOR HIGH PROFIT

many government bodies, frequently one individual is the most influential (i.e., the power center) with respect to the final response to requests for rezoning. Knowing his attitudes is particularly important. Your time will be well spent.

A $1 OPTION, SYNDICATION, AND REZONING PUTS $30,000 PROFIT IN ENTREPRENEURS' POCKETS

For five years, Chris B., a draftsman for the city's engineering department, had prepared maps for the planning commission as one of his assignments. He had gradually become acquainted with the complexity of zoning and the original master development plan for the city. His active interest in the subject had included attending a few recent hearings by the zoning board.

The planning commission asked him to prepare a map showing zoning, variances, exceptions, and the dates of any zoning actions for three blocks each way from the intersection of A Street and Z Avenue. The zoning board had asked the planning commission to make a recommendation on an application for a zone change from "Single Family Residential" to "Apartments." The request was for a large corner lot one block north of A Street (a heavily traveled boulevard) on Z Avenue (a major street). The primary reason a map was needed was that during the past twenty years a number of variances and exceptions had been granted in the area; the zoning board needed up-to-date information in order to make decisions consistent with past actions. They were also raising the question of whether the entire area should be rezoned and whether the master development plan should be updated.

While preparing the map, Mr. B. made it a point to become better acquainted with the thinking of the planning commission members. He also was present at the zoning board hearings relating to the requested zone change. It was granted. He estimated it would be at least one and more likely two years before any blanket rezoning would be done for the area.

Mr. B. canvassed the area for a property which might be rezoned to allow apartment construction. The owner of a large inside lot on Z Avenue near A Street had built a one bedroom unit over three garages at the rear of the lot. The structure was fifteen years old. He had applied for a zone change twice; the later attempt was two years ago, but it was denied. A primary reason for the denial was that several neighbors had objected. The owner told Mr. B. that he had given up any thoughts of getting it rezoned and was thinking of selling it. He said it should be worth $42,000.

Chris B. returned to the city hall and compiled a list of recent sales of single family residences within two blocks of the property he had just discussed. He had the same attorney who had handled the application which rezoned the corner lot prepare an option to purchase the property with the contingency that a rezoning request be granted. He had left blank the sales price, the price to be paid for the option, and the duration of the option.

He made a verbal presentation to the owner. He showed the market (sales price) comparison he had compiled. He stated that he believed the property would be saleable for a maximum of $37,000 (at least $5,000 below the value asserted by the owner) within 120 days, but that he was not interested in buying even at the lower price. He then reviewed the written offer (still with blanks to be filled in) with the seller. Mr. B. said that he planned to apply for rezoning immediately, but that because of the expenses and effort involved he would want an eight month option for a payment of $1. He said he would be willing to share possible profits with the owner by making the option price $10,000 higher than the $37,000 estimated market value with the present zoning. He reemphasized that the owner would not be responsible for any expense. The owner would need only to review the application with Mr. B's attorney and be present at the hearing. The owner signed the option agreement.

Chris B. returned to his attorney's office with the signed option. He frankly admitted that he did not have cash to follow up on getting the property rezoned and selling it or building seventeen additional units on it. He offered one-third of any future profits in exchange for the attorney's service in getting the property rezoned, and the attorney was to pay all expenses. They finally agreed on a fifty-fifty split of profits with out-of-pocket expenses to be reimbursed before dividing the profit. If the zone change request was rejected, Mr. B. would have no obligation for the expenses.

After some frustrating delays, rescheduled hearings and objections from neighbors, the zone change was approved. A key factor which the attorney used in his argument for the change was that both ends of the block were now zoned for apartments and that probably the entire block would be rezoned in the near future.

Within three weeks Mr. B. and the attorney sold the option for $32,000. They split more than $30,000 profit. By recognizing an opportunity and that the time was right, Chris B. had pocketed $15,000 profit and his total risk was only $1. He had combined:

1. the use of an option to gain control,
2. rezoning to remove the restriction which was keeping the property from being used to its highest and best use,

3. the formation of a small syndicate (a two-man general partnership) to cover the expenses and take the risk of a turn-down by the zoning board, and
4. sale of the property for its true market value.

This venture was Mr. B.'s first in real estate. With his knowledge and the increased confidence which comes from a successful deal plus $15,000 in working capital he is on his way to financial independence by other such ventures.

THE FUTURE IN ZONING

There does not appear to be a trend toward decontrol of the way in which private property is used. Although there are cities which do not attempt to exercise such control, they are small ones (except, of course, Houston, Texas). To the best of my knowledge, there have been very few communities which have eliminated zoning once it was set up. If, however, there is an effort underway in your community to eliminate zoning and if you predict it will be successful, look for properties which have been held down (with respect to realizable market value) by the still existing zoning. There should be several opportunities.

I believe the most likely course of events in zoning the next fifteen years in most communities will be to continue as is. Government in some communities will conduct extensive studies and adopt new master development plans. In the majority of communities, I believe that requests for exceptions, variances, and rezoning which are granted will simply create or add to a crazy quilt pattern of property uses. Locating a property which offers profit opportunity in such communities can be time consuming. The profit opportunity, however, means it is well worth the effort required. The key is to find property which is not being put to its highest and best use because of zoning restrictions. If your subsequent investigation indicates that you can get it rezoned then you have an opportunity.

SEVEN KEYS TO FORTUNE BUILDING THROUGH REZONING

1. Become an expert in rezoning. Many entrepreneurs avoid involvement if there is a need for rezoning. They don't know the insider's secrets of rezoning for profit and they avoid hassles. Their avoidance means less competition for you.
2. Zoning prevents land from being put to its highest and best use. Fortunes are made by locating such land, gaining control of it, and getting the zoning changed. The key is to recognize

property which is being restrained by zoning and to predict whether you can get the zoning changed.

3. Even though you have been using an attorney regularly on your previous real estate transactions, check his explicit experience on zoning applications. If he is relatively inexperienced, you may decide to use him on all except the zone change application itself. Ask him to recommend another attorney for the rezoning; the importance of successful experience in rezoning cannot be overemphasized.

4. Learn the philosophy of zoning. Study the master development plan if one exists for your community. Attend zoning hearings. Become acquainted with the way each member of the zoning board thinks and acts. Learn the basis for decisions for approving or rejecting zone change applications. Particularly, try to determine if one individual on the zoning board is the power center.

5. Make a personal effort to stay up-to-date on zone changes, variances, and exceptions in your community. Upon occasion, a single variance or exception can be the signal for you to canvass nearby properties for opportunities.

6. Entrepreneurs who repeatedly make profits by getting property rezoned are risk takers, but they are not wild gamblers. They don't assume anything. They check and double check zoning particulars. They know the insider's secrets given in this chapter. Unless they somehow have inside knowledge of future zone changes, they do take the risk of having an application denied. But their potential profit makes the risk worth taking.

7. An experienced entrepreneur stays abreast of changes in a growing community. Zoning which was consistent with the highest and best use five years ago may be totally out of date today. Getting parcels rezoned in such a case can put large profits in your pocket.

REMEMBER THESE POINTS

- Zoning limits the purposes for which private property may legally be used.
- Frequently, zoning prevents the highest and best use of real property and keeps its market value artificially low.
- Zoning ordinances are the controlling documents.
- Zoning variances, exceptions, and rezoning are means of removing the zoning barrier to better utilization of property.

- Many communities have a master development plan; theoretically, it is used as a guide for zoning and rezoning decisions.
- A thorough understanding and intimate knowledge of the prior five items, the philosophy behind them, and a knowledge of their applications will speed your progress toward profits.
- Rezoning does not create value, but it can remove a restriction which is keeping you from getting full market value for your property.
- Many entrepreneurs avoid rezoning effort. Your competition is thereby lessened.
- An attorney with a track record of success is an invaluable aid. Choose one with great care.
- Ask your attorney if he knows of potentially purchaseable parcels of the type land you're seeking.
- Attend zoning hearings. Become acquainted with the attitudes of each member of the board. Learn why they accept or deny applications.
- Determine whether one individual on the board is the most influential.
- Determine whether zoning in your area is out of date; you may discover opportunities.
- Rezoning for profit has built many fortunes. Profits can be very large.

18

HIGH LEVERAGE METHODS FOR MAKING PROFITS ON OUTLYING PROPERTY

Raw land, including farmland and other outlying property, is another area of real estate investment which can yield excellent profits. Many entrepreneurs specialize in dealing in such properties; some buy a large parcel (many acres) and sell in comparatively small parcels. Others specialize in resort or recreation areas or in buying acreage in the path of growth of a city.

The timing of your investment in outlying property is of utmost importance. For example, if it appears that certain outlying acreage is a likely candidate for construction of a large manufacturing plant and if you wait until it is announced, then your timing is off; you should have purchased and/or obtained options on acreage in the area months ago. On the other hand, if you're overly optimistic with respect to future development of an area, you might have to hold land many years before it would become possible to sell it for a good profit.

Your personal time frame for turnover of land investments depends upon your goals as an investor. Generally speaking, the greatest increase in land value is when its highest and best use changes from raw land or farmland to a higher use, e.g., industrial sites or acreage plots for other use. When it later changes from acreage plots to lots, the increase in market value and potential return on your investment is usually somewhat less. And, further, when the change is to building sites and/or tract housing, the land value increase is still less. Strictly from the viewpoints of greatest increase in land value and the most leverage of the cash you invest, investing in raw land is the best. But you must be accurate in your evaluation of future development and in predicting its timing.

How an investor with a special goal in mind made a profit and achieved a secondary goal is described in the first example in this chapter. He bought a much larger parcel than he needed for his personal "get away from it all" retreat and sold portions of it to others with a similar desire. The second example shows how an entrepreneur (who likes fishing and boating and making money in real estate) took care of both his goals. He assumed control of a site development project in a resort area where he wanted to live.

Also, see Chapter 4 for other examples of high profits and high return on investment by entrepreneurs dealing successfully in raw land.

HOW A FAMILY MAN MADE $10,000 PROFIT AND KEPT FIVE ACRES

As vice-president of a corporation headquartered downtown, Arthur N. and his family were city dwellers. Usually twice per month, Mr. and Mrs. N. and their two sons went camping or driving in the country. They finally decided to look for a few acres, perhaps with an old house they could renovate. They narrowed their search to an area within ten miles of a new, Interstate highway. A local broker showed them a forty-six acre parcel with a battered three bedroom house and a chicken house. The broker explained that it was what remained after the elderly owners had sold more than 200 acres of adjacent good farm land and that the price per acre was very low. The terrain was rough and it was heavily wooded on most of the farm; it was not suitable for farming, hence the low price.

It was a larger parcel than Mr. N. had in mind, but he thought he could sell portions to others who had similar interests. He checked the zoning to be sure that he would be free to sell and found that there were no restrictions except that he would have to comply with the law on subdividing if he split it into more than four parcels.

To make a long story short, he purchased the property for 10 percent down with an agreement to pay off proportionate amounts of the loan carried by the seller if he sold any of the acreage. He obtained a five year second mortgage on his home to make the down payment.

Mr. N. had the forty-six acre parcel surveyed and platted to show four smaller parcels (one twenty-six acre, one ten acre, and two five acre parcels). He sold three parcels (retaining ownership of one of the five acre parcels) for $10,200 more than his investment, including survey and escrow costs, in the forty-six acres. He not only owned (at no cost) the five acres he originally set out to buy, but he had a handsome profit as well.

Arthur N. had discovered one of the insider's secrets known to experienced investors in real estate. He had learned that a good profit can be made by buying a large parcel of land and selling small parcels.

HOW TO CHOOSE OUTLYING PROPERTY

Appraisers for very large land investment companies and developers who have the entire country as their operating territory say that the three most important factors in choosing property are location, employment opportunities, and climate. They are right, of course, but there are other important considerations. A discussion follows, but some factors may not be pertinent in your case. Every pertinent factor should be carefully considered. Pertinence will be determined by your goals in investing in raw land. Even for an individual, pertinence and the relative importance of each factor may change if his goals change between two successive deals.

Location

An experienced entrepreneur in dealing in raw land asks himself two fundamental, related questions when considering a purchase: "Will it or can I make it increase in market value?" And: "Can I make a profit on it within my time frame?" Other features, such as beauty, view, and end use are of secondary interest.

Employment opportunities

If a parcel of raw land is in an area where there are employment opportunities of a nature that will last into the indefinite future, then the parcel's present value certainly should increase. The uncertainty of employment in large plants with huge government contracts means that investment in raw land near such plants is risky unless it is land that can be resold within a comparatively short time. The market value of raw land can drop sharply if there is a large layoff. The short turnover requirement applies also to recreational property of various types; such properties are usually much in demand when prosperity is high. A downturn in the economy can mean a serious reduction in the market value of recreational land. People find they can get along without a vacation home, but they will move into areas with employment opportunities.

Climate

Very large investment companies can choose areas with desirable climates. Most of us must, however, choose land within a reasonable distance from our home base or office. The relatively small investor settles for investing in the climate he's in unless he chooses to move to another area.

Higher education

An example wherein higher education facilities were considered was given in Chapter 4; Mr. L. was the investor. Other corporations in the area employed many well educated personnel and Mr. L. wisely sought corporate buyers for whom a nearby university would be an asset. Nearby colleges may be a factor in your raw land investment; it depends upon your planned end use and the needs of potential buyers.

Recreation and cultural facilities

Nearby facilities for recreation and cultural activities generally add to the present market value of raw land and will usually make it more readily saleable in the future. The four day work week at some companies has resulted in an increased interest in cultural events and recreation facilities. People have the time and money for using their increased leisure time as they choose. Depending upon the intended end use of your raw land, the availability of leisure time facilities may be important, but location, employment opportunities, and climate are almost always at the top of the list.

Developability

The price you can afford to pay for raw land and the future market value (for your specific intended end use) will depend upon the cost and ease of developing the land. In addition to the factors already discussed, the following may be used as a checklist for developability:

- *Topography*—rough and wooded land, not suitable for farming, may be best for your purpose.

- *Soil*—soil fertility may not be a factor for your purpose; but look out for adobe soil, it's difficult to build upon.
- *Subsurface Geological Structure*—inclined slippage planes can mean no structures should be erected; if in doubt, call in a geological engineer.
- *Size and Shape of Parcel*—check to insure that the size and shape of the parcel suits your planned use.
- *Police and Fire Protection*—be sure you have police and fire protection if necessary for your purposes.
- *Telephone Service*—if telephone service is not presently available at the property, find out how much it would cost to obtain it.
- *Water, Gas, Electricity, Streets, Sidewalks, and Curbs*—determine the necessity, availability, and cost of each of these factors if you need them.
- *Freeways, Railways, and Airports*—not so important for recreation area development, but necessary for land planned for future industrial sites.
- *Schools*—schools are almost always important; check their availability and accessibility.

An example wherein all of the above factors were considered was a venture by Mr. L. (see Chapter 4). He purchased raw land which was being used as farmland and sold it to a buyer who would utilize it for a higher use, i.e., manufacturing. Although he considered the cost and ease of putting in streets, sidewalks, and utilities, he did not add any of these improvements himself. His profit was made possible by using the insider's secret of buying property being used below its highest and best use and finding a buyer who would use it more intensively. Mr. L. had no development costs per se; he had only his original investment tied up plus the carrying costs of taxes, interest, and lack of current income on cash invested.

Financing availability

Availability of financing for your purchase and for your planned sale of the property is a key factor. Experienced entrepreneurs always consider money availability at both ends of their ownership of property. When you are selling, the problem of financing is as much yours as it is the buyer's. If he cannot get acceptable financing, he simply will not buy. If your interest is to sell the property to a developer who will add improvements, then financing must be available to finance his purchase and pay for the improvements.

The government(s)

In recent years, the multiplicity of regulations concerning use of land has increased enormously. One major East Coast corporation obtained an option on raw land on the West Coast. They planned to build a large manufacturing plant. Their option, of course, contained contingencies relating to being able to use the land for their desired purpose. They found that they would have to file dozens of applications with various agencies and at various government levels. Some of the applications were costly to prepare with much "justification" required. They finally surrendered their option and abandoned their plans.

A relatively small investor must also check both existing and probable future regulations and restrictions on a property of interest. I personally try to be aware of government actions, but regulations and restrictions are too numerous and complex for the small investor to handle and have any time left for the usual activities of an entrepreneur. An attorney who specializes in this area is a necessity.

Summary—choosing outlying property

Entrepreneurs who are familiar with the inside secrets of making money on outlying property first make sure that they have their own personal goals in mind and then seek properties which promise to satisfy their goals. They keep uppermost in their analyses the three most important factors, i.e., location, employment opportunities, and climate. Many have built their fortunes by investing in outlying property. Many more fortunes will be made by those who make the necessary effort to locate desirable properties.

HOW TO CHOOSE THE RIGHT OUTLYING PROPERTY

In bullish or bearish times, real estate is always for sale. A local newspaper always has advertisements for properties offered by brokers or directly by owners. Finding the right property for you to buy in good times or bad requires time and effort. Ideally, the property you select to buy will:

- meet your investment goals
- have only foreseeable and removable obstructions to your intended end use

MAKING PROFITS ON OUTLYING PROPERTY

- allow you to have a quick turnover or will meet your longer range value appreciation goal
- have only such encumbrances as you can handle
- be priced right for your purchase and
- have favorable financing available for selling.

Although this list does seem ideal, it is so important that professional investors familiar with insider's secrets will shy away from buying a property unless it meets all six criteria.

For example, note that Arthur N., in the example presented previously in this chapter, had only the urge to get away to the country when he began looking for a four or five acre parcel. Only when he was shown a forty-six acre parcel did he get the idea of selling to others with desires similar to his own. His first venture with its handsome profit and with five acres held out at no cost to himself has resulted in a new and pleasurable avocation. He also learned, by chance, one of the insider's secrets of professional dealers in buying farming acreage for splitting and selling to city dwellers. He learned that one should ask for a cheap farm (i.e., one that is low priced because of its relative unsuitability for farming). Mr. N. is a man of high ethics and integrity but he sees no need to tell a local real estate broker of his intended use of a cheap farm (and I agree). He merely expresses an interest in buying a cheap farm.

Your goals may be much different from Mr. N.'s. The type land you buy may be different and the actions you must then take in order to achieve your goals may be far more complex. Whatever your goals are, after they are defined, the six criteria given in this section will apply to complex situations as well as Mr. N.'s relatively simple requirements.

DIVIDING YOUR LAND—LEGAL CAUTIONS

It is an understatement to say that life is not as simple as it used to be. Certainly it is true if you are dealing in raw land or other real estate. Not very many years ago, I would have used an attorney mostly to write or review a purchase contract and to insure that I would have a clear title to a purchased parcel. Today and in the foreseeable future, an attorney's services are needed to help assure that you will be able to utilize your private property in the way you plan.

Self-styled ecologists and environmentalists have accelerated the already existing trend toward more controls on land use. Governmental control at all levels, sometimes by law and sometimes by bureaucratic edict ("pursuant to law"). It is now necessary to check and double check as to *what* you may do, *when* you may do it, and even *if* you may develop the land you own or wish to purchase. An attorney who specializes in this aspect of real estate, i.e., all of the myriad laws and regulations, can save you from buying land which some govermental agency would forbid you to develop.

On the other hand, entrepreneurs will continue to make fortunes in raw land. Those who make it will be those with the expertise and the determination to develop land in the face of increased difficulties.

HOW TO GO FISHING AND BOATING AND MAKE MONEY IN RAW LAND

As is true of many entrepreneurs, Martin L. had "too little time" to devote to fishing and boating. Two years earlier, he had even sold his cabin on a lake when he received an exceptionally good offer. He finally decided to move to a lake resort area and retain his townhouse for occasional trips back to the city. After considerable searching, with time out for fishing at various lakes, he found a developer in distress. The developer had improved 15 acres of a 90 acre parcel and sold the lots for a profit. He was not in danger of bankruptcy, but adverse developments on another project of his had consumed every cent at his disposal and were requiring his everyday presence in the city. The rolling option he had on the remaining 75 acres provided for a payment of $10,000 if purchase of the next 15 acres were to be postponed a maximum of one year. He and Martin L. agreed to an equal partnership with Mr. L. to borrow the necessary immediate amount to make the $10,000 payment and to manage the development of the 75 acres. After signing the agreement, Mr. L. borrowed on his townhouse to pay the necessary sum to the owner of the land. The agreement called for repayment of the $10,000 to Mr. L. out of first profits.

Mr. L. rented a nearby house and moved to the lake. He plans to build a home for Mrs. L. and himself as a first step. Thus, without investing any of his cash on hand and with the $10,000 to be paid before additional profits are paid to the partners, Mr. L. had achieved his goal of living in an area with fishing and boating outside his door. And, he had a fifty percent position in a highly promising resort development.

LIVING BETTER—ENVIRONMENTALLY AND FINANCIALLY

Anyone who combines his leisure or spare time interest with a profit-making activity is either lucky or has deliberately set his goals to achieve such a great setup. For example, one man I know put his love of constructing models and writing to work in publishing a hobbyist's

MAKING PROFITS ON OUTLYING PROPERTY 213

magazine. Similarly, Mr. L. is continuing his career in real estate while fishing and boating. Also similarly, Mr. N. (see first example in this chapter) retained his position in the city, but he is avidly pursuing his new-found avocation in country real estate.

By setting one's goals appropriately, it is indeed possible to live better environmentally while building a fortune in real estate ventures.

SIX KEYS TO MAKING HIGH PROFITS ON OUTLYING PROPERTY

1. Real estate investors with knowledge of the insider's secrets of making money in outlying or farm property follow the practice of buying large and selling small. That is, they buy many acres in a single purchase and divide it to sell in small parcels.
2. The time required for selling of outlying property, whether in one to five acre parcels or small building sites, will frequently depend upon financial terms offered. Easy payment terms usually mean much faster sales.
3. For most ventures in outlying property, the three most important factors in choosing property are:
   - location
   - employment opportunities and
   - climate.

   An exception is resort or lake acreage.
4. A professional investor who is still building his fortune is objective. Even though he may have set as one of his goals to live better environmentally, he still evaluates a possible purchase using all pertinent profit-making criteria. He keeps in mind that his primary purpose in investing is to make a profit.
5. Real estate investors who specialize in buying larger parcels for splitting and selling to users who want a "get away to the country" parcel look for land with special features such as streams, woods, and somewhat rough terrain. In farming areas, such land is sometimes the lowest in price because of its unsuitability for farming. The key to buying such property is to ask local brokers for a "cheap farm." It is better not to reveal what you intend to do with the farm.
6. Putting land to its highest and best use is a key in dealing with outlying as well as urban property. Some of the restrictions on use of outlying property are similar to zoning restrictions in urban areas. A key to making outstanding profits on outlying property is to get restrictions changed to suit your goals. For example, if there exists a twenty acre minimum restriction and

you can get it changed to 2 ½ acre minimum, then you may be in a position to make outstanding profits.

REMEMBER THESE POINTS

- Put your goals in writing. Seek outlying property which will meet your investment and personal goals.
- Review criteria for choosing outlying property and apply those which are pertinent to your goals and the intended use of the property.
- Generally, the three most important criteria for selecting property are:
  - location
  - employment opportunities and
  - climate.
- Secondary, but important, criteria for selecting property are:
  - higher education availability
  - recreation and cultural facilities
  - developability
  - financing for purchase
  - financing for selling and
  - laws and regulations by government and others.
- The six essential requirements for outlying property selection which apply for almost every possible intended end use are:
  - must meet your investment goals
  - will have only foreseeable and removable obstructions with respect to your intended end use or disposition
  - is a possibility for a quick turnover or to meet your long range appreciation goal
  - must have only encumbrances you can handle
  - must be priced right and
  - must have potential for favorable financing for selling.
- The emotional appeal of a property may be important, but the professional investor who is seeking a profit will carry out his evaluation objectively.
- In areas used for farming the cheapest farm can well be the one most suited for your purpose.
- Buying large acreages and selling small parcels is usually a fundamental aspect of making money on outlying property.

MAKING PROFITS ON OUTLYING PROPERTY

- Choose an attorney who specializes in real estate of the type you wish to buy. Governmental regulations are extensive and are in seemingly constant flux. A new regulation may have gone into effect while you were seeking property.

19

HOW TAX AVOIDANCE HELPS YOU USE OTHER PEOPLE'S MONEY

For many years the federal government has given preferential treatment to real estate investors by encouraging building with favorable financing and by tax laws which favor real estate investment. Tax advantages are still a strong factor but, as always, tax laws and IRS regulations and rulings are in flux. As in government control of the use of land, the effect of taxes can change while you are spending your time finding a property for acquisition. The effect of taxes in your evaluation may not be the same for a property you're now considering as it was for your previous venture. It is essential for each new proposed venture that you consider up-to-date tax information and the effect taxes will have.

Tax attorneys and tax accountants spend an appreciable part of their time in keeping up to date on all taxes affecting their clients. I personally like to stay abreast of tax changes myself. The real estate or tax section of financial newspapers and real estate magazines are excellent for non-technical reporting of new tax information. A daily newspaper in a large city is another source. Also, you may be able to borrow from your tax adviser copies of bulletins put out by tax information services; they tend to be couched in more technical language, but are not difficult to understand.

Sixteen ways of increasing your profits and speeding your progress toward a fortune in real estate are given in this chapter. If use of any of them appears to offer financial advantages for your real estate investments, the time spent to explore them should pay off handsomely.

How to avoid taxes in the way you structure a deal is discussed and illustrated in this chapter. The time to set the stage for the best deal in all respects, including tax effects, is when you begin negotiations.

How to postpone a seller's taxes to a future year by avoiding present tax liability is a powerful technique described in the first example in this chapter. In addition to tax postponement, the second example shows how a seller expects even more benefits if his ordinary income is lower, as he predicts, in future years.

USE OF TAX AVOIDANCE AND AVOIDANCE OF TAX EVASION WILL INCREASE YOUR PROFIT

According to the Internal Revenue Service, tax avoidance is legal and tax evasion is illegal. One way of achieving tax avoidance in real estate sales is by structuring the contract for the transaction in such a way as to *avoid* liability for taxes. Tax *evasion* occurs whenever a taxpayer reports false information on the size of profit of a transaction or simply omits including any information on the transaction in his annual report. In most states, although income taxes on real estate profits are lower than the federal government's tax, the same interpretations apply with respect to state laws and the state income tax.

The above discussion relates to tax avoidance whenever a profit is made upon the sale of a property. Other ways of avoiding taxes during your ownership of a property will be discussed in the following sections. In the real estate area, as in other types of businesses, taxes have increased to such a high level that tax consequences (taxes on profits from a sale and other taxes) must be considered in every deal.

Attorneys and Tax Advisers

The advisability of using an attorney who specializes in real estate (even by entrepreneurs who are familiar with the insider's secrets of real estate investing) was mentioned in prior chapters. Actually, two

TAX AVOIDANCE

specialists can be used for added profits by either experienced or beginning entrepreneurs in real estate. One is an attorney with considerable experience in legal matters relating to real estate. The second specialist should be an individual who is highly experienced in taxes affecting real estate management and transactions; this adviser is usually either a tax attorney or a public accountant. There are, of course, individuals who first obtain a degree in accounting and then one in law. Some of them later specialize in real estate. It is rare, however, to find the desired experience and knowledge combined in a single individual. A good tax adviser will help you get financial benefits equal to several times the cost of his services.

Seller vs Buyer vs Taxes

Contained within the phrase "seller versus buyer" is the implication that seller and buyer are antagonists. It is true that a buyer wishes to buy for a low price and a seller is seeking a high price. But once an experienced buyer and experienced seller have agreed upon a price, each turns his attention to structuring the agreement for legality and for tax consequences.

During the analysis of a desired property, an experienced buyer takes into account the probable effect of taxes upon the seller as well as the tax benefits he, as the buyer, will enjoy during his ownership of the property and the probable tax consequences when he subsequently sells the property for a profit. In fact, if the buyer is creative and innovative enough and if he is familiar with the insider's secrets of real estate investment, he will suggest a structured sales contract and point out the tax advantages contained in it for the seller. A buyer who has the creativity and knowledge to structure contracts with built-in tax advantage for the seller has an advantage over less creative competitors; he should close more deals per year and will surely build his fortune at a faster rate.

SIXTEEN WAYS TO TAKE ADVANTAGE OF TAX FACTORS IN REAL ESTATE

The following ways of taking advantage of tax factors are the ones most used by investors familiar with the insider's secrets of real estate invesment and management.

1. Capital Gains Treatment of Increased Property Value

Build up the value of your property by making tax-deductible repairs and by tax-free improvements made by tenants. Get capital gains tax treatment, when you sell, on the additional profit you make as a result of these repairs and improvements.

2. Ordinary Loss Treatment

If you sell an investment property for a loss, you most likely can deduct the loss from your ordinary income even though a profit would have qualified for capital gains treatment.

3. Costs of Carrying Real Estate

In highly leveraged deals, property which is highly mortgaged or is obtained with a lease with option for purchase, the investor will reap the full benefit of any increase in value. Yet the costs of carrying the property, whether he's leasing or paying interest, are fully deductible against ordinary income.

4. Carrying Costs—Your Choice—Deduct or Capitalize

In almost all cases I know of, wherein a buyer of real estate incurs out-of-pocket carrying costs, the buyer has chosen to deduct the costs. In some cases, you can elect to capitalize interest, taxes, and other costs (such as legal fees). Analyze and choose to your own best interest.

5. Tax Free Exchanges

Many entrepreneurs use the techniques of building up the market value of a property, exchanging it for a larger property, building up the value of the newly acquired property, and so on. Thus they pyramid upward to the point where they have a substantial equity in a major property. By conforming with the Tax Code, they avoid payment of taxes until they finally make a direct sale.

6. Depreciation Deductions

Your ordinary income, from a real estate investment or from other sources, can be sheltered by depreciation deductions. Accelerated methods of depreciation can be used.

7. Tax Deferral by Installment Sale

The critical figure to qualify for tax deferral in an installment sale is that the amount paid to the seller the first year be less than 30 percent of the sale price of the property. Be careful that additional payments (such as prepaid interest) do not boost the first year payments to more than 30 percent.

TAX AVOIDANCE

8. Tax Deferral by an Option Agreement

If you give a lease with an option for purchase, it may qualify for deferral or postponement of taxes. Check the documents carefully; the IRS might regard it as a "disguised sale" and tax you accordingly.

9. Tax Deferral by Deferred Sale

A deferred sale (i.e., one wherein title to the property is to pass at some future date), provided it is carefully structured to meet the requirements of the Tax Code, will allow you to defer taxes to a future date. Double check to be sure your deal will qualify. Note that the IRS may require that a portion of the payments be treated as ordinary income by "imputing interest" if no interest or an "unusually low" interest rate is specified.

10. Other Tax Deferral Possibilities

Lesser known ways of deferring or postponing tax consequences from the sale or transferral of control of real estate include:

- Contingent sales price arrangement (the actual sales price depends upon some factor not determinable until a future date).
- Conditional sales contract (consummation of the sale depends upon a condition to be satisfied in the future).
- Special terms and conditions in escrow agreement (check your state laws for latitude in terms and conditions in escrow).
- Give title to property in exchange for a private annuity ("buyer" promises to pay you an annual amount for the rest of your life. You are taxed on the annuity income. Gain or loss is recognized only as payments are received.)

11. Security Deposit

It is possible to postpone taxes on a security deposit until the end of a lease. The Tax Code spells out conditions which must be met to qualify for this benefit.

12. Tax Deductions for Cost of Land

Improvements to property are depreciable for tax purposes but land is not. The cost of the land portion of property you buy can be made tax deductible by a sale-leaseback. Analyze to see if you can benefit by selling the land and leasing it back for a long period of time. The cost of leasing is fully deductible against ordinary income.

13. Form of Ownership

The four principal types of ownership of real estate are personal, partnership, corporate, or in a trust. Each deal you enter into should be analyzed to determine which is best for you with respect to taxes.

14. Accelerate Tax Liability

An unusual situation may occur wherein you wish to accelerate tax liability after perhaps one or two years into an installment sale you have made. Check it out—you may be able to accelerate tax liability by disposing of installment obligations.

15. Sell to Offset Operating Loss

If you have an operating loss (in a non real estate operation) which cannot be carried back for tax purposes, consider selling your real estate for a profit within the same tax year. You may get tax (and dollars) benefits which would not otherwise be realizable.

16. Convert Home to Income Property

Before selling your present home it may be to your advantage to convert from an IRS classification of "Personal Residence" to "Income Property." A key requirement by the IRS is that you succeed in renting it or make a "serious," sincere attempt to rent it. If you do not succeed in renting it, the IRS has the power to disqualify your property as income property.

The following example shows how an astute and experienced tax accountant restructured a deal to the satisfaction of both buyer and seller. The accountant was that rare individual—one who is highly knowledgeable and creative. The tax consequences to the seller were serious enough that the deal would probably have died except for the accountant's effort.

HOW A SELLER STRUCTURED A LEASE WITH PURCHASE OPTION TO ALLOW SELLER TO DEFER TAXES

David S., a marketing consultant specializing in small, product oriented companies had purchased a small, one story, suburban office building with ample parking in front. At the time of purchase, his return on total investment (his own small down payment plus borrowed money) exceeded 13 percent. Inflation plus appreciation in value had increased the market value of his property by more than 25 percent during his three years of ownership. He had increased rents proportionately and was presently receiving a return of 13 percent of the *current* market value.

The owner of a similar but older and slightly smaller property next door asked David S.'s opinion of the market value of his (Mr. S.'s) property. The owner said that Mr. S.'s estimate of $145,000 seemed in line with other property he had checked on and that he estimated his own to be worth $105,000 to $110,000. The owner mentioned that he was retiring and moving "back home" to the Midwest. He was thinking about selling for 29 percent down and carrying the balance himself. Mr. S. expressed a possible interest.

Three days later they met and verbally agreed upon a price of $100,000 with $20,000 down and the balance to be amortized over 15 years at 9 percent interest; they agreed that their verbal accord would be subject to approval of the final contract including the seller's satisfaction with the tax consequences.

The seller's tax accountant reviewed the proposed transaction and pointed out the large taxes (federal and state) the seller would have to pay because of his low cost basis. He mentioned that the seller, who was sixty-five years old with a wife of fifty-one, would most likely have a much lower income ten years hence. He suggested that the deal be restructured as a ten year lease with an option to buy at any time during the last six months of the lease period.

When the seller proposed the lease-option approach, the buyer objected—he said he had agreed to the purchase price of $100,000 in part because of the tax shelter he would have as the owner. He and the seller finally agreed for their individual tax counselors to get together to work out terms of an agreement which would enable the seller to obtain net benefits at least equal to what he would have enjoyed as the result of an immediate sale at $100,000 and still allow the seller to realize the benefits of a sale (along with its tax consequences) ten years later when his income and tax bracket would be lower. Mr. S. agreed that he would adjust his own analysis to take into account that he would still have the $20,000 cash which he had intended to use for a down payment.

To make a long story short, the two tax accountants were successful and Mr. S. signed a ten year lease with option to buy. As a matter of fact, Mr. S. had made use of one of the insider's secrets of real estate investing; he had gained control and use of a property without actually owning it. Furthermore, he had no cash invested and could use his $20,000 cash for another venture. Also, he believed that properties in the area would appreciate in value and he would profit thereby when he exercised the option. He had essentially no doubt that his net worth would increase substantially upon exercising the option.

The seller also achieved his goal with respect to taxes and had freed himself of responsibility for the property so he could return to his home state.

LEGAL TAX AVOIDANCE—USE THE GOVERNMENT'S MONEY

A statement I've heard many times is "Use the government's money to make money." The statement is usually made in connection with a transaction which avoids present payment of taxes by postponement or deferral. It is true that if the seller in the last example had sold his property at the outset, then he would have had to pay taxes on the profit. By legally avoiding immediate taxation he retained the built-in profit and he was making money on money which otherwise would have become government money. Any legal tax avoidance technique which an investor can use to retain any profit he makes or to postpone its taxability will speed the building of his fortune.

HOW TO USE AN INSTALLMENT SALE TO DEFER TAXES

Many advertisements of real estate for sale include the phrase "29 percent down." The reason is that if a seller has a property which will yield him a handsome profit upon sale and if the seller wants to defer payment of taxes on the profit to future years, he can do so if he accepts a down payment of less than 30 percent of the sale price and if further payments on the principal are made in succeeding fiscal years. The portion of the total profit which is "taxable income" each year is proportional to the amount of principal paid within each of the seller's tax years.

A secondary benefit is that spreading his profit over a number of years usually means that the seller is in a lower tax bracket than he would have been if he had accpeted more than 30 percent in the year of the sale. If, however, more than 30 percent is paid during the first (tax) year then the seller must pay taxes on the entire profit; the tax will be the same as it would have been if the buyer had paid all cash. For example, I know of one case wherein the seller accepted 29 percent down payment on a sale made in December (the seller's tax year was the calendar year) but he also accepted prepaid interest on the balance at the same time. When his tax return was audited, the IRS claimed that the prepaid interest was actually a part of the down payment. The two payments, combined, were more than 30 percent of the purchase price; the IRS

TAX AVOIDANCE

demanded that taxes be paid on the entire profit as if the seller had sold for all cash. Double check to be sure that you will qualify for tax deferral with respect to the 30 percent factor.

SELLER DEFERS TAX PAYMENTS AND AVOIDS HIGHER TAX BRACKETS BY INSTALLMENT SALE

A young attorney, Marvin F., purchased a vacant, multiple-residential lot at what he was sure was a bargain price. He had not been active in real estate but he "couldn't afford not to" buy the lot. The purchase price was $19,500 with $5,000 down. His intent was to form a syndicate and build ten or twelve apartment units. For months after purchasing it, new clients left him no time to work on the syndication. Seven months later, a local builder offered $40,000 for the lot. Mr. F. decided to sell, but did not want to pay taxes on $20,000 profit in a year when his taxable income from his law practice was up appreciably. He sold for 25 per cent down ($10,000 with the balance payable in twenty quarterly installments of $1,500 each plus interest of nine percent).

Thus, in the year of the sale Mr. F. will pay taxes on $5,000 profit and in each succeeding year for five years he will pay on $3,000 profit. By selling on an installment plan with less than thirty per cent down, he deferred payment on $15,000 of the total $20,000 profit and at the same time kept himself in a lower tax bracket in the first year when his taxable income was relatively high. He will, of course have interest income on the unpaid principal. He also has an asset in the form of an interest bearing note for $30,000. If he needs cash, he may be able to pledge the note as collateral for a loan.

HOW TO OPTIMIZE USE OF SERVICES OF YOUR TAX COUNSELOR

As with any specialist you may engage, the costs and benefits of his services depend in large part upon you. The following checklist will help you to get the most benefits for the least cost.

Action Checklist—Working With Your Advisers

The procedure given below will help you use the services of tax or legal advisers effectively, efficiently, and economically.

- In each important or complicated proposed venture, talk with your advisers at the outset. If you don't need them to help you develop the deal, touch base with them on major points.
- Carry out your own research, including referral to your own library of reference books, before major sessions with your advisers. Document your data.

- Prepare your questions and information on major points before your next conference with your advisers. Idle conversation is costly.
- Listen carefully to their comments and suggestions. Be sure they understand that you expect them to take the devil's advocate position.
- Keep in mind that you're not in a joint venture with them. They're working for you. They get paid whether or not your proposed venture turns out to be profitable.
- You are the responsible party, both financially and legally. Listen to them, but make up your own mind.

It's Your Money and Your Responsibility

The last item in the above list cannot be overemphasized. The most successful entrepreneurs in real estate never really become *dependent* upon anyone. They depend only upon themselves to know and protect their own interests. A well selected, knowledgeable, and experienced pair of advisers will work to your best interest but, still, you have the responsibility and you are risking your money.

Tell All to Your Advisers

I've known of cases wherein a principal in real estate, for some incomprehensable reason, withheld information from his tax and legal advisers. In the foregoing discussion, I assumed that your tax adviser had full knowledge of your financial position. If he does not, use the following format to furnish him with the personal and financial data he must have if he is to do a good job for you.

PERSONAL DATA SHEET

Name:	John Alphonso Doe Date: 23 XXX, 19XX
Address:	2100 Maple Drive, Anytown, OH 43614
Telephone:	123-4567 (home); 765-4321 (office)
Age:	42
Marital:	Married seven years to Jane. One child; John II; age 5. One ex-wife; no children; divorced, 19XX; property settlement; no alimony.
Employment:	ABC Corp., 493 Oak Street, Anytown, OH. Employed 11 years; now, Vice-President, Engineering. Wife not employed.
Annual Income:	$27,000 per year at ABC. Net taxable income of $1,900 per year received from six unit apartment building.

TAX AVOIDANCE

BALANCE SHEET
23 XXXX, 19XX

ASSETS

Cash and checking accounts	$_____
Savings account	$_____
Stocks and Bonds (see detail sheet)	$_____
Cash surrender value of life insurance	$_____
Receivables (see detail sheet)	$_____
Real estate (see detail sheet)	$_____
Automobiles—market value	$_____
Miscellaneous personal property (see list)	$_____
Other assets (see detail sheet)	$_____
Total Assets	$_____

LIABILITIES

Notes payable (see list)	$_____
Real estate mortgages (see detail sheet)	$_____
Automobile, Furniture (see detail sheet)	$_____
Other accounts payable (see list)	$_____
Taxes owed	$_____
Other liabilities (see detail sheet)	$_____
Total Liabilities	$_____
Net Worth	$_____
Total Liabilities and Net Worth	$_____

With the above information your advisers can do a better, more comprehensive job of helping you. These data sheets should be updated at the beginning of every proposed new venture.

NINE KEYS TO USE OF TAX BENEFITS TO SPEED YOU ON THE ROAD TO WEALTH

1. Tax laws and rulings are still favorable to real estate owners and entrepreneurs. An entrepreneur who learns how to reap the benefits from real estate tax laws will progress faster to his fortune.

2. Taxes are in a constant state of flux. Don't rely upon their being the same for your new venture as in your last, similar venture. Examine each new proposed venture carefully to be sure you have covered the effects of income taxes and other taxes.

3. Tax avoidance is legal. Structure your deals, whether you are buying or selling, in order to avoid becoming liable for taxes.

4. You are taxed upon profits. Take all the deductions which are legal. Be sure you have supporting documentation for all deductible expenditures.
5. An increase in market value of your real property is not subject to income tax unless you sell it for a profit. Taking out a loan on a property gives you cash, but with no tax consequences. If you need cash, analyze to determine whether you should sell one of your properties and pay a tax or borrow on it and pay interest.
6. If in doubt on any item involving the IRS, check it carefully. The IRS considers you guilty until proven innocent. The IRS has legislative, executive, and judicial power. Appeals to the Tax Court are seldom won by the taxpayer and even if you win, your legal expenses can be high.
7. A good tax adviser (usually a tax attorney or tax accountant) is essential to help you build a fortune in real estate. The IRS is only one of the taxing agencies which impedes your progress; *all* taxes should be analyzed to improve your profits and cash flow.
8. It is not necessary to own property in order to benefit from it. A long term lease approach can give you your desired benefits and enable you to close more deals with a given amount of capital.
9. Your advisers should fulfill the role of devil's advocate on each proposed deal. Advisers who give rubber stamp approval to your ideas are a waste of money at best and they are possibly harmful.

REMEMBER THESE POINTS

- Tax avoidance is legal. Tax evasion is illegal. Learn the difference.
- Structure your deals to avoid or defer or postpone taxes.
- Choose your tax adviser (a tax attorney or tax accountant) with great care. Find the best one available. Be sure he's a specialist in real estate.
- Consider all taxes at the outset—while you are analyzing a new, proposed venture.
- Consider every possible way of maximizing your profits by knowledge of taxes. Check the following list of frequently used methods wherein taxes are an important factor.
- Capital gains treatment of increased property value.
- Tax treatment of a loss as an "ordinary" loss.
- Deduct costs of carrying real estate.

- Consider capitalization of carrying costs.
- Use tax free exchanges whenever appropriate.
- Use depreciation deduction.
- Get tax deferral by an installment sale.
- Defer taxes by using an option agreement.
- Defer taxes by means of a deferred sale.
- Postpone taxes with a contingent sales price arrangement.
- Postpone taxes by means of a conditional sales contract.
- Postpone taxes with special conditions in an escrow.
- Give title to property in exchange for a private annuity.
- Postpone taxes on security deposits.
- Sell and lease back the land portion of your property.
- Choose form of ownership for best tax advantage.
- Accelerate tax liability whenever it benefits you.
- Sell property for a profit to offset an operating loss.
- Convert a private residence to income property before selling.
- Give your tax adviser your personal data sheet and balance sheet. Update it whenever you begin analysis on a new deal.
- Have your advisers play the role of devil's advocate.
- Your investments are your responsibility (legally and financially) and it's your money you're investing. Don't become *dependent* upon advisers. Listen to them, but make your own decisions.

SPECIAL NOTE

Your knowledge, your drive, and other people's money can make you rich. The insider's secrets given in this book can help insure your success and speed you on your way. The many examples given herein show how others have used these insider's techniques to make money in real estate in the past. By *doing,* by action, you can be one of the thousands who will make their fortunes in the future.

INDEX

Ability to pay, 99
Acceleration clause, 136
Advertising
  caution, 60
  controls, 60, 62
Agreement
  lease with option, 93, 110, 223
  rolling option, 59
Agricultural land, 37
Alexander P., 143
Andrew K., 43, 114
Anthony A., 101
Apartment
  land contract, 130, 134
  lease purchase, 94
  leveraged, 143
  limited partners, 121
  negative leverage, 146
  option, 43
  second mortgage, 150
Arthur N., 206
Avoidance of taxes, 218, 224

B

Balance sheet, 99, 227
Barterer, 188
Benjamin G., 48, 91, 146
Best bets, 28, 54
Bill D., 68
Blight
  creeping, 49
  neighborhood, 49

Brick R., 26
Bruno W., 64

C

Capital gains, 219
Carrying costs, 220
Cash flow, 99
Caution
  advertising, 60
  leveraging, 145
  outlying property, 211
  presentation, 83
Checklist
  best bets, 28
  developable outlying property, 208
  investment review, 104
  land contracts, 132, 133
  lessee qualifications, 91
  loan application, 100
  potential option buyers, 78
  sales presentation, 82
  syndicate prospects, 30
  tax advantages for seller, 110
  tax counselors and advisers, 225
Chris B., 199
Commercial property, 63, 123, 163
Conditional sales contract, 221
Contingent sales contract, 221
Contract for deed, 129
Contract to purchase, 123
Control by escrow, 27, 29
Corporate ownership, 111

INDEX

Cosmetic improvement, 115
Counselor, legal, 23
Counselor, tax, 23
Creeping blight, 49

D

Dale R., 187
Data sheet, personal, 226
David S., 222
Deception, 83
Deferral of taxes, 220
Deferred sale, 221
Depreciation, 220
Disintermediation, 43
Donald J., 163
Downside protection, 52, 57, 62, 63
Due-on-sale clause, 136

E

Edward H., 150
Edlerly seller, 67
Elliott U., 76, 125
Escrow, 66, 221
Evading taxes, 218
Evaluation, 49
Exchange, tax free, 220

F

Finance, *109*
    analysis, 36
    by land contract, 21
    by limited partners, 20, 120, 122
    by savings and loan, 98
    by second mortgage, 21
    by seller, 20, 110, 123, 141
    by syndication, 26
    by tenant, 101
    by using seller's credit, 113
    organize investor information, 31
    outlying property, 209
    shopping for money, 164
    sources, 97
    wrap around mortgages, 21, 169
Flexibility, 44

G

George J., 94
Goals, investment, 34
Government
    controls on seconds, 160
    intervention, 60
Gross multiplier, 94

H

Hard money seconds, 160, 165
Harry C., 123

Herbert L., 54
Highest and best use, 198
Higher usage, 54
Home conversion, 222
Horse trader, 188
Houston, Texas, 195

I

Industrial option, 63, 125
Industrial property, 67, 71, 125
Industrial property cautions, 71
Installment purchase, 59, 110, 112
Installment land contract, 110, 129
Integrity, 98
Interest rates, 98
Interim loan, 102
Investment goals, 34
Investment review checklist, 104
Investor candidates, 30
Investor information, 31, 32

J

James G., 121
Jerry T., 175
John P., 33, 130, 140
Joint tenancy, 39

K

Kenneth E., 111, 134

L

Land, 37, 53
Land contract, 110, 123, 129, 133
Lease, 19
Lease option agreement, 94
Lease purchase, 19, 85, 125
Lease with purchase option, 110, 223
Lessee qualifications, 91
Leverage, 21, 25, 51, 54, *139*
    advantages, 141
    apartments, 41, 143
    build equity, 36
    definition, 139
    disadvantages, 144
    lease, 85
    negative, 146
    outlying property, 205
    raw land, 54, 205
    second mortgages, 149
    wrap around mortgages, 169, 174
Limited partners, 120, 143
Loan documents, 100
Loan fee, 160
Loan, interim, 102
Loan, takeout, 102
Loan-to-value ratio, 100

INDEX

M

Marginal property, 49
Marvin F., 225
Master development plan, 195
Master lease, 76
Medical property, 76, 80
Merger and acquisition, 69
Michael N., 103
Mismanaged property, 28, 51

N

Neighborhood blight, 49

O

Office building, 76, 86, 101, 172, 222
Option, 18, *41*, 52, 56
   agreement, 45, 49
   apartment, 42, 48
   assignment, 71, 76
   buyers, potential, 78
   commercial property, 63, 67, 68
   cost of, 64
   how to use, 45
   industrial property, 63, 67
   lease purchase, 110, 111
   legal format, 45
   progressive, 57
   purchase, 42, 80, 222
   raw land, 55
   rolling, 59
   selling, 44, 75, 78, 80
   to control land, 56
   to optimize, 52
   to provide downside protection, 52
   urban property, 200
   when to use, 50
Organize investor information, 31
Other people's money (OPM), 17, 19, 31
   investor information, 34
   key sources for money, 119
   land contracts, 131
   lease, 85
   lease purchase, 85
   leverage, 139
   wrap around mortgages, 169
Outlying property, *205*
   choosing, 207, 210
   financing, 209

P

Packager, 76
Partner, limited, 120, 143
Partnership, 66
Pay as you go, 58
Personal data sheet, 99, 226
Personal residence, 222
Placement fee, 160
Points, 98
Portfolio, 100
Presentation checklist, 82
Presentation to buyer, 82
Profit sharing, 127
Progressive option, 57, 58
Progressive option agreement, 59
Projections - cash flow, 99
Prospectus, 27
Purchase leaseback, 91
Purchase money second mortgage, 151, 166
Purchase option, 42, 80, 222

R

Ralph D., 196
Randolph Q., 153
Raw land, 37, 53, 55
Real estate broker's license, 76
Refinance vs. second mortgage, 154
Refinance, when to, 155
Remember these points
   apartments, 52
   commercial/industrial property, 72
   financing, 108
   installment land contract, 137
   land, 61
   leverage, 147
   on property you don't own, 84
   other-people's-money sources, 128
   outlying property, 214
   purchase leaseback and lease purchase, 95
   second mortgages, 158, 167
   seller financing, 117
   selling second mortgages, 191
   taxes, 228
   wrap around mortgages, 179
   zoning and rezoning, 202
Remodel, 47
Rezoning, *193*, 195, 199
Richard S., 46
Robert B., 58
Roe, Robert 162
Roger Z., 106
Rolling option, 57, 59
Ronald W., 165

S

Sale-leaseback, 88, 96
   advantages, 89, 90
Sales contract, 129
Sales presentation checklist, 82
Samuel M., 172
Savings and loan associations, 98
Second mortgages, 21, 110, *149, 159*
   best sources for seconds, 159, 161
   costs of financing, 160, 166
   discounting seconds, 182
   hard money, 160, 165
   low cost, 166

Second mortgages: *(cont.)*
  pitfalls, 156
  purchase money, 151
  selling a second, 181, 183, 185, 189
  trading-in seconds, 187, 189
  12% vs. 8¾% interest, 153
Security deposit, 221
Seller finances, 109, 124, 133, 141, 170
Seller, elderly, 67
Share the profit, 127
Shopping center, 33, 64
Steven C., 86
Syndicate, 18, *25*, 26, 38
  apartment, 26
  definition, 39
  high leverage, 25, 37
  investors, 30
  medical building, 106
  office building, 102
  raw land, 37
  shopping center, 33
  special-purpose building, 106

T

Takeout loan, 102, 103
Tax, *217*
  acceleration of tax liability, 222
  advisers, 218, 225
  attorneys, 218
  avoidance, 23, 217, 218, 224
  counselor, 23, *225*
  deferral, 220
  deferred sale, 221
  depreciation, 220
  evasion, 218

Tax: *(cont.)*
  installment sale, 224
  records, 80
  sixteen advantages, 219
Tenant financing, 175
Tenants in common, 39
Tight money, 43
Tom T., 36
Tucker vs. Tucker Savings and Loan Association, 137

U

Undermanagement, 77
Unimproved land, 53

V

Victor V., 80

W

Wrap around mortgages, 21, *169*, 181
  advantages for lender, 174
  finding investors, 173

Y

Yankee trader, 188

Z

Zoning, 18, *193*, 195
  ordinance, 194
  variance, 80